KNAVES, FOOLS AND HEROES

Knaves, Fools and Heroes

IN EUROPE BETWEEN THE WARS

by

Sir John Wheeler-Bennett

G.C.V.O., C.M.G., O.B.E., F.B.A.

ST. MARTIN'S PRESS

D
15
.W45
A 34
1975

Printed in Great Britain

Library of Congress Catalog Card No. 74–83586
First published in the United States of America in 1975

For
IRENE
with my love
JACK

Contents

List of Illustrations

Introduction

I OFFER this book with some diffidence. It is always hard for me to write about myself for, by reasons of circumstance, I have, generally speaking, been a privileged observer rather than a member of the cast in the drama. I have been lucky enough to watch at close quarters a variety of episodes of considerable historical importance and this has enabled me to chronicle them with a certain degree of authority. This is really my only excuse for writing this book – to explain how and why I wrote others.

But one cannot, of course, please everyone. My dearest and severest critic, my wife, has said of it: 'These aren't memoirs; this is just history', whereas I recall a somewhat carping and anonymous reviewer once writing something to the effect that the truth was that I was not really a historian at all but a first-rate writer of memoirs. This present volume has pretension neither to an autobiography nor to a historical treatise. It merely records some recollections and reflections over the first thirty-seven years of my life. These deal almost exclusively with Europe, but in later volumes I shall write of my experiences in the Orient in the late twenties and in the United States and Britain before, during and after the Second World War.

I have never kept a copious day-to-day diary but, as occasion demanded, I recorded impressions of men and events, descriptions of incidents I had witnessed, and conversations with persons of interest. This I did whenever it was both possible and expedient – which was not always the case – and unfortunately some of these memoranda were destroyed when my house in Bolton Street was bombed during the war. I had already used these records, however, in the writing of my various books, though they did not appear as personal experiences. I have also preserved my annual engagements books over a period of some forty years and these have proved a most valuable means of stimulating 'total recall'.

At any rate, I have tried, I hope successfully, to resist the temptation which assailed the great Latin historian (was it Lucan?) who admitted that he would have made Pompey win the battle of Pharsalia had the effective turn of a sentence required it.

I should apologise to my readers both for a certain overlapping in

1

the narrative and also for having cut the historical background to a bare minimum. Those who wish to have greater detail are, with all modesty, referred to my more serious works, including *Disarmament and Security Since Locarno*, *The Disarmament Deadlock*, *The Wreck of Reparations*, *Hindenburg*, *Brest-Litovsk*, *Munich*, *The Nemesis of Power* and *The Semblance of Peace*.

I am indebted to many who have assisted me in checking dates and details, more particularly the ever willing and helpful staff of the London Library, and the research staff of the Imperial War Museum, and I owe a great measure of obligation to those who have been good enough to read the typescript of the book in whole or in part and to comment on it. These include my wife Ruth and my friends Harold Macmillan, Harold Caccia, Anthony Nicholls, Edward Crankshaw, Jock Colville and Frances Coulson. I greatly appreciate their kindness in this and have accepted their criticisms most gladly and gratefully and always with benefit. Finally, my very sincere thanks are due to Mrs Sybil Cook for her efficiency, first in reading my handwriting and then translating it into type.

JOHN WHEELER-BENNETT

Garsington Manor,
Oxford

CHAPTER ONE

Myself when Young

I

THAT peerless and fascinating statesman the Prince de Talleyrand, whose span of experience stretched from the reign of King Louis XV, the last King of France to live and die an absolute monarch, to that of Louis Philippe, the Citizen King of the French, once remarked that 'no one who had not known France before the Revolution could understand, in its true sense, *la douceur de la vie*'. I shall not be the first to remark that this is perhaps also true of anyone who did not know England before the First World War. Harold Macmillan has made this point in the final volume of his autobiography and has emphasized 'the sense of peace and security which, in the course of this century, has been taken from us'. This is essentially true. One has only to read the opening chapters of his first volume, or Barbara Tuchman's *The Proud Tower*, or Stephen MacKenna's immortal novel *Sonia*, or to leaf through the issues of the *Illustrated London News*, to recapture that deep sense of peace and security which went to make up *la douceur de la vie*. I have vivid childhood memories of that golden period, memories which I cherish and would not for the world have forgone, but because I am of that age-group which just missed active service in the First World War – though I was myself a war casualty – I had the added advantage of having been able to enjoy the amenities without realizing the discords which lay beneath the glittering surface.

To be sure I was aware of certain divisive issues – the People's Budget of 1909, the Parliament Act of 1911, the Home Rule Bill of 1913 together with the incipient civil war in Ireland, and the industrial unrest caused by unemployment; but these only disturbed the domestic peace of my childhood by reason of the fact that my father would become choleric, speaking of His Majesty's Government of the day as 'a pack of confounded radicals', and of Mr Lloyd George as 'a howling yahoo'. I also recall that my mother would on occasion say to us: 'I think we'll keep the papers from your father until after lunch, my dears; they're so bad for his blood pressure.'

I did not therefore reach man's estate until after the close of the First World War, and there was much in the early days of the inter-war years to experience and enjoy. The war was over and we had missed it. Our hearts were young and gay, 'nightingales sang in Berkeley Square' and our hopes for peace were as yet unsullied by disappointment. Yet by 1922 the Chanak Incident had brought us to the brink of war once again. From then on, save for a brief period from the euphoric myopia of Locarno to the crowning folly of the Kellogg–Briand Pact, there was neither peace nor security in these years, and my contemporaries and I experienced the tragic and hideously remorseless acceleration of tempo from one World War to another. As the pace increased with the advancing thirties, one felt a terrifying, helpless fatalism, which darkened our skies and forced many of us towards a recklessness of life, being certain that, given the existing trend of circumstance, a second world cataclysm was inevitable.

All the same, for one just emerging into full manhood – even though handicapped, as I was, by a very bad stammer, the immediate post-war period was not without its attractions. There were still dances to which one wore white tie and tails; there were jolly little parties at the Hyde Park coffee-stall (which we once persuaded to remove itself to Belgrave Square in the middle of a ball) and the intimate welcome of Sovranis in Jermyn Street; the Berkeley, under the amiable authoritarianism of Luigi, was still in Piccadilly; there was tea-dancing in the Palm Court of the Ritz; the Savoy was in its glittering heyday. Michael Arlen, in a style which defied imitation, was, we felt, immortalising our generation. André Charlot purveyed for our delectation the new and rising talent of Gertrude Lawrence, Bea Lillie, Jack Buchanan and Noël Coward, the last of whom was shortly destined, with the initial assistance of C. B. Cochran, to become the Prince of Entertainers. Somerset Maugham and Freddie Lonsdale entertained us with sparkling comedy, and the choreographic fantasies of the Diaghilev Ballet were an added delight.

Moreover, I was presented by Major-General Sir Neill Malcolm to King George V at a levée at St James's Palace in 1931, and a magnificently glittering affair it was, with high-ranking soldiers and sailors in full fig and decorations, and the civilians in the romantic attire of court dress. To walk up St James's Street from the Palace today in black velvet knee-breeches and dress coat, silver-buckled shoes and silk stockings, cloak, sword and cocked hat would be the cause of raised eyebrows (if nothing else) but forty years ago it was not unusual for young men thus arrayed, or in the uniform of their service, to lunch at their clubs after having been presented to their Sovereign.

Thus for me it was 1939 rather than 1914 which saw the deluge that swept away my world, destroyed our civilisation and killed many of my friends in many countries.

II

I was born in Keston in the county of Kent on 13 October 1902, the youngest son of elderly parents, my father being over sixty-five and my mother some twenty years younger. We lived in a large and some-what rambling house called 'Ravensbourne' surrounded by some seventy acres of grounds and gardens. I survived what used to be termed 'a delicate childhood', which involved a good deal of illness and plenty of time for reading.

I think it was an intensive course of the novels of Dumas *père*, plus a strong injection of Henty and Brereton, which gave me the itch to become a historian. It developed further as a result of an unrealisable desire to be a soldier, and when I found that this ambition was vain and futile because of my health I became the more determined to find out why and how things had happened in the past and might well be repeated in the future.

My earliest recollection of the inescapable undertow of history was listening at a tender age to my father telling me the story of the Battle of Waterloo. He was a brilliant and vivid raconteur and so animated and realistic were his descriptions of the carnage of the Sunken Road and the desperate courage of the last charge of the Old Guard that I was both terrified and fascinated and spent many a sleepless night in consequence.

The year 1914 was momentous to me not only as a landmark in history but also for an important change in our domestic life. My father had retired from active business the year before at the age of seventy-three but had retained his directorships in a number of rail-ways and other concerns and also his membership on the boards of various charities. These mercifully took him to London one or two days every week, otherwise I think we should all have gone round the bend! His whole life had been bound up in business: he had no hobbies and was not a reader. Too old to acquire new interests or to continue riding a horse, which was his sole relaxation – and he had been a superb horseman – he was utterly miserable at home, where he roamed about finding fault with his family, with the domes-tic staff and with the gardeners and chauffeur. I am confident that but for the outbreak of the war, which brought fresh fields of ener-getic activity, he would have died in a year or two after his retire-

5

ment, having previously worried my mother into the grave also. As it was he lived another twelve years in excellent health.

In a desperate effort to provide him with occupation and distraction, my mother suggested that he take herself and me (my sister Irene, having completed a year at a finishing school at Dresden, was then at another in Paris) for a tour on the Continent in the spring of 1914. This was a daring proposition and one not at once received with favour. My father was an Englishman to his fingertips. His travelling had taken him mainly to the New World and though he had more than once visited the continent of Europe he had not been favourably impressed by it. To him 'Asiatics began at Calais', a sentiment to which he did not fail to give expression. It took all my mother's persuasive powers to win her cause, but she eventually succeeded and we left England in April as soon as my Easter holidays began.

It was a memorable experience for a boy of twelve and, though I have subsequently travelled throughout the world, the romance of that first contact with Europe is still with me, though in later years I find I have inherited much of my father's xenophobia.

At my special request our itinerary included a visit to the battle-field of Waterloo, with which I had been so long familiar in abstract, and I listened spellbound to the guide's account of the battle, though I was somewhat disappointed to find it less clear and vivid than my father's.

Apart from the fact that he would habitually look up the trains for departure from a place as soon as he arrived at it, my father really took the whole thing remarkably well. He led us at a smart clip through the cathedral towns of Belgium, then to Berlin where we witnessed the last review of the Prussian Guard by the German Emperor, and at length to Vienna where, during a performance at the opera, I was made aware, as the audience rose, of a shadowy figure in the Imperial box which betokened the presence of the aged Emperor Franz Joseph. When I next returned to Europe Belgium was in ruins and the German and Austro-Hungarian Empires had ceased to exist.

I had entered my preparatory school at Westgate-on-Sea some years before, and the summer term of 1914 was interrupted for me by permission to come home for my sister's coming-out ball in June. To my young eyes it was the loveliest thing I had ever seen. A ballroom under a marquee was built out over the lawn with access from the french windows of the drawing-room. Thousands of fairy-lights illuminated the grounds, and in the middle of the lake the boat was moored, its shape outlined in lights. It was a warm moonlit night and the orchestra played 'Destiny'. There were fireworks and lovely things to eat, and I was allowed to stay up till midnight; altogether it was a dream of delight for a twelve-year-old, who did not know enough to realise that we were even then dancing on the brink of a volcano.

Unlike many Englishmen, my father had realised to the full the potentialities of the shots at Sarejevo. He anticipated war from the first, and I learned later that during these weeks between the assassination of the Archduke Franz Ferdinand and the actual outbreak of war, he completely reorganised the basis of his fortune, getting out of all European interests and re-investing in Australian and Canadian securities. He also transferred his American holdings to Canada. It was a singularly wise decision.

When war actually came he took on a new lease of life. Here was something which called for all his natural ability, energy and leadership. He threw himself with passionate zest into the work of recruiting, touring the country in a series of mass meetings, to some of which I was allowed to go, and at which he spoke with remarkable eloquence and a surprising lack of that cant and sentimentality which were so prevalent at the time. Later he became identified with the Red Cross, first in the county of Kent and later as chairman of the Finance Board of the national organisation, and when conscription was introduced he became chairman of the county tribunal of appeals and a member of the City of London Committee on Manpower. When, however, at the close of the war, he was offered a peerage he refused it.

To me that summer holiday was the most exciting I had ever spent, and I took a very good view of the war. Hitherto it had been something I had read about in history books or played at with my friends or, in the case of the Balkan Wars, followed with keen interest in the newspapers and on war maps, on which I moved particoloured flags as the fronts ebbed and flowed with the tide of battle. Now, however, there was some new and exciting happening every day. Within six weeks of her ball, Irene and her friends had been mobilised as V.A.D.s and were scrubbing and cleaning the halls and buildings which had been hastily requisitioned as hospitals. A few days later these places were filled with British and Belgian wounded, and the girls who nursed them were called upon to experience the harrowing ordeals of the operating-theatre, the dressing of wounds, and the less romantic aspects of the sickroom.

And then there were the Belgian refugees. These unfortunates, driven from their homes like spume before the wave of German aggression, brought to Britain the first evidence of the new totality of war. Wounded soldiers and sailors were recognised as tragic concomitants of hostilities, but this wholesale flight of a civilian population before the flood of war was something which England had never seen before. As a result it evoked popular outpourings of generosity and sentimentality. In the first flush of enthusiasm these innocent victims of German barbarity, bringing with them blood-curdling stories of atrocities committed in their country by the Kaiser's legions, were welcomed into British homes as honoured guests, their needs ministered to, their destitution relieved and provision made for the schooling of their children. Complete responsbility was assumed for them.

My mother shared this riot of emotion, but she knew better than to import any Belgian refugees into Ravensbourne. My father's reaction could be very easily predicted. An intensely patriotic Englishman, he would gladly have given his last penny for his country, but an equally strong tenet of faith with him was that 'an Englishman's home is his castle'. So my mother had to find another outlet for her generous impulses and very grateful she subsequently was for my father's pragmatic, if self-centred, common sense.

She and a group of friends rented and furnished a house in the village of Keston, which had recently been vacated, and in this several families of Belgians were installed and a fund raised for their welfare. Thus we were spared at Ravensbourne the unfortunate incidents which occurred all too quickly as the tide of enthusiasm ebbed and a general disillusionment set in as to refugees in general. The planting in English homes of men, women and children of a different nationality, religion, language and, in many cases, of social background, was and experiment which, though successful in a number of cases, seemed doomed to general failure. The foreign guests took much for granted, often giving too little in return, and there rapidly developed a situation in which their hosts and hostesses would meet to discuss in a competitive spirit the relative unlikeableness of 'my refugees' and 'your refugees'.

In the case of my mother's refugees, they solved the problem for themselves with comparative rapidity. Bitter dissension broke out between the families inhabiting the furnished house and so acute did hostilities become – I believe that some were Walloons and some Flemings – that one night they all levanted in several directions and we never saw them again.

To me, of course, this was only one more excitement in the swiftly moving kaleidoscope of conditions that was rapidly changing the shape of the life and world I had known. The Belgians were romantic figures to me because I had very recently visited their country but they paled in romance beside the British Tommies who were now filling the beds of all available hospitals. These were heroes whom I could comprehend, and my greatest delight was to visit them, bringing with me cigarettes and sweets, and listening to their stories which, no doubt, were suitably embroidered for so appreciative an audience. Later, when Irene was transferred as a V.A.D. to the Third London General Hospital, then housed in a large orphanage at Wandsworth, I was allowed to attend the concerts which were organised for the entertainment of the wounded at week-ends. The best concert and variety artistes of the day gave their services at these affairs and I recall the exhilaration of sitting among that vast audience in their hospital 'blues' and joining in the choruses of every popular music-hall song, ancient and modern. The songs of the First World War were infinitely superior to those of the Second, and 'Tipperary', 'The Broken Doll' and 'Roses of Picardy' still bring a lump to my throat.

Back at school I found that war had also wrought its changes. Most of the younger members of the staff had volunteered, and the Headmaster had become the personification of a British jingo. He gave us long patriotic exhortations, urged us to accept with goodwill the, at that time, very small privations which were imposed upon us, and read to us daily the front-line despatches of Sir Philip Gibbs and others which appeared in the newspapers. He read very well, and his rendering of the account of the landings at Gallipoli, for example, moved me greatly.

My first experience of actual warfare was lying on the lawn of the school garden and watching with feverish excitement an aerial dogfight between a British and a German airman. The day was warm, the sky blue and cloudless, and in this firmament the two combatants swooped and rolled as they manœuvred for position, their bursts of gunfire being clearly audible. At length the British pilot got on the tail of his opponent and poured bullets into him. Black smoke poured from his plane and he dived headlong into the sea amid our youthful cheers. We were to see more of these aerial invaders later.

Gradually the war brought other changes into my life. Because of the growing shortage of petrol, difficulties of rationing and the increasing inability to get servants and domestic fuel, my parents decided to close Ravensbourne during the war winters and migrated to the Alexandra Hotel at Hyde Park Corner, from which my father was able to conduct with greater facility his governmental and Red Cross activities. It was here that I became acquainted with London in wartime, for I roamed the city at will during my holidays, and it was here that I came to know that doughty old warrior, the Maharajah-Regent of Jodhpur, Sir Pertab Singh, an old friend of my parents who with his suite had likewise taken up quarters at the Alexandra. This magnificent octogenarian had brought over his own contingent of Indian cavalry but these had been temporarily immobilised by the adoption of trench warfare. Pending the day when the great breakthrough should come – alas, it was long postponed – the old gentleman with growing impatience rode daily in Hyde Park despite the fact that he had broken both legs pigsticking and was as bow-legged as a cowboy. He took a liking to me and would tell me long stories about India to which I listened with attention though without complete comprehension, for his English was both 'pidgin' and broken.

By the summer of 1915 conditions at Westgate had taken on a new aspect. The military authorities were now contemplating the possibility of a large-scale raid, or even of an invasion, by German forces on the east and south-east coasts of England and were taking their precautions accordingly. In so far as we were concerned locally these involved the potential evacuation of all civilians from the Isle of Thanet, in which Westgate was situated. It was considered unnecessary to remove the many schools in this area prematurely, as this, it was thought, might produce alarm and despondency in the country as a whole, but all arrangements had to be made to leave at a few hours' notice.

I had by this time become head of the school and thus occupied the unenviable position of a sort of quasi-adjutant to the Headmaster, who described himself as our commanding officer. I must confess, however, that I thoroughly enjoyed the planning which went on in some degree of secrecy so as not to alarm the younger boys, and actually the preparations were very efficient. The object of the exercise was to effect the evacuation across the river Stour, which threads the marshy land between the Isle of Thanet and the rest of Kent. Once across we were to proceed to Southborough, there to be housed in another school kept by our Headmaster's brother. Provisional transportation was arranged with the local military and police authorities, but an emergency ration had to be prepared for each boy, who was also supposed to carry a knapsack with him containing a change of underclothes, toilet articles, etc.

I was made privy to the whole plan, and my especial duty was to organise the boys in sections under my fellow-monitors (whom we called 'captains' – I was 'head captain'). Since only the captains were allowed to have a limited knowledge of the plan it was impossible to have any form of rehearsal. The knapsacks were stored in a secret place and were to be issued and filled by the captains at the first warning of departure and I bound my subordinates to me by an oath of deepest secrecy, with blood-curdling penalties for violation, unvisualised by the modern Official Secrets Act.

Fortunately, as I have no doubt – for the thought now of shepherding some sixty small boys on trek in the grey dawn fills me with horror – we were never called upon to put the efficiency of our planning to the test; but it was fun while it lasted and I took the whole thing very seriously.

The threat of invasion, however, was followed by one of very real and imminent danger. Our coastal area was plentifully supplied with airfields and other military installations, and the naval depot at Sheerness was not far distant. These became the targets of ever-increasing air-raids by the enemy, and we were in the direct line of attack. Zeppelins, Taubes and Fokkers seemed to stream over our defenceless heads, and we became intimately acquainted with the sound of bombs, 'flak' and machine-gun fire.

Why the authorities did not see fit to evacuate the many schools in the area or why the respective headmasters did not insist on our being moved I shall never know. If the attitude of our particular Headmaster was any guide to the general feeling of his colleagues, they hung on out of sheer obstinacy, masquerading as courage. The only precaution for our safety was the fitting up of the cellars as a primitive air-raid shelter with bunks for the younger boys and benches for the rest of us and there we spent a number of depressing nights.

It was now, however, that our original planning for evacuation bore some fruit. The sectional organisation was made an integral part of our regular air-raid drills and each captain was responsible for getting the boys of his section down from the dormitories into the cellars. I exercised an overall authority and responsibility.

The end of this really shocking situation came about one early dawn in the April of 1916. An attack was made, as I afterwards learned, by a lone raider on the R.F.C. post at Manston. Driven off by the 'flak' and pursued by our fighters, the German accelerated his flight by jettisoning his remaining bombs as best he could as he made for the coast. Our school raid alarm sounded, and I awoke to the noise of bombing which drew steadily nearer as I herded my sleep-drunk charges down the stairs.

Then followed a hideous nightmare. I went from cubicle to cubicle shaking the occupant awake and seeing that my fellow captains did likewise. As soon as we got them aroused they were asleep again, for this was the third successive night we had spent in the shelter, and we were all very tired. Finally we got the last of them under way and after making a quick round of the dormitories to see that there was no one left I made for the stairs at a run. I was now thoroughly frightened, for the last bomb had seemed to be very near indeed. The next one was nearer still. It fell in the school yard with a tremendous detonation which pitched me down the stairs and into oblivion.

No one was killed, indeed there were no physical injuries, and I was the only one to suffer serious repercussions. I was badly shell-shocked, and when I recovered consciousness it was to find that I had been afflicted with a bad stammer. As a child I had had a nervous hesitation, but this had disappeared with the passage of time and I had been an eager participant in amateur theatricals and had taken pleasure in reading the lessons in the school chapel. Now, however, I was virtually inarticulate, and there began for me fifteen years of hell until a final cure was effected by the aid of Mr Lionel Logue, who also effectively cured King George VI.

My health also suffered. For a year I was a prey to nervous disorders, internally and externally, including a facial tic which was disfiguring. I had been entered by my parents for both Rugby, where my brother had been, and for Charterhouse, but I was too unwell to go to either. Both schools generously kept a place open for me for two terms, but when I was still unable to enter they were compelled to fill them. It was for this reason that, when in the summer of 1917 I had sufficiently recovered, I was sent to Malvern College.

III

It was at Malvern that my decision to become a historian finally took shape and meaning. I received an excellent grounding and won prizes. My masters were men of infinite understanding. They did not concentrate on dates and reigns of kings and battles; they taught me the broad scope of history, 'splashing at ten-league canvas with brushes of comet's hair'. I discovered the romance, the brutality, the ruthlessness and the sentiment of history. Nor was scandal avoided. I remember that one splendid work read in the History Sixth was Coxe's *House of Austria* in several volumes in which nearly every page consisted of some ten or twenty lines of text, and the rest footnotes à la Gibbon recounting the more scandalous doings of the

Habsburgs. I never forgot a word, and many years later took infinite pleasure in recounting some of them to Frau Sacher in Vienna, in exchange for enlivening and even spicier stories of her own of some of the more modern vintages of Archdukes.

It is only fair to say that at this same time I also discovered that I had not the smallest or most elementary ability to absorb arithmetic, algebra or geometry. It has always seemed to me ironic and vaguely unfair that, whereas the two men who gave me my invaluable historical grounding have passed into obscurity and have died, the two others who presided over this mathematical débâcle in my career both became bishops and still live.

A further bout of ill-health prevented my going up to Oxford, where I had been destined for Christ Church, and thus, though I do not wholly endorse the remark of Michael Arlen, my old friend and fellow Malvernian (we called him in those days by his original patronymic of Dikran Kouyoumdjian), that 'I went to an English Public School and am therefore entirely self-educated', the fact remains that my formal education terminated with my leaving Malvern. I was bitterly disappointed at missing Christ Church, and my happiness and gratitude may be imagined when in 1949 I was made a Master of the House with the privilege of calling myself, for domestic purposes, an M.A. Ch.Ch. Three years earlier, in 1946, I had been made an M.A. of Oxford by decree in order to be considered eligible to teach returning warriors who were flooding the colleges, and in 1961, when Harold Macmillan was installed as Chancellor of the University, he was kind enough to include me in his first 'Honours List' as an Hon. D.C.L.

IV

My career as a historian has been influenced to a major degree by four men of very varied personality. The first was Anthony Eden, though he was ignorant of it at the time as we had never met. In those years after the war when our enthusiasm and our optimism were still pristine, my contemporaries and I came to look upon Anthony Eden as the one person in public life who represented our ideals. From the moment he entered the House of Commons in 1924 and became P.P.S. to Austen Chamberlain, then Foreign Secretary, Anthony was the Golden Boy, slim, handsome and charming. My generation looked upon him as typifying the generation who had survived the war to become the champion and defender of our pathetic beliefs in what proved to be those ephemeral

Wilsonian shibboleths of 'a war to end war' and 'let us make the world safe for democracy'. Though he did not succeed, we knew it was no fault of his, and he retained our confidence. So impressed was I by his courageous struggle for sanity in diplomacy, so imbued with the ideals which I felt to be an integral part of those policies which he favoured and pursued, that I felt impelled to chronicle the narrative of that anguished period of the twenties and thirties which terminated in the Second World War.

Thus began my career as a serious historian, born of a desire to place on record the story of what may be called the Eden ethos, together with its failures and its triumphs. The result was a series of books dealing with the closely associated problems of Security, Disarmament and Reparations which, though written between forty and fifty years ago, are today being republished in the United States as essential text-books – largely because nobody else seems to have written on these subjects. I am also happy to say that a further lasting result is the warm friendship which I then formed with Anthony Eden and which has continued ever since.

My second influential benefactor was Sir Neill Malcolm, as whose P.A. I acted on several occasions on governmental missions in the Orient. In the course of these events we travelled together across Asia on the Trans-Siberian railway from Chang-Chun to Moscow and Berlin, and it was at this time that my interests became directed towards Germany. Neill Malcolm, for whose kindness to me for so many years I am ever grateful, had been head of the British Military Mission in Berlin immediately after the Armistice of November 1918 and had witnessed the birth pangs and the early struggle for survival of the Weimar Republic. He had known many Germans of influence and importance of that period and he was certain that the centre of interest for Europe lay in and around the catalytic agency of Germany. To this end he advised me – and there is plenty of time for advice in a ten-day railway journey – that, whereas what I had been writing heretofore had been of historical importance, the time had now come to study Germany intensively and specifically, for upon what she did or did not do in the next decade – we were then in 1929 – would depend the issue of peace and war. He certainly convinced me, and on our return to London I made a decision which was to influence the whole future course of my life – to devote myself to the study of modern Germany, and to observe the business of German men and events at first hand.

My friendship with Malcolm and Eden led me, I suppose naturally, to Sir Robert (later Lord) Vansittart, then Permanent Under-Secretary at the Foreign Office, and the chief director and designer of all its activities. Neill Malcolm's advice to me may not have been professionally entirely disinterested because, in the course of my four-year stay in Germany, I became in effect an alternative and purely unofficial channel of communication between leading German politicians and public figures (excepting Nazis) and London. As later pages will show, I was able on occasions to make some contributions of my own. I was neither a professional diplomat nor in any sense a 'secret agent'. I was paid neither salary nor expenses. Perhaps the best, though not the most flattering, description of my international role is that of a 'convenience'. My role, however described, was I think as useful to my German friends at that time as it was to my friends in London.

I was recently delighted to find among the Foreign Office papers which had just been released to the Public Record Office the minutes of some of my colleagues, written in June 1943, on a paper I had written on some form of German future policy. One of them asked in evident bewilderment what the present position and status was of Mr Wheeler-Bennett, and back came the answer to the effect that I had long made a study of German affairs. 'It *is* Mr W.-B.'s personal trade,' this minute continued, 'and he does it *con amore*, as he has for 20 years past; praise and thanks would surely be welcome.'

Thus began, too, the second period of my career as a historian, which resulted in a further series of books dealing with Hindenburg, the Treaty of Brest-Litovsk, the Munich Agreement and the German Army in Politics. It was now that I came under the influence of one of the greatest of the historians of our time, Sir Lewis Namier. I never sat under him *in statu* pupillari, though I should much have liked to do so. We met at 'Baffy' Dugdale's house, took a liking to each other – not always the immediate result of meeting who was undeniably a prickly character – and became fast friends. Thereafter, until his death in 1960, he read and criticised every manuscript I wrote, with highly beneficial results to myself and my work. He was not an easy mentor. Slovenly writing and 'purple passages' were ruthlessly excised : statements were challenged, necessitating the adduction of facts; praise was sparingly awarded. It was a tough and gruelling apprenticeship, but I would not have missed a moment of it – at least not in retrospect. Even when hardest pressed one felt Lewis's intellect at work, striving, however brutally, to evoke some responsive chord within oneself, moulding one's mind along lines more brilliant than one had known, fascinating one by the very working of his own mind and his vast knowledge and, above

15

all, never withholding merited encouragement or 'rebuking one's genius'.

I owe Lewis Namier much, both as master and friend, and not least for the fact that it was he who brought me to Harold Macmillan, then a young rising Member of Parliament, already marked for office, although as yet something of a rebel. He has remained my friend, my guide and my father-confessor for forty years. It was he who persuaded me to write, with Tony Nicholls, *The Semblance of Peace* – and it is he who has stimulated me to write this present book and in this particular form.

V

But I was not content with writing books. I wanted to *know* the people of whom I was writing and the events which I was essaying to describe. In 1924, therefore, when I was twenty-two years old, I took the somewhat unusual step of establishing my own intelligence service, known as the Information Service on International Affairs. This, as may be imagined, was received with considerable scepticism – not to say hostility – by my father, who wanted me to follow in his footsteps in a commercial career and dismissed my passionate interest in international affairs as 'ephemeral nonsense'. I found myself therefore in somewhat straitened financial circumstances, having to pay out of my own income office rental, staff salaries and general expenses. However, I raised the wind somehow, and the period of stringency did not last too long. We had a remarkably rapid success, and when men at his club began to ask my father if he was any relation of mine he began to realise that there was something in the whole thing and made a generous contribution to the funds of the Information Service – but it was tough going for a time.

I was exceedingly lucky in my supporters. I persuaded Lieut.-General Sir George Macdonogh, a former D.M.I. and later Adjutant-General, to become chairman of an executive committee of which the other members were 'Baffy' Dugdale, a niece and fanatical admirer of Arthur Balfour; Dame Adelaide Livingstone, who although born an American – she was a Stickney from Boston – had married an Englishman, and during the War had done remarkable work at The Hague in arranging the exchange of prisoners of war. She was the first woman to hold a major-general's commission and one of the first D.B.E.s to be created. The honorary treasurer was Oliver Brett, later Lord Esher, who never failed to enliven our meetings. I was vice-chairman.

We issued a fortnightly publication called *The Bulletin of Inter-*

national Affairs, consisting of articles (chiefly written by me) and a chronology of events. At first we gave it away free to our subscribers and it was a good advertising 'gimmick'. When it ceased publication in 1955 it was not only paying its own way but also the not insubstantial salary of its professional editor. I travelled extensively on behalf of the Information Service, enlisting the help of many of my friends in various countries as honorary correspondents, who sent us summaries of their local national press and other useful information, and in the course of these travels I met and grew to know a wide variety of the leading figures in Europe, the Orient and America. I also developed a special sense whereby I instinctively knew where the next trouble spot was going to occur. This earned me the sobriquet of 'The Vulture' from my friends.

I established myself in A14 Albany, which I still believe to be the most comfortable and desirable bachelor's quarters in London, and there the strangest variety of persons forgathered. Looking through the visitors' book which I kept for luncheon and dinner parties recalls a sort of 'Mist Procession' of memories. Faces emerge from the past, faces of European cabinet ministers, Jesuit Fathers, foreign journalists, propagandists from every corner of the earth, English friends who 'liked meeting foreigners', and ambassadors such as Eduard Raczynski of Poland and Quo Tai-chi of China. Most of them are dead, and it is still tragic to remember how some of them died. Albrecht Bernstorff was shot by the Nazis after the abortive coup of 20 July 1944. Colonel Gregori Putna, the Soviet Military Attaché, was liquidated by Stalin in the great military purge of 1936, and Jan Masaryk was hounded to his death by Czech Communists in 1948. All were my friends.

Gradually the Information Service established a reputation for purveying accurate information. Journalists would consult our reference staff, M.P.s would solicit our aid in drafting questions to the Foreign Secretary. At length the Foreign Office itself gave us its cautious approval, and the day came when the Royal Institute of International Affairs at Chatham House, of which I was a Founder, made overtures to us. They had never succeeded in establishing an information service department of their own and they now proposed a merger. We drove a good bargain. Sir George Macdonogh and I went on the Council of the Institute, of which Sir Neill Malcolm was Chairman. Our committee of management became its information committee, our staff were transferred *en bloc* and I was appointed Director of Information, a factor which opened many doors to me in Europe.

This then is the story of how I became a historian and intimately acquainted with the politics of Europe and particularly Germany. This stood me in good stead during the Second World War, when I eventually became the Assistant Director-General of the Political Intelligence Department of the Foreign Office.

In order that the book may be exonerated from any intent of being an exercise in name-dropping, I may perhaps be allowed to quote – with some bashfulness – the following excerpt which was written by H. R. Knickerbocker, a Pulitzer Prizewinner whose untimely death in an air crash in 1949 was an irreplaceable loss both to his many friends and to the world of international journalism where his integrity and ability were deeply respected. 'Knick' wrote in an introduction to the American edition of one of my books:

John Wheeler-Bennett has not confined himself to the study of treaties. He has studied the men who make the treaties. He is personally acquainted with and trusted by virtually every Minister of importance and State executives in Europe. His indefatigable travels from capital to capital precede or parallel the historical moments which punctuate his chronicles. Not a few of these moments have been influenced by the information which he has exchanged with prime movers of European politics. His insatiable curiosity drives the scholar from study to battle-field. Berlin police-men, nervously fingering cocked automatics, were acquainted with the tall, slim form of this young Englishman imperturbably wandering in and out of the beams of search-lights on the bullet-ridden Bülowplatz. The *Stamm-Tisch* of the Anglo-American journalists in Berlin's *Taverne* has made him an honorary member. At least one famous plan of international action derives from him. Not a few of the witticisms which blast an international conference have been his invention, yet no parley for peace is complete without him. The corridors of Geneva, the castles of Hungarian nobles, the hiding places of political exiles, are equally familiar to this his-torian whose scholarly retreat is behind purple-liveried doormen of the Albany, Piccadilly.

Even allowing for native American hyperbole, I could wish for no more gratifying an epitaph.

CHAPTER TWO

Winter of Discontent in Weimar Germany, 1929-33

I

I⊤ has always seemed to me that the most remarkable thing about the Weimar Republic is not that it existed for only fifteen years but that it ever survived the circumstances of its nativity. Never was the idea of a republican form of government less welcome. The birth pangs of the ill-fated French Third Republic in 1870 were at least suffered to the accompaniment of demonstrations of enthusiasm, but the natal processes of the German republic in November 1918 were not only lacking in acclaim but were attended by more 'bad fairies' than darkened any of Grimm's gruesome tales. Inimically, reluctance and lack of popular support were among the 'evil spirits' with which the infant Weimar Republic had to contend, but these were not all.

From the first the Weimar system was tagged with two terrible indictments which rendered it vulnerable to attack from all quarters. In the first place, because the Provisional Government was largely composed of Socialists at the outset – the right and left wings of the Social Democratic Party – this party came to be held responsible for the 'stab in the back' which, by undermining the loyalty of the home front, had betrayed the front-line soldiers and rendered defeat in the field inevitable. This in turn engendered the complementary myth that Germany had not been defeated by the Allies in the field but only by the machinations of her own traitors at home.

The second indictment was that the new democratic form of government, so alien and unsuited to the German political way of thought, had been forced upon Germany by the victorious Allies – led by President Woodrow Wilson, whose demands for the abolition of the monarchy and the substitution of a democratic republic were held by many in Germany to have been welcomed all too warmly and implemented all too pliantly by the Social Democrats. Those who held these views knew little of the agony of spirit which assailed the chiefs of the S.D.P. when it was revealed to them that they must assume the burden of government or surrender to a Communist régime. They would have far more willingly retained a monarchy with a regency and a Socialist Chancellor.

When I first went to Germany in the middle twenties, the republic had traversed its early stages of uncertainty – which comprised the agony of the peace terms, the Kapp Putsch, the collapse of the Reichsmark, the deadlock over reparations and the occupation of the Ruhr – and was luxuriating in the artificial affluence and the chronic euphoria derivative from the Dawes Plan and the Locarno Agreement. Field-Marshal von Hindenburg was in the model era of his first term of office, Gustav Stresemann was in the heyday of his career as Foreign Minister, and it seemed as if a new Germany, enlightened in outlook and democratic in its political institutions, had been re-admitted to the polity of Europe. She had even been elected to the League of Nations.

Above all Lord D'Abernon was still British Ambassador in Berlin, though approaching the conclusion of his term of office. Rarely can any foreign diplomat have occupied such a position as D'Abernon did in Germany. He was a virtual viceroy. His very appearance was vice-regal. Well over six feet tall and built in magnificent proportion, his bearded face usually a study in enigmatic impassivity yet capable of breaking into the most delightful of smiles, he was a man of greatness, and with his beautiful wife Helen he dominated Berlin. In the many cabinet crises which assailed the republic in its early days he always played an effective and not infrequently a decisive role. No political leader if asked by President Ebert or President von Hindenburg to form a government would fail to consult D'Abernon on the composition of his cabinet, and the first courtesy call which every Reichskanzler paid on assuming office after presenting his cabinet to the President was upon the British Ambassador.

Indeed D'Abernon has been credited with 'godfathering' the Locarno Agreement, and the story as told to me *si none vero* may very well be *ben trovato*. For some considerable time this wise and astute man, whose record fully qualified him for the more devious type of diplomacy, had been contemplating the possibility of a Western Security Pact between Britain, France and Germany, directed not against a one country *per se*, but against aggression itself, from whichever direction it might come, and that this might pave the way for the conclusion of a general disarmament agreement as envisaged in the Treaty of Versailles and the Covenant of the League of Nations.

He was also convinced that the chances of success for this revolutionary manœuvre would be greater if the proposal were to come from Germany. How then was the Ambassador to sell the idea to the Foreign Minister? Difficult in itself, there was the added obstacle that, whereas both were good talkers, neither was a good listener.

D'Abernon's ingenious mind hit upon an original solution. Stresemann was one of the most unlovely-looking men I have ever seen. Porcine of feature, his little eyes set close together, his hair cropped close over a nearly bald pink skull and the inevitable roll of flesh behind the neck, he was a caricature of a German as depicted in the wartime cartoons of *Punch*. Yet he was a man undismayed by his own appearance, and when D'Abernon suggested that he have his portrait painted by Augustus John he jumped at the idea. It was arranged, moreover, that the sittings should take place at the British embassy, but a stone's throw from the Ministry of Foreign Affairs on the Wilhelmstrasse.

Having therefore created, as it were, a captive audience, D'Abernon ranged and paced about the room, expatiating on European affairs in general and dropping ideas, grain by grain, into the mind of the perforce listening Foreign Minister. Suddenly, when the portrait was almost finished, this policy bore fruit. At the conclusion of a sitting Stresemann drew D'Abernon aside and said that he had a proposal of the greatest importance and the highest secrecy to communicate. Would it not be a possibility that if Germany proposed to Britain and France a pact of security against aggression it might prove acceptable? The Ambassador evinced amazed delight at so unique a project and warmly congratulated Stresemann on his inventive and ingenious plan. The two began to exchange views, and the Ambassador, as was his wont, made notes on his shirt cuff, which in the manner of many Edwardians – including my father – he wore starched from wrist to elbow to ensure the set of the coat sleeve.

An hour or so later Stresemann returned to his Ministry with his mind agog at this new plan and its possible far-reaching results. He summoned his Permanent Under-Secretary and outlined to him the gist of his talk with D'Abernon, referring, *en passant*, to notes which the Ambassador had made. Where, asked the professional diplomat, were these notes? To his unfeigned horror, the Foreign Minister confessed that they were on the shirt cuff of the British Ambassador. A colloquy followed as a result of which a very junior member of the Foreign Ministry staff was sent to ask if he might be given a sight of the Ambassador's shirt-cuff. It was now after luncheon and D'Abernon habitually played tennis in the afternoon. His discarded shirt which he had worn in the morning had been consigned to the laundry basket, which might or might not have gone to its appointed destination. A frantic search, however, yielded up the historic garment, and, after a slight difficulty in transliteration, the notes were borne back triumphantly two doors down the Wilhelmstrasse, where they became

21

the origins of the Agreement initialled at Locarno in October 1925.

D'Abernon was fortunate in having a well-selected and very competent embassy staff, but perhaps his most valuable asset in this respect was a non-career diplomat, Tim Breen, whom he had inherited from Neill Malcolm, on whose British Military Mission Tim had served. Tim had gone over to France with the original B.E.F. in (I think) the Irish Guards, and had been captured at Le Cateau, being for the next four and a half years a prisoner of war. During this time he acquired a fluent and valuable knowledge of the German language not only in its purer and more polite forms, but also in its argot and the vernacular. When, after the signing of the Armistice in November 1918, the Germans merely opened the prisoner-of-war camps and shooed the inmates on to the roads with no other form of transport than their feet, Tim Breen tramped from Silesia to Berlin and was promptly co-opted by Neill Malcolm on to the staff of his mission.

Tim's linguistic knowledge and his native astuteness were of the greatest value. The fact that he spoke German fluently but with an Irish brogue caused him to be accepted by all Germans as a fellow countryman coming from another part of Germany; a Rhinelander would take him for a Bavarian and a Saxon for an East Prussian, and this he turned to the best possible intelligence purposes. So completely was he accepted that he managed to play an important part in drafting the constitution of the Free City of Danzig. Neill Malcolm passed him on to D'Abernon and he became an established figure at the embassy, acting as the 'eyes and ears' of successive ambassadors until shortly before the outbreak of the Second World War.

The story of Tim which I liked best was of an occasion during a period of disturbances in March 1919. The Commandant of the Berlin Garrison, who was, of course, loyal to the Provisional Government, had set up a machine-gun post on the top of the Brandenburger Tor, commanding in its field of fire the Unter den Linden, at the top of which, near the old Imperial Palace (now destroyed) the rioters were massing. Neill Malcolm wanted a first-hand situation report and sent Tim Breen to make it.

He found a well-positioned post with three machine-guns and plenty of ammunition under the command of a sergeant, whom Tim addressed in German, until he suddenly observed on his left sleeve a regimental ribbon marked 'Ireland'. This could mean but one thing. The wearer must have been a member of that ill-fated and abortive attempt of Sir Roger Casement to raise an 'Irish Brigade' from among the prisoners of war taken from the Irish Regiments of the British

Army. Like Tim Breen, this young man had been captured early in the war; bored to death with the monotony of prison-camp life and attracted by German promises of pay and promotion, he had been one of the few who had responded to Casement's blandishments, had achieved non-commissioned rank and, when the German Army had disintegrated, had drifted into one of the Free Corps and thence into the Reichswehr. Tim, now speaking in English, asked why he had not gone back to Ireland and, if he really disliked the British, had not joined the Sinn Fein forces.

At this moment there was a forward movement of the rioters and the sergeant, at once responding to the call of duty, swung his machine-gun into position, opened fire, and with his thumbs glued to the firing buttons replied politely over his shoulder to Tim's question: 'Och, sir, you know very well we've got to be on the side of law and order.'

II

When I first arrived in Berlin I had only one introduction, a letter to Harold Nicolson, then Counsellor of Embassy and at that particular moment Chargé d'Affaires. He was kind to me, invited me to dinner and laid himself out to be his entertaining best. Indeed that dinner *à deux* laid the foundation of a lasting friendship which ended only with his death in 1968. It was also directly responsible for my being appointed by Her Majesty the Queen to write the life of her father.

On this evening Harold brought proceedings to a close by asking if there was anyone in Berlin whom I particularly wanted to see.

I replied at once, 'General Hans von Seeckt.'

Harold looked perplexed. 'It won't be easy,' he said. Then he looked pensive. 'Isn't there *anyone* else in the whole Weimar Republic that you want to see?' he asked.

'Only General Max Hoffmann,' I answered.

'Oh dear,' said Harold. 'These soldiers; they're so difficult. And why on earth do you want to see them?'

I told him that in my view they were the two ablest soldiers whom Germany had produced during the war. In the case of von Seeckt, I added, he had created the most efficient volunteer army on the Continent and, if rumour were true, he had laid the foundation for the expansion of this army at the pressure of a button.

'That', said Harold, 'is something which you have no business to know anything about.' But, having administered this official rebuke, he became again his urbane self. 'We'll try von Seeckt first,' he said.

'But I warn you, he is said to be anti-British and doesn't take to strangers. If he sees you at all it will be for only ten minutes. But I'll tell him you're a great admirer of his. All soldiers are vain, vainer than diplomats,' he added with a whimsical smile. 'I'm told he's more approachable since he's retired. I'll send a message to your hotel before lunch tomorrow.'

He was as good as his word. I duly received a message that the General would receive me at eleven o'clock on the following morning.

I must explain briefly about Hans von Seeckt. My admiration for him as a soldier was based on the fact that he had shown brilliant leadership in both victory and defeat. His highly successful use of the 'breakthrough' tactics at Gorlice on the Eastern Front had broken the deadlock of trench warfare and 'wiped the eye' of Hindenburg and Ludendorff, who had based their strategy on effecting a 'Cannae' manœuvre and encircling the Russian armies. Later in the war von Seeckt, as Chief of Staff of the Mackensen Army Group had conducted the invasion of Romania with considerable skill, and later still had extracted the German forces co-operating with the Turkish Army thereby showing the loyalty of his men in retreat as well as in victory. He also performed the difficult and unpopular feat of moving the German forces out of the Baltic Provinces.

When, as a result of the Treaty of Versailles, Germany's defence forces were drastically curtailed in manpower and armament, it was to Hans von Seeckt that the command of the new Reichswehr was assigned, although it was known that he was a monarchist at heart and had little faith in the republic. However, after one moment of weakness, at the time of the Kapp Putsch, when he simply went on leave and waited to see which side would win, he remained loyal to the republic and for a year he even virtually governed it.

This was in 1923–4. When the Stresemann Cabinet decided on 26 September 1923, to call off passive resistance and thus terminate the state of deadlock in the French-occupied Ruhr area, it was expected that there would be national resentment and unrest, and how this was prevented was one of Stresemann's favourite stories. The President of the Republic called an emergency cabinet meeting and invited von Seeckt to attend it. It was in the early hours of the morning. The Ministers arrived in varying degrees of disarray, some with hair unbrushed, some unshaven, some with their ties awry, and some without ties at all. Fearfully they took their places around the cabinet table. One chair at the far end remained empty. Suddenly the great double doors were thrown open and there entered Hans von Seeckt. Cool and collected, his uniform and his appearance were immaculate;

Myself when young

In court dress

On The Witch

H. R. Knickerbocker

Sir Neill Malcolm

his riding-boots shone in the electric light, his spurs jingled, his rimless monocle was held firmly in his eye. Bowing he sat down, remaining silent, and the President explained the situation; at the end he asked the all-important question: 'General, will the Reichswehr stick to us?' And von Seeckt, speaking for the first time, replied: 'The Reichswehr, Mr President, will stick to me.' Then he paused and speaking with great emphasis said: 'No one but I in Germany can make a Putsch, and I assure you I shall make none.'

The effect was electric. Courage returned; apprehension faded. The necessary articles of the Constitution were called into effect and for practical purposes the government of the Reich was placed in von Seeckt's hands for one year. At its close he surrendered these emergency powers with the same military correctness with which he had accepted them. He had governed well.

Moreover, von Seeckt had rearmed Germany, both in collaboration with Soviet Russia and with the co-operation of heavy industry. While he was in command this process was a closely guarded secret, but later, after he had been dismissed from office as a result of a cabal headed by his own protégé, Kurt von Schleicher, security became relaxed and reference to the subject of 'secret rearmament' was openly made in the political cabarets of Berlin.

For example a compère would tell the following story: a man, whose wife had just had a baby, complained to another that he could not afford to buy a pram. His friend, who worked in a perambulator factory, offered to bring back the parts, piece by piece, so that the impoverished father could assemble it for himself at home. Some months passed before they met again, but when they did the father was still carrying the baby. His friend, who had completed the delivery of the permabulator parts, asked the reason. 'Well, you see,' was the reply, 'I know I'm very dense and certainly the least mechanical of men, but I've put that damned thing together three times, and each time it turns out to be a machine-gun.'

It was with some trepidation that I rang the door-bell of General von Seeckt's flat on the Lichtenstein Allee punctually at eleven o'clock. Punctuality may be the courtesy of kings, but unpunctuality is a criminal act in the eyes of soldiers, and I was taking no chances. I was shown into a typically Prussian sitting-room, decorated with bronzes of horses and naked warriors and elk-horns, and antimacassars on plush- or leather-covered furniture. Yet there was something different. There were some good Impressionist paintings and a grand piano, none of which were usual habiliments of a Prussian general officer's quarters. Nor was the owner of the room less surprising in contrast.

Von Seeckt liked dramatic entrances, and he made one now. I had been in the room alone for some ten minutes when the curtained glass door into an inner room opened suddenly and von Seeckt stood motionless on the threshold. He was in civilian dress, and wore it to better advantage that most German officers. There was a cluster of decoration ribbons at his button-hole, among which I recognised that of the coveted Pour le Mérite Cross, which the Kaiser had awarded him after his victory at Gorlice. At first glance he seemed like a typical Prussian officer, with his thin, red turkey-neck, his inscrutable face and its inevitable monocle. Just another general, one thought, as he stood in the doorway, but that impression only remained until he took his hands from behind his back, and one was amazed at their beauty. Long, thin, sensitive, they might have belonged to a Cellini, and, indeed, in his military genius von Seeckt combined the precision and accuracy of the general staff officer with the vision and imagination of the creative artist.

I was determined not to take the first step. It was his house, he was my host and it was up to him to go through the motions of welcoming me. Eventually he did so in a militarily correct manner, without shaking hands, then he offered me coffee, and when it had been served, asked me what I wanted with him. I replied unblushingly that I had wanted to meet Germany's most brilliant soldier. This piece of outrageous flattery produced a perceptible rise in the temperature. Was I a journalist? No, I replied, I was a historian, an observer of men and events. And what events did I expect to get from him? asked von Seeckt a trifle suspiciously. I introduced the word 'Gorlice', and it proved the 'open sesame' to a cavern of precious jewels.

Not only did I get a first-hand account of the great victory over Russian armies but thrown in for good measure was an acrid and abrasive estimate of Hindenburg and Ludendorff as military strategists. Hoffmann he spared, even praising his genius, but for the two top commanders on the Eastern Front, whom he had temporarily displaced and who had never forgiven him for it, he had little but contempt.

We passed from this to other events in his war-time career. A question here, a comment there, and I was able to elicit his views on the defeat of Romania, the mishandling of the Balkan Front, the final débâcle in Turkey. He spoke vividly, with precision and without hyperbole. I sat fascinated, until I glanced at the clock; it was twelve-thirty; I had been warned that I could expect only ten minutes. I rose hastily with apologies. But he would not let me go. He insisted that I stay to lunch and rang for his manservant to inform Frau von Seeckt of this fact. He proffered a glass of schnapps as an apéritif. Nothing could be less like the cold and barely veiled hostility with which he had entered the room an hour and a half before. He could not have been warmer in his invitation.

At luncheon I was introduced to Frau von Seeckt, who was a very different cup of tea. There was little charm here and much pomposity. One was reminded of 'Mrs Chubb was very portly, Mrs Chubb was very grand.' She was as wholly a *Frau Oberst* as it was possible to imagine and had never forgotten the status of a *memsahib*, which had deeply impressed her during their visit to India before the War. Moreover she was a crashing snob and for some obscure reason had convinced herself that the hyphen in my name was in some way an indication of nobility. She was alternately patronising and syco-phantic, and, as I later discovered, a very bad influence on her hus-band. Her political ambitions were boundless, and she ardently desired that the General should succeed Hindenburg as President of the Reich, and with this end in mind she brought him into contact with the least desirable elements of the Right. It was Frau von Seeckt who propelled her husband into the Nazi orbit, though only for a brief period.

After luncheon there was more talk, but we kept firmly off politics as I felt I should not press my luck too hard – but this came later.

When I reported next morning to the British Chargé d'Affaires, Harold Nicolson was frankly incredulous. 'It can't be true,' he said. 'Von Seeckt has never talked to any foreigner like that before.'

'Well,' I answered, 'next time you see him ask him about it.'

With his usual amiability Harold later told me that he had done just this and that my story had been confirmed.

I am also happy to record that there now began for me a friendly relationship with General von Seeckt which I greatly valued. I saw him whenever we were in Berlin concurrently, and when I was writing my biography of Field-Marshal von Hindenburg he was of the greatest help to me. An evening at his house was always something to look forward to, for it was an essentially civilised atmosphere. His *savoir faire* gave him a particular charm; he was well and widely read, and his appreciation of beauty in every form – music, art, women and nature – afforded an ampler vision than could ever have been achieved by, for example, Ludendorff, whose war-time doctor once told me that he used to treat the General 'for his soul'. Apart from admirable food and wine, von Seeckt's dinner-parties were distinguished for his excellence as a host. An accomplished conversationalist, he would so vary his company that the talk might range from horse-breeding and military history to politics and the arts. Or he might sit down at the piano and would drift off into something enchanting of Chopin, something sparkling of Mozart, something exhilarating of Liszt or something romantic of Johann Strauss. There was never a *longueur*. Years later von Seeckt himself confessed that vanity, a sense of beauty and the cavalier's instinct were the three salient traits of his character, but in this he did himself an injustice. He possessed all these characteristics admittedly, but in addition he was a master of war and a true friend. When my Life of Hindenburg was published in 1936 it was banned in the Third Reich, but a bootleg traffic went on through Holland and von Seeckt became possessed of a copy. By a similarly devious route he sent me word that he had read it from cover to cover and endorsed every word. He died in the same year, a saddened and disillusioned man.

III

When in 1929, at the instigation of Neill Malcolm, I decided to study the German situation *in situ*, I also decided to 'black myself all over for the part'. I had loved horses ever since I had overcome my early fear of them, and I was a passable rider. I had always wanted to breed but had found it too costly a pastime in England. I determined therefore that, in so far as my life in the countryside was concerned, horse-breeding and racing should be my ploy, and I therefore rented a little stud near to Fallingbostel on the Lüneburg Heath (where the Second World War ended). This was a good strategic position, partly because there were some good stables nearby and partly because it formed one apex of a roughly equilateral triangle of Fallingbostel–Verden–Celle.

Verden was the heart of the horse-breeding region of the Weser and the Aller, two rivers which wound their peaceful way through lush and dreaming water-meadows, with a lime soil. It was also the training headquarters of the German Army Olympic team and the centre of horse-trading. At Celle was one of the two German national studs, the other being at Trachen in East Prussia.

Verden was a delightful little town, with many half-timbered houses and a mighty cathedral in the nave of which Charlemagne was said to have slaughtered a large number of Saxons. In the cathedral precincts was one of the most moving monuments I have ever seen; a small memorial shaft surmounted by a bronze rampant steed and dedicated to the horses in all armies who had been killed in the Great War.

The principal event of this small township was the annual horse-fair to which stock was brought from all over Europe. It was an early summer affair, and for weeks one could hear but one remark bandied about in general conversation : 'The horses are coming.' And then at length they came, usually in the breaking of the dawn. The thunder of their hooves echoed through the narrow streets as they cantered to their encampments, and on the following morning one would go down to inspect them. Superficially they presented a pretty bedraggled lot, with dusty coats and tangled manes and tails, for some of them had come from as far as the Hungarian Pusta. But in forty-eight hours a miracle occurred. Every coat shone with grooming and curry-combing, tails and manes had been combed and brushed, the weariness had gone and every horse seemed aware of being on show, with ears pricked and arched neck. It was a wonderful and unforgettable sight.

As I have said, the other importance of Verden was the training of the Army Olympic team, and to watch this many prominent personages came from Berlin. Von Seeckt put in an appearance, and I also met there Franz von Papen, who had been champion gentleman-rider of Germany in 1911, and also Kurt von Schleicher, the evil genius of the Reichswehr. Both these men became Reich Chancellors in later days and my acquaintance with them, as will be seen, was not unuseful. A constant visitor, too, was General Walther von Reichenau, the chairman of the German Olympic Committee, who later became one of Hitler's Field-Marshals. He it was who later made to me the classic remark about Germany's attitude towards Italy. This was in the spring of 1934, when he held an important Wehrkreis command and we were discussing the various possibilities of the next war. I asked him if Germany needed allies. 'Allies!' he replied with utter contempt. 'Do you realise that we lost the last war because we were tied to a lot of rotting corpses? No, we don't want allies, we need benevolent neutrals.' I asked about the position of Italy, and he answered with all the scorn which the Teuton has felt for the Latin since Arminius the Cheruscan destroyed the legions of Quintilius Varus. 'Mark my words, my friend, it does not matter on which side Italy begins the war, for at its close she will be found playing her historic role of "The Whore of Europe".'

Of the team itself I grew to know and like two members very

well: Lieutenant Count Hans-Viktor von Salviati and Lieutenant Hans von Brandt. Hans-Viktor's sister made a morganatic marriage with Prince Friedrich-Wilhelm of Prussia, the eldest son of the former German Crown Prince, and this so enraged his grandfather the Kaiser that he compelled the young man to renounce his rights of succession to the Prussian throne – not perhaps in practice a very heavy sacrifice. Friedrich-Wilhelm died of wounds received in action in June 1940, and so great was the popular demonstration at his funeral in Charlottenburg that an infuriated Hitler ordered all members of former German royal families to resign their commissions and accept assignment to civilian war-time jobs.

Hans-Viktor von Salviati himself, a most likeable man and not unintelligent, became A.D.C. to Field-Marshal von Rundstedt, and was also involved in the conspiracy to assassinate Hitler on 20 July 1944. When this plot failed he was among the many of my friends who were executed.

Hans von Brandt was a delightful person and one of the most superb horsemen I have ever seen. He was a veritable centaur and could establish an absolute empathy with any mount he was given. Alas, his charm of manner and equestrian ability were not matched by his cerebral capacity. One could not help liking and admiring him and he had enough brains to pass the General Staff examinations, but when it came to *Bauernschlauheit* (peasant cunning) he was wanting, and this has assured him an important if little-known place in history.

Hans was essentially a gentleman and with all the right instincts. He too thus gravitated naturally into the ranks of the conspiracy, and his position as a member of the Führer's personal staff was of value to the plotters. But because they did not entirely trust his ability to do the right thing at the right moment he remained on the periphery of the plot, knowing little of the details. His colleagues' anxieties were more than justified; at the historic moment he did the wrong thing at the wrong moment. On the morning of 20 July 1944 when, at the Führer's headquarters conference at Rastenburg, Claus von Stauffenberg having placed his briefcase with the activated bomb inside it beside the Führer's place at the conference table left the room, Hans von Brandt, finding it in his way, moved it to the other side of the wooden baulk supporting the table, so that when it did explode Hitler was thus protected from the impact. Von Brandt died of his wounds received that day.

As for myself I was exceedingly happy in these surroundings. I owned three horses, a black gelding, a huge grey stallion, who could jump a house and had a profound equine sense of humour in that, when I rode him through the streets of Fallingbostel, he would take large mouthfuls from the laundry baskets usually carried on the heads of washerwomen and would proceed on his way with a sort of beard composed of intimate articles of feminine apparel.

I also had a bay mare called The Witch, and never was a horse better named, for she was indeed bewitching. She was the sweetest dispositioned horse I ever knew and would come to my whistle across the pasture, whinneying her welcome. I recall so well when I was assisting at the birth of her first foal and raised the little thing in my arms on to its long shaky legs to take him to her. Just for one moment she was all atavisitic maternal protection. Her ears went back, she bared her teeth and for an instant I thought she was coming for me. Then she suddenly realised that I was her friend and signified the fact by nuzzling us both, first her foal and then me. It was a moving moment.

I also possessed a piebald Great Dane, of great canine nobility, called Argon von Huntermayer, whom I brought up to be a vegetarian for experimental purposes, and I have never seen a fitter dog. He used to accompany me riding and would take jumps with me with the greatest of ease.

It was all in all a good life: constant practice in equitation, regular attendance at the friendly, jolly little race-meetings which were held every Sunday in the adjoining villages and where one found excellent half-blood and three-quarter-blood entries. I also met many interesting, and, on the whole, pleasant people.

I became a competent horseman because I learned the hard way. I used to ride with my friends and fall off at the jumps which they cleared with ease. Finally I managed to jump sufficiently well to keep a monocle in my eye without rim or cord. But I never came anywhere near the heights of their achievements, which included jumping with a glass of water on a tray without spilling a drop!

I also learned a lot beside equestrian proficiency and met many people who were subsequently of great service to me in Berlin.

IV

It is not true, as some of my friends alleged, that I kept a flat, a car and a dog and – I have little doubt that some then added – a mistress, in every capital in Europe. There was a moment however, when I had a flat, a car and a Great Dane in London; a stud, three horses, a car and a Great Dane in Fallingbostel; and an apartment and a car in Berlin.

I knew a number of people there from previous visits and they passed me on to their friends. I also had a number of introductions and my connection with the Royal Institute of International Affairs was an added advantage. It was indeed ironic to find what influence the word '*Königliche*' carried in this republican state.

I took up my quarters in the old Kaiserhof Hotel in the Wilhelm-platz, an establishment not unlike Brown's Hotel in the old days, where provincial nobility had stayed for generations on their periodic visits to the capital, along with the German equivalent of county families. Lord Beaconsfield and Lord Salisbury had also put up there during the Berlin Congress of 1878. The Kaiserhof had not the glamour of the Adlon, nor the sparkle of the Bristol, but it suited my purposes admirably, for a variety of reasons. It was exactly opposite the palace of the Reich Chancellor in the Wilhelmstrasse and adjacent to the Foreign Ministry. It was also the social headquarters of the Nazi Party and a special large table was reserved each afternoon at tea-time for the highest ranking Party hierarchy. Adolf Hitler himself often came there, and it was interesting to note who from outside the Party were recipients of Nazi hospitality. I remember that Hjalmar Schact was a not infrequent caller and also a certain Major von Marcks, who was said to be the intimate adviser of General Kurt von Schleicher.

Minor royalty also stayed at the Kaiserhof, and here I must record an odd experience which has dogged me for years. Quite unrecognised by myself, I appear to have resembled one or more members of the House of Hohenzollern. Unfortunately my *Doppelgänger* at the time was Prince August-Wilhelm, the youngest son of the Kaiser and so violent a supporter of Hitler that he not infrequently appeared in S.A. uniform and was elected a Party deputy to the Reichstag. The likelihood of our being mistaken for one another when he was wearing a brown shirt was comparatively slight – I seldom wore Nazi uniform! – but in civilian clothes we were apparently very much alike and I have been frequently, and obsequiously, addressed as *Kaiserlicher Hoheit*.

This absurd confusion, which led to the rumour that I was in some degree not entirely legitimately connected with the Hohenzollerns, pursued me into the war and after, and on one occasion Mr Winston Churchill himself – primed, I have always believed, by his puckish, mischievous but wholly delightful young private secretary, Jock Colville – made enquiry as to whether 'there was anything in it'. A somewhat embarrassed Foreign Office official was assigned the delicate task of asking me this question, to which I, needless to say, answered that it was totally false and that my dear mother had never even met a Hohenzollern in her life !

But the rumour persisted, and once, when my wife and I were at a dinner-party in the country, another guest, as we entered the drawing-room, swept me a curtsy and uttered the bewildering greeting of 'Sire, may I kiss your hand?' She turned out to be a Romanian lady, of more emotive imagination than sense, who had mistaken me for King Carol II of Romania, who was, of course, a Hohenzollern-Sigmaringen, the Catholic branch of the House. This again was not an entirely felicitous confusion of identity, but it certainly caused a stir in an English country drawing-room. I have always wondered whether she thought that my wife resembled more closely Zizi Lambrino, Hélène Lupescu or Princess Helen of Greece !

V

At this time in 1929 the Great Depression, which struck the United States in October of that year, had not yet manifested itself in Germany. To be sure there had been warnings and portents. In successive annual reports Mr Parker Gilbert, the Agent-General for Reparations appointed under the Dawes Plan of 1924, had drawn attention to the fact that the German economy was unsound, largely by reason of irresponsible municipal spending. As a result of this the Young Committee had produced its plan for the 'final settlement' of he reparation programme and successive conferences at The Hague in 1929 and 1930 gave legality to their proposals.

But in the everyday life of Germany, and especially in Berlin, these were halcyon days, and the Locarno spirit was still in being, albeit as an hallucination. The capital had good music and opera, an indifferent theatre – except for Brecht – and a night life which had become notorious throughout Europe. Berlin had become the vice centre of the Continent. Every sexual appetite was catered for, whether heterogeneous or perverse. Visits to such famous homosexual cabarets as the Eldorado and the Blue Jockey figured among the attractions advertised on sightseeing tours, and other perversions could easily be satisfied. The many-tiered Wunderbar Café provided attraction for the more innocent if unaesthetic.

Nor was the political underworld untroubled. Intrigue – and no one could intrigue more deviously or with less security than the Germans – was seething in all quarters. Already the great divisive factors which were to ruin Germany and destroy Europe were becoming manifest. The extremists of the Right and the Left were mobilising their forces, and between them the parties of 'respectability' raged furiously together.

I was lucky in having some useful centres of information, though I gained them under what later proved to be somewhat dubious auspices. Franz von Papen put me up for the Herrenreiterverband (The Gentleman Riders' Club) and Hjalmar Schacht for the Union Club. The first of these institutions was a possible parallel with the Turf in London and the second a curious amalgam of the Athenaeum and Brooks's. I was also made an honorary member of the Herrenklub – a sort of Prussian White's.

My two sponsors were men of very different calibre. Franz von Papen was extremely good company, a wickedly accurate mimic and quite the most politically bird-brained chap imaginable. He was an 'Uhlan in politics'. A man of irresponsible decisions and careless thought, he had considerable charisma, and his period as military attaché in Washington during the war, though it had ended disastrously with his expulsion, had given him an extra polish and a fluent use of English, which made him easy and attractive in conversation. His capacity for misjudging a situation was unexcelled. It had been said of him that his only fault as a rider was that he 'rushed his fences', and he certainly carried this failing into his conduct of political affairs. I was to have later dealings with him of some interest.

Hjalmar Schacht, Governor of the Reichsbank, on the other hand, was a very different type. Tough, shifty and witty in a curiously unpleasant way, he was undoubtedly one of the greatest financial wizards of the century. I could never bring myself to like Schacht, though he went out of his way to be helpful to me. To talk with him was always stimulating. There was nothing wrong with his brain, it fairly radiated brilliance; what he did lack was manners. I remember some time later sitting next to Frau Schacht at a luncheon party at the German embassy in Washington, during a lecture tour of her husband's. She was a repressed and rather frightened lady and not an easy luncheon partner. I essayed various subjects of conversation without the least success and at last I fell back on the banal. Was she, I asked, very fatigued after her long trek across the United States and back? She paused a moment and then, speaking with great sincerity, she said: 'Well, I do get very tired of sleeping in the upper berth.' This seemed an interesting comment on the hymeneal bliss in the Schacht household.

Both von Papen and Schacht played vitally important parts in bringing Hitler to power, the one by political intrigue, the other by financial support at a crucial moment. I considered this so shocking a complicity that I felt no pangs of post-prandial disloyalty when, in 1946, I found them both in the dock at Nuremberg and myself attached to the British Prosecution. I have been told that my appearance on the floor of the court caused considerable perturbation among those of the accused whom I had known. However, the International Military Tribunal, in its wisdom, concluded that to have helped Hitler to power, reprehensible though it might have been, did not constitute a crime within the terms of the Tribunal's charter, with the result that both were acquitted.

Lest it should be thought that I was *lié* only with the forces of re-action, I must add that I had many of the Left among my acquaintance from the Chancellor, Hermann Müller, downwards, and even a Communist or two, among them Ernst Torgler, who figured prominently in the Reichstag Fire Trial. Karl von Ossietsky, the courageous pacifist and editor of the *Weltbühne*, I also met, and in a later age Hubert Knickerbocker and I went to see him in the Oranienburg concentration camp.

Thus from my observation post in the Kaiserhof I watched the fragile structure of German democracy first crack, then crumble and finally disintegrate. It was a tragic process for which none of the political parties were wholly without responsibility and in which world events played a disproportionate part. If the Nationalists had shown one atom of political sense or decency; if the Social Democrats had displayed greater foresight; if the economic crisis had not happened at just that moment; if the American, British and French governments had been more understanding of the danger which faced Germany and Europe. If – if – if. It is the saddest word, and, as one looks back, it becomes the more credible that, had any one of these happenings occurred, the chances of avoiding Hitler's coming to power and its ghastly consequences were not too meagre. What was lacking was the slightest modicum of luck.

The situation was a peculiar one. Because of the Hague Reparation Conferences of 1929 and 1930 the Chancellor, Müller, the Foreign Minister, Stresemann, and the Finance Minister, Dietrich, were absent from Berlin for months at a time. The government of the Reich was carried on by a kind of rump cabinet, presided over by the Defence Minister, General Wilhelm Gröner, who was very much in the hands of his trusted *chef de cabinet*, Kurt con Schleicher, whose evil influence was thus given free licence.

Of General Gröner I have written elsewhere.[1] He was as fine, courageous and honest a man as I have ever known. His chief fault was that he was too trusting; too trusting to the point of naïveté. His chief virtue was that he never shirked an issue, however unsavoury or unpopular it might be. He alone in November 1918 had had the courage to tell Wilhelm II in so many words that the Emperor no longer commanded the loyalty of his troops and, when challenged with arguments that they had taken an oath to the Sovereign, replied clearly and sadly: 'Sir, in times such as these, oaths are but words.' It was Gröner who had told President Ebert a year later that the government of the Republic had no choice but to accept the Allied peace terms, when all Germany was clamouring for their rejection. And he was to make further momentous decisions. There was about this good, stolid Swabian with his non-commissioned officer family background, something which compelled respect. His integrity was impeccable; his record unassailable.

How different a man was Kurt von Schleicher. Good-looking, amusing, gallant with women, an amiable companion, all these were undeniable; but behind the façade was a mind consumed with ambition, not for position but for power. This ambition justified everything and every means. There was no vestige of loyalty or innate decency in him. He operated in the dusk behind the throne, spying on all and sundry, tapping their telephones, bugging their offices. He betrayed patron after patron, including von Seeckt and Gröner, to whom he owed everything. Friendship with von Schleicher was the Kiss of Death.

I used, however, to keep in touch with him – after all he was the best informed man in Berlin – and we used occasionally to ride in the Tiergarten together. I also made a point of cultivating his exceedingly able and much more likeable public relations officer, Major Erich Marcks, whose capacity for calculated indiscretion was limitless. If Schleicher was the *Eminence grise* of the Reichswehr, Marcks was his father confessor, but with little regard for the secrets of the confessional.

It was from this period that I date the beginning of my friendship with Heinrich Brüning, which became sincere and intimate. He was at this time forty-three years old – a young man if judged by the standards of German politics where the parties made little or no attempt to attract young men – and it was never his original intention to enter a political career. Of a very sensitive nature, he was at once a romantic and a paladin, a dreamer of dreams and a man of courage.

[1] See 'Men of Tragic Duty' in A *Wreath to Clio* (London, 1967).

36

A devout Catholic, he came of a middle-class Westphalian family, and, a delicate, shy and brilliant young man, he was about to complete his doctoral thesis at the University of Bonn when the outbreak of the war destroyed the sheltered life which till then had been his. The glamour of war appealed to him; the paladin and the romantic were merged into one and sent him unhesitatingly to volunteer. To his dismay he was rejected for defective eyesight, and returned disheartened to complete his doctoral thesis which won him a brilliant degree in economics, but he still hankered for active service. He volunteered again. The inroads of war upon the manpower of Germany had made the medical authorities less particular, and Brüning was accepted. It was May 1915 and he was then twenty-nine.

Wounded almost immediately, he was invalided home and was granted a commission in the Machine-Gun Corps, with whom he fought in the great battles of 1916 and 1917 and in the March 1918 offensive. Brüning proved himself a good soldier and a capable officer, with a natural ability and a cool courage which belied his studious appearance. He and his unit were more than once cited for 'unparalleled heroism' and he himself received the Iron Cross (First Class).

His war experiences had wrought a great change in Brüning. Much of the romanticism of youth had been burned out of his soul, and in its place there was a certain mysticism of comradeship. He had learned to command men and to earn their respect and loyalty, and he himself had come to know the spiritual satisfaction of following a leader in whom he had confidence. Military discipline in its finest sense appealed to him, and he carried out of the war an abiding devotion to duty and public service.

Brüning entered the Reichstag as a deputy of the Catholic Centre Party for a Silesian constituency in the general election of 1924 and at once achieved a reputation as an expert in economics and finance. His speeches in budget debates soon commanded respect and admiration, even from his bitterest political opponents, for it was obvious that this tall, slight figure, with the thin lips and nose, the receding hair and clear, blue eyes twinkling through gold-rimmed spectacles, knew what he was talking about. He was marked for rapid promotion and in December 1929 he was elected leader of the parliamentary group of the Centre Party.

I had met him a year or so before this, and we had immediately taken to one another. We shared a love of horses – though he was no great horseman – and of history, and I learned from him the company commander's view of the war which so rarely finds its way into history books. Moreover he was willing to talk about German politics and political problems with an unusual frankness which characterised our relations. He was one of the first to see the writing on the wall in respect of the perils assailing the Republic from the extreme Right and Left. He understood earlier than most men the vital connection between the economic dangers inherent in the present state of German economy and the question of Treaty Revision in respect of reparation payments and disarmament. He believed that, in accepting the Young Plan, Stresemann had paid too high a price for the completion of the evacuation of the Rhineland. In all, he had vision and foresight. One felt instinctively that he was waiting in the wings for a call to play a heroic role in history.

I was not alone in this belief. Von Schleicher thought similarly! Stresemann, when he went to the first Hague Conference in 1929, was already a dying man, dedicated to the fulfilment of his post-war ambition of freeing German soil from occupation by allied troops. He achieved this goal on 29 August 1929, in exchange for German acceptance in principle of the Young Plan. On 3 October he died.

Stresemann's death created a vacuum in the German political structure which von Schleicher had been anticipating with some impatience and certainly greeted without sorrow. His idea was to get rid of the Social–Democratic coalition dominated by Hermann Müller – that man of fateful destiny whose tragic duty it had been to sign the Treaty of Versailles and who was now about to make formal acceptance of the Young Plan – and replace it by a government based further to the Right which could cope with Nationalist opposition, command the uncommitted support of the Social Democrats and contain the rising tide of extremism on Left and Right. To such a government, von Schleicher persuaded Gröner, the Army would give its support; for, whereas von Seeckt had regarded the Reichswehr as the supreme protector of the Constitution, von Schleicher saw its role as the maker and breaker of governments.

Much of this was told to me by the invariably informative Major Marcks, but it was Brüning who told me of what followed.

Von Schleicher proposed to Brüning that he should encompass the downfall of Müller in the Reichstag and himself form a government on the lines indicated. This proposal Brüning uncompromisingly rejected. He was loyal to Hermann Müller, whose friend he was, and would enter into no cabal against him. He did, however, tell von Schleicher that the support of the Centre Party for the ratification of the Young Plan was dependent upon the simultaneous presentation to the Reichstag by the Müller Government of measures to meet the most urgent of the many financial reforms necessary to meet the near-crisis situation.

With this von Schleicher had to rest temporarily content, but with an almost diabolically acute reading of Brüning's character and his weakness for hero-worship he arranged for him to meet Hindenburg. It was a historic moment – the veteran octogenarian Field-Marshal and the former Machine-Gun Captain. An affinity was established which at the time perhaps both of them believed would endure. The Field-Marshal, himself emotional in the inherent German manner, also knew how to 'ham it up'. Suddenly he began to weep, those facile tears of old age, and clasped Brüning's hand in both his own. 'So many have forsaken me; give me your word that now, at the end of my life, you will not desert me.' Though deeply moved, Brüning would not commit himself to a betrayal of Müller. He replied, a trifle enigmatically perhaps, that the Centre Party would always support the Field-Marshal so long as he remained loyal to the Constitution.

Müller, however, having won his struggle for ratification in the Reichstag on 13 March 1930, realised that his political career was at an end. He resigned with his cabinet on the 27th, and Brüning accepted the mandate to form a government on the following date. The Marshal greeted him warmly: 'You shall be my last Chancellor and I will never give you up,' and old Oldenburg-Januschau, the veteran Conservative leader, declared that: 'Brüning is the best Chancellor since Bismarck.' He was certainly the best of Konrad Adenauer's predecessors.

There now began an even closer relationship between the new Chancellor and myself. When I was in Berlin during his term in office I saw him nearly every evening. I would walk across from the Kaiserhof Hotel to the side door of the Reichskanzlei, and, when he became his own foreign minister, I had ready access to his State-Secretary, Berhard von Bülow. I was thus able to occupy a ringside seat for the poignant penultimate act of the Weimar Tragedy.

VI

There were other observers of a more professional nature than I. With the exception of the period of the London Blitz in 1940–1, I do not suppose there has ever been a more extraordinary display of co-operation and confraternity between Anglo-American journalists than in Berlin during the last months of the Weimar Republic and the first of the Third Reich. There was competition of the healthiest nature in obtaining stories, but there was also a pooling of facts and figures and personal reactions which made for greater accuracy and double-checking. They met regularly each evening at the Taverne restaurant (in, I think, the Lutherstrasse). Under the Nazi regime, when censorship was imposed in varying degrees of stringency, this collaboration made it considerably more certain that at least one 'shared story' would find its way to its parent newspaper if others fell victim to the censor's blue pencil.

In addition to their generosity of spirit the corps of correspondents were a galaxy of genius. Norman Ebbutt of *The Times* was the outstanding British member; a benign, roly-poly, figure with a brilliant mind and a fine sense of journalistic morality, and with him were often also Douglas Reed and Donald Maclachlan, also of *The Times*. Darcy Gillie, cadaverous and sardonic, and later on Hugh Carleton Greene of the *Daily Telegraph*, and Frederick Voigt of the *Manchester Guardian* were 'regulars'. Among the Americans I can still see the faces of friends who were to be household names in years to come. Hubert ('Knick') Knickerbocker of the Hearst Press, a gangling red-haired, raw-boned Texan and my special 'buddy'; Edgar Mowrer, of the *Chicago Daily News*, who looked like Abraham Lincoln in his earlier years; an ebullient, round-faced young man called John Gunther, also from Chicago, and Raymond Gram Swing from Philadelphia. William Shirer of C.B.S., whose diaries were to become famous, and William Birchall of the *New York Times* were less regular attendants, and on one or two occasions the meetings were graced by Dorothy Thompson and 'Red' Lewis.

Nor must I forget the one regular woman member of the circle, that gallant lady Elizabeth Wiskemann, who forsook the academic life of Cambridge to become a freelance journalist and also rose to the top of her profession as a historian of the period, despite partial blindness. Few things gave me greater pleasure than when Oxford gave her an honorary degree of Doctor of Letters shortly before she died in 1971.

There was another British correspondent, Sefton (Tom) Delmer, of the *Daily Express*, who adopted a unique and totally different technique of his own. On the perfectly sound principle of 'know thine enemy', he established such good relations with the Nazi Party that he had an entrée to their headquarters which was unequalled. Indeed so completely did he infiltrate the inner circle of the hierarchy that he was more than once invited to accompany Hitler on the famous 'Freedom Flights' (*Freiheitsflüge*) by means of which he conducted his election campaigns. Tom Delmer was, I believe, the only foreign correspondent to be afforded this privilege, and his knowledge gained thereby of the leading Nazi personalities proved of the greatest possible value to us when he was a member of the Political Warfare organisation during the Second World War. At the time, however, Tom, who was a lone wolf, was somewhat suspect in the Taverne circle, who were to a man openly anti-Nazi, and of whom more than one member was later expelled for his outspoken criticism of the regime; these included Norman Ebbutt and Edgar Mowrer.

The composition of the group was strictly confined to working journalists – with two exceptions, Jim Passant, a Cambridge don then on sabbatical leave for the purpose of German historical research, who subsequently became Librarian of the Foreign Office, and myself. We were included for different reasons; Jim because his historical knowledge could supplement the journalistic contemporary information, and I partly because they all happened to be friends of mine and partly because I had access to sources which were denied to them. Although I never abused a confidence which had been made to me by a German, I was able, on occasion, to confirm somebody's story or to indicate when I thought somebody else had been given what in American slang is known as a 'bum steer'.

Night after night we met to eat and drink – or just to drink – in the smoke-laden crepuscule of the Taverne, where a big *Stammtisch* (club-table) was always reserved for us. Some brought their wives and some their mistresses, and a warm feeling of comradeship pervaded all, even though most of what we talked about became increasingly gloomy as time drew on. When the Nazis seized power we came periodically under police surveillance. But as the Gestapo in its infancy was not too well organised and always sent the same man to sit alone at the next table to ours we very soon came to recognise him, and when he showed up we would talk spectacularly ridiculous nonsense in loud voices. He really became something of a tame pet, and we even once asked him to join us for a drink. He accepted and 'a good time was had by all'. But this was in the very early days of Nazidom. Life was soon to be far more realistic and much less pleasant.

In the latter years of the Weimar Republic, however, we were not, so far as any of us knew, ever spied upon. The proprietor, who cashed our cheques with financial intrepidity and flattering confidence, was a rabid anti-Nazi and, alas, paid for his freedom of speech with a period in concentration camp; but this was some time after I had left Germany.

Our increasing pessimism was but a reflection of the political and economic situation in the world at large and in Germany in particular. Heinrich Brüning came to office at a homeric moment in German history, though there were few who recognised its true significance at the time. Brüning himself, though he saw further ahead than most of his countrymen and certainly than most of those in Europe and America, yet did not see far enough. He failed to estimate the abysmal villainy of the Nazis and the growth of their grip upon the imagination of the German people, he failed to gauge the stupidity and the obscurantism of the Social Democrats, he failed to comprehend the duplicity and disloyalty of von Schleicher, and he failed to envisage the pusillanimity and shiftiness of Marshal von Hindenburg. These failures were largely due to the salient virtues of his character. His own outstanding sense of probity blinded him to the essential evil and the evasive dishonesty of others. A man of deep loyalty himself, he could not plumb the mendacity of those to whom he had given his trust.

The essential problem with which he was faced on assuming office in March 1930 was simple to define but hideously complex to deal with. The ailing economy of Germany demanded, at least according to the canons of orthodox finance, immediate attention and drastic reforms; sacrifices more Draconian than the Germans had ever endured before. To make this treatment more palatable, more endurable, Brüning sought to give his countrymen compensation in the sphere of foreign affairs by bringing off diplomatic successes in the fields of reparation and disarmament, which should at once expand the ego of the German people and afford them economic relief.

What he sought, in effect, was the abandonment of the Young Plan schedule of payments, which extended into the distant future of the eighties, and to replace it by an agreement for a final settlement of reparation on the basis of 'the clean slate'. In the field of armaments Brüning sought the abandonment of the restrictions placed on Germany by the Treaty of Versailles as a preliminary to the voluntary disarmament of the other Great Powers. Since it was obvious that these powers had no intention of reducing their armaments to the level imposed upon Germany, it was Brüning's thought that a new start should be made at the forthcoming General Disarmament Conference at Geneva with the adoption of an agreed scale, down to which the former Allied Powers should reduce their armaments and up to which Germany would increase hers.

So much for Brüning's hopes; hopes which he was never destined to see realised. Fate seemed to be working against him, for by September 1930 he had allowed himself to become involved in a general election from which the only party to benefit were the National Socialists, who emerged with 107 seats in the new Reichstag as opposed to 12 in the old. From that moment Brüning realised that he was engaged in a race against time in which he knew that he was competing against the Nazis, making it the more imperative to obtain concessions from the Great Powers, who, if they did not make them to him, would be called upon to conciliate a far more dangerous successor.

Of these facts Brüning spoke frankly to me in our not infrequent talks. What, however, he did not know, or even suspect, was that he was also competing against Kurt von Schleicher, who, with the emergence of the Nazis as the second largest party in the Reichstag, began that series of intrigues with Hitler which were ultimately to lead to his own murder.

Moreover the whole world economic situation was confederate to Brüning's failure. By 1931 a serious monetary crisis was developing in Central Europe. In May of that year the most important of the Austrian banks, the Kredit Anstalt, closed its doors, to be followed into bankruptcy three months later by the large German Darmstädter und National Bank. The Reichsmark fell in relation to other countries' currency, and there was a flight of German capital to London and New York. At the same time political violence had been steadily on the increase in Germany. As economic confidence waned and financial misgivings increased, the two political extremes reflected the hatred and fear which underlay all German society. Sunday after Sunday throughout the Reich was marked and marred by clashes between the Nazi S.A. and the Communist Red Front Fighters, resulting in dead and wounded on both sides. In the months of April and May 1931 alone, for example, there were fifteen deaths, two hundred serious casualties and over a thousand minor casualties, and never have I admired a constabulary more than the Prussian police force at this time. Weekend after weekend they stood between these warring factions armed only with pistols, which they seldom used, and rubber truncheons (*Gummiknüppel*), which they wielded to great effect. I witnessed many of these encounters, which would have resulted in much greater casualties were it not for the dispassionate and patient conduct of the 'Blue Police'.

At this time it wrung one's heart to watch Heinrich Brüning fighting his losing battle with his back to the wall and a prayer in his teeth. He used every weapon and artifice available to him, but always it seemed that his sword broke off at the hilt or his planning went awry. His attempt to effect a Customs Union with Austria was frustrated by the opposition of Pierre Laval and the operation of French gold. At this moment France held over a quarter of the world's supply of this valuable commodity, and Laval did not scruple to use it to fish in troubled waters, to trouble the waters still further and to cause an imbalance in any scales which he considered to the advantage of France.

In June Brüning undertook the first of the visits abroad which he made during this *Annus Terribilis*, in his efforts to awaken European statesmen to an awareness of the dangers with which Germany and Europe were now faced. On 6 June he met at Chequers with Mr Ramsay MacDonald; each principal had some of his cabinet colleagues with him, and at the conclusion the British Prime Minister passed on to the United States Secretaries of State and Treasury, Mr Stimson and Mr Mellon, that which Brüning had told him. But the conversations did not result in any definite conclusions.

On the night of 8 June I dined at the German embassy in London as the guest of the Ambassador, Freiherr Konstantin von Neurath, who proved to be another of my acquaintances with whom I was confronted at Nuremberg before the International Military Tribunal. It was a small party, and the only non-Germans were the head of the German Department of the Foreign Office and myself. He seemed surprised at my presence. Brüning was profoundly depressed at the inconclusive results of his Chequers conversation. He did not hesitate to give expression to his disappointment.

After dinner we had a few words together and he asked me when I was coming again to Berlin. I said in about a week's time. Could I not, he asked, come back with him tomorrow in the *Europa* to Bremerhaven. There would be an opportunity to talk on board, he added.

So, after the quickest packing job imaginable, I did just that. I did not join his party but travelled by myself on the same train to Southampton, having secured a good cabin at the last moment. I remember that the German ministerial party was officially seen off at Waterloo by 'Van', as Permanent Under-Secretary, immaculate as ever in short black coat, striped trousers, black soft hat and yellow chamois leather gloves so pale that they appeared white. Though we passed within two feet of one another, he gave me no sign of recognition, but, as we steamed slowly out of the station and my carriage, out of which I was looking, passed him, I detected a perceptible wink on that impassive, saturnine face of old ivory.

On my arrival on board the *Europa* from the tender there was a surprise. Returning from leave in his native Kentucky was the American Ambassador to Berlin, the Hon. Frederick Sackett, an honest, intelligent and delightful man and a great breeder of horses.

It had been his intention to leave the ship at Cherbourg and return to his post via Paris, but hearing that the German Chancellor was travelling from Southampton to Bremerhaven he remained on board for a talk.

Now Brüning had invited me to dine with him and his party in his suite, but on the advent of Mr Sackett I at once told the Chancellor's secretary, Erwin Planck, that I would forgo this pleasure so as to give more time for the great men to talk together. Back, however, came a message that the Chancellor and the Ambassador had already got down to it and that I was still expected to dinner. I went, and Mr Sackett was there too. I had known and liked him in Berlin and we had horseflesh in common.

Later that evening Brüning talked to me alone. He said that before Mr Sackett went on leave he had asked him to take a special message to President Hoover giving him much the same information as he had given to the British Prime Minister at Chequers and urging that *some* gesture be made by America to encourage not only Germany but Europe as a whole. That afternoon the Ambassador had said that he had seen the President on two occasions and had given him Brüning's message. There was, however, no good news from Washington. The President had vouchsafed no gleam of hope.

'And, by the way,' said Brüning as he bade me good night, 'there may be an attempt to assassinate me tomorrow at Bremerhaven. The Chief of Police has reported that they have word of a plot, but so far have not been able to make any arrests.'

I was up betimes next morning, and as we entered the harbour of Bremerhaven I saw that the end of the pier, which was always painted white, had been decorated in gigantic letters of red and black with the Nazi slogan of *Deutschland erwache* (Germany awake!). I imagined that this had not been unobserved by the Chancellor, who, I knew, was also an early riser.

As the great *Europa* moored alongside the pier and the gangways came aboard, I watched as Brüning and his suite prepared to disembark. As the Chancellor paused at the moment of descent, there was a sudden stir in the crowd below, and I saw a police inspector knock up the arm of a young man. A shot rang out harmlessly, a pistol hurtled over the heads of the crowd and the would-be assassin was pinioned. Brüning proceeded to disembark with absolute composure.

The effect of returning empty-handed from Chequers was a grave blow to the Chancellor's political stature. It had been confidently hoped that a moratorium on reparation payments would result from the conference, and when it did not he was under great pressure to make it unilaterally. Crisis rumours dominated Berlin – in the clubs, in the drawing-rooms and around the smoke-tiered *Stammtisch* of the Taverne. Would Brüning resign? If so, who would succeed him? Would the President send for Hitler? Were the Nazis planning a coup? Could the Reichswehr be trusted? Chaos reigned on the stock exchange and in the money markets. During this week of panic over a milliard gold marks were withdrawn from the Reichsbank, which tended to increase rather than diminish the volume of the crisis.

It was at this time that Hans Luther, who had been Chancellor at the time of Locarno and had been appointed President of the Reichsbank on Schacht's resignation, asked me to lunch at the bank. He was remarkably calm, considering the circumstances, for his opening conversational gambit was a statement of some importance. 'This is a historic day in German banking,' he said quietly, 'for the first time in our history we have not enough gold to cover our paper.' Everything is, of course, relative. Today, when international finance has become so complicated that few can fathom its intricacies, this remark might be of little significance, but in that more conventional period it was of staggering importance, and, in fact, very shortly thereafter an international rediscount credit of £20,000,000 was necessary to help the Reichsbank over the end of the month.

But Brüning did not lose his head – he 'kept his cool', as we say today. He had, he assured me, no intention of resigning but he did mean to reconstruct his cabinet further to the Right and take the portfolio of foreign affairs himself. He also admitted that he did not quite know what would happen next.

It is difficult to recapture or to describe the climate of despair which settled over Germany in these June days. It was like being suspended in a vacuum, isolated from reality, waiting for some cataclysm to occur which should break the spell which held everyone in thrall. On the evening of Saturday, 20 June, the German people went to bed with a sense of impending catastrophe, and awoke with no reason to hope for its relief. I rode in the Tiergarten that Sunday morning and on my way to the park I noted that larger congregations than usual seemed to be attending churches of all denominations. Their faces were grey and drawn. Men and women had reached the conclusion that prayer and divine intervention were their only source of salvation now.

An hour or so later as I rode home the long-prayed-for miracle had happened. As the congregations streamed out into the streets they were greeted by newsboys selling special newspaper editions announcing President Hoover's proposal for a year's moratorium of payments of reparation and inter-Allied debts as from 1 July. The effect was amazing. A grey blanket of depression seemed to have been lifted from the German souls; a blanket which had suffocated for days all processes of thought and hope. People smiled and laughed and shook hands. Some went back into the churches to give thanks to God. It occurred to few that this miraculous act might not betoken a new dawn in international affairs.

And yet it was not to be. The whole psychological impact of the Hoover proposal, especially for Germany, depended upon its instant acceptance by all interested parties. This to Brüning offered a new lease of life, a breathing space in which to give the German people an opportunity to recover their sense of balance and not to hurl themselves in desperation into the arms of either the Nazis or the Communists. But this was exactly what did not happen. Pierre Laval ruined the effect of the President's proposals by adopting dilatory tactics based on the need for firm assurances that when the Hoover Year was up there would be no doubt about the resumption of reparation payments by Germany under the Young Plan schedule. Now everybody knew, including probably Laval himself, that once these payments had been discontinued they would never be resumed; this we all believed would follow as the night the day. Yet for two mortal weeks he dragged out negotiations in Paris before France would give her assent on 6 July, a full week after the date set by the President for its coming into force. By that time, though the moratorium had become a living fact, much of the gilt had been rubbed off the gingerbread. Its psychological effect had greatly diminished.

Nor did Laval stop at wrecking the psychological benefits of the Hoover moratorium. His manipulations, blackmail, pressures and cajoleries; his unscrupulous use of French gold to achieve all that French chauvinism could desire, continued throughout the summer and autumn, until it received a substantial setback at the hands of the new British National Government which Ramsay MacDonald had formed with Tory support. On 20 September 1931, the inevitable but incredible happened. In order to place herself out of reach of a direct attack by France upon sterling, Britain abandoned the gold standard and devalued the pound.

I am not likely to forget that day. In the dog-days of August I had moved my little establishment from Fallingbostel to Garmisch-Partenkirchen, where I had rented a villa in the grounds of the larger establishment of the former Crown Princess Cecilie of Prussia. I had two reasons for doing this; it was time that my horses had a change of air, and the mountain breezes of the Bavarian alps were beneficial to both of us, and I also thought it timely to test the climate of ideas in southern Germany, more particularly in Munich, the Nazi Party headquarters.

In those dear dead days of international confidence one did not even have to have a letter of credit from one's bank. I had standing drawing accounts wherever I found it convenient to do so, and it was always an accepted thing that one could cash an English five-pound note at any branch of the Reichsbank. All this delightful dream world disappeared in a flash on the morning of 21 September 1931. I had the unnerving experience of having my five-pound notes rejected and I was also refused any form of currency exchange. And there was I with no other resources than the money I had in my pocket-book and with the rent of a villa drawing near, a feed bill for three horses, a petrol bill for the car, wages for a groom and two house-servants and the usual tradesmen's accounts coming in at the end of the month.

It was an unenviable dilemma, and took some thinking out. I had just enough cash for a one-way air-ticket to England, and I discovered that, though one could not get marks in exchange for sterling in Germany, one could buy them on the open market in London. I therefore telegraphed my faithful secretary, Margaret Dunk, to purchase a substantial amount on twenty-four hours' credit. I then interviewed my landlord and employees and told them that I proposed to fly to London and obtain the necessary funds to carry on and would return immediately. In the meantime they could have the horses and the car as security, the sale of which, in the event of my levanting, would cover more than comfortably the collective sum which I owed them. They proved willing to take what was, after all, a pretty safe gamble, and by the twenty-fifth I had returned to Germany once more solvent.

In the months which followed it did not require any major degree of observation to reach the conclusion that, politically, economically and financially, the situation in Germany was rapidly deteriorating. Brüning was governing, albeit constitutionally, by means of decrees, which required subsequent ratification by the Reichstag, and a majority for this was only forthcoming because the Social Democrats, seeing at last the folly of their earlier opposition to Brüning's reforms and aghast at the consequences thereof, gave him their support. Hitler's star was in the ascendant; the country in sheer desperation was responding more and more to Nazi propaganda, and an imminent confrontation was inevitable on account of the impending presidential election, consequent upon the termination of Marshal von Hindenburg's term of office in March 1932. It was virtually certain that Hitler would stand as a contestant.

It was now that Kurt von Schleicher began to assert himself, even coming somewhat into the open. His conversations began to betray his objectives and his ambitions. One evening in the early spring of 1932 I was dining with a group of friends, of whom 'Knick' was one, at the Königin Restaurant on the Kurfürstendamm when von Schleicher's party arrived at the next table. The general was resplendent in full uniform, with a scarlet-lined cloak which he removed with a flourish, and in excellent spirits. His bald head gleamed in the harsh lights, and he laughed a good deal. Suddenly the dance-band stopped with the abruptness of syncopation and von Schleicher, whose voice had been raised to be heard by his friends above the music, was overheard declaiming: 'What Germany needs today is a strong man'; and he tapped himself significantly on the chest.

When I told Brüning of this incident at our next meeting, adding for good measure though perhaps inelegantly that I wouldn't trust the General further than I could throw a bull by the tail, it was the occasion of our only disagreement – at least until many years later when, after the Second World War, he withdrew both his friendship and his confidence from me. On this occasion he rounded on me with some asperity, saying that I had always been prejudiced against von Schleicher and implying indirectly that I was trying to make mischief. I took this in silence, for I knew that his nerves were badly frayed, and his ill-humour soon passed. I only wish to God that he had been right and I wrong.

Brüning, had he known it, was now entering on the penultimate stage of his battle for the soul of Germany. In the forthcoming presidential election he knew that, once Hitler had declared his candidacy, there was one man, and one alone, who could beat him and that was Hindenburg, even though he was then in his eighty-fifth year, and with infinite difficulty he persuaded the Marshal to stand again. The full burden of the campaign fell upon Brüning, and never have I admired more greatly his unflagging endurance, rising to the emergency with magnificent courage. For the first time it was discovered that he was an orator. I attended a number of his meetings in Berlin and in Silesia where he spoke to vast audiences, compelling their attention with magnetism and personal charm. He suddenly became a warm public figure, which he had never been before, and I was impressed beyond measure with the masterly and gallant way in which he dealt with the truly vitriolic tactics of his Nazi opponents, who employed every vulgarity and ballyhoo of the circus parade.

Unsparingly Brüning flogged his weary spirit forward, and his gallant single-handed struggle is among the epic performances of modern politics.

For this was no ordinary election. Never was there a more reluctant candidate than Hindenburg, and for a very understandable reason. At his first electoral contest in 1925 he had been the candidate of the Right, the darling of reaction, the man who should redeem the Republic from the taint of socialism. Seven years later the whole position was reversed and all his traditional affinities were ranged against him behind his opponent. To Hitler's banner rallied the upper classes of the Protestant north, the German Crown Prince, the great industrialists of the Ruhr and the Rhineland and the powerful agrarian interests of the *Landbund*, while behind them, in the dusk of the corridors of power, Kurt von Schleicher wove his intrigues. Behind the Marshal were the embattled forces of the very elements he had fought and defeated in 1925: the Centre Party and the Roman Catholic Church, the Social Democrats and the trade unions and the Jews.

Thanks to the indefatigable efforts of Brüning, the Marshal was re-elected on 10 April 1932 after a second ballot, and by a handsome majority. But he was ungrateful. In the course of the hard-fought campaign he had been subjected to much insult and vilification from his old associates, who had not scrupled to call him a traitor to his class, his caste and his traditions. This had wounded him deeply, and he found little comfort in the fact that he had now become the idol of the Left, who looked upon him as their protector against the terror which the Nazis promised to let loose once they came to power. In his muddle-headed octogenarian thinking his resentment centred upon the one man who had sweated blood to bring him victory – Heinrich Brüning – and in his growing disenchantment with his Chancellor, whom he had once agreed was 'the best since Bismarck', he was titillated by Kurt von Schleicher.

Wearied though he was by the rigours and strain of the election campaign, Brüning now prepared for his final encounter abroad in his desperate rearguard action to protect the freedom of the German people against the growing menace of National Socialism. He went to Geneva to make his last bid for an adjustment of the restrictions on German armaments. I tagged along. On 26 April he met Ramsay MacDonald, Mr Stimson, the American Secretary of State, Norman Davis, American Ambassador-at-large and Dino Grandi, the Italian Foreign Minister. André Tardieu, the French Prime Minister, had returned to France to take part in an election campaign, but it was felt that if an agreement among the others was reached in principle he could be called back to Geneva in an emergency.

And indeed an agreement was reached in principle. Brüning made a brilliant and persuasive plea for German equality in armaments with a detailed plan as to how this should be accomplished. The British, Americans and Italians agreed that his contention was both justified and reasonable and that his proposals were practical and workable. A formula had therefore been found which satisfied four out of the five former Allied Powers and for just a moment a gleam of hope rejoiced our souls. Brüning made a hit at Geneva with all whom he encountered. He was recognised as one of the leading statesmen of Europe; a worthy successor to Stresemann.

An urgent message was sent to Tardieu to return and set the seal of general approval on the agreement, but here fate again intervened. Kurt von Schleicher, meeting with the French Ambassador, André François-Poncet, at a dinner-party in Berlin, had tendered him private advice that France would be well advised not to negotiate with Brüning, who was 'on the way out' and whose successor, whom he named, France would find more amenable. Acting on this intelligence, Tardieu made more of an attack of laryngitis than he otherwise might have done and remained in Paris. Brüning's last hope was dead.

He returned to Berlin on 1 May to find that von Schleicher, despite all Brüning's faith in him, was now openly against him. By machinations of his own, he devised the elimination of Gröner, by the time-honoured euphemism of telling him that he no longer 'enjoyed the confidence of the Army' as Minister of Defence, thereby rendering his resignation inevitable. Not even an appeal by the Chancellor to the newly elected President could reverse the verdict of the generals bewitched by von Schleicher. Gröner retired with great dignity and reserve.

The scales had at last fallen from Brüning's eyes, and he now saw von Schleicher in his true colours. Characteristically he took the first opportunity of confronting him. Some months later, when he himself was in retirement in the hospital of St Hedwiga, he told me of this interview. Disillusioned and therefore the more shocked and embittered, especially at von Schleicher's treatment of Gröner, who had treated him as a son, Brüning spoke his mind in no uncertain terms. He added that having undermined the confidence of the army, von Schleicher must now himself become Defence Minister and restore it. 'I will, but not in your Government,' was the reply.

In the Chancellor's library, where Bismarck had once planned the greatness of the German Empire, they talked for hours. Brüning, the scholar-paladin, with the light of honest anger in his eyes; von Schleicher, the dandy officer, who could not meet the other's stern gaze. At last, as the new day broke in a grey dawn, Brüning brought the conversation to a close on a note of prophecy. Von Schleicher was leaning against a book-case, his face pale and haggard, sweating slightly under the lash of the castigation he had received. Brüning stood in front of him.

'The difference between us as soldiers', he said, 'was that I fought in the line and you served on the staff. In the line, with the machine-gun corps, we learned to control our nerves and to hold our fire sometimes till the enemy were almost on us. At the end of the war it was G.H.Q., not the army, that lost its head in a panic. We could have fought on, it was you who threw up your hands. And when the time comes, General von Schleicher, you will give up your battle before it is lost and you will become caught in your own intrigues.' He spoke truly.

With the departure of Gröner from the Cabinet on 12 May 1932, Brüning's own days were numbered. I saw him nightly during these final two weeks of his Chancellorship, and he told me much, of which I made copious notes and which I used in the writing of The Wooden Titan later. The story is too complicated to repeat here for von Schleicher was as envious as a fox and, as Mr Jorrocks remarked, 'a damned unpleasant fox at that'. Brüning himself was stoical, even fatalistic. He had done all that he could and had failed. Fate had been against him almost from the start, but he was not above self-questioning and realised some of the errors and miscalculations into which he had unwittingly fallen.

The end came on 30 May when he had his final interview with Hindenburg and emerged from it Chancellor ad interim until his successor had been appointed. I saw him the following day and he gave me a graphic account, but he also added that the unkindest cut of all had come on his return to the Chancellery from the President's Palace. There awaiting him he found an urgent message from the American embassy. The American representative at Geneva, Hugh Gibson, had met secretly with the new French premier, Edouard Herriot, at Lyons and had obtained his approval for the terms which Brüning had proposed, and which Tardieu had rejected, as a sound and honest basis for the negotiation of a new international armaments agreement. The message from the embassy was: 'Persuade Brüning to return to Geneva as soon as possible, for there is every prospect of his speedy success there.' But Heinrich Brüning was no longer in a position to reap the harvest that he had sown.

For me it is an article of faith that the tragedy of Brüning is the tragedy of Weimar. He wished to do so much, he was allowed to accomplish so little. He was fated to be the undertaker rather than the physician. In his desire to carry on the policy of reconciliation he was no less eager than Rathenau and Stresemann, yet it was his role to initiate the policy of repudiation. There was no greater believer in German parliamentary institutions than he, yet under the irresistible pressure of events it was he who struck the first blow at their foundations by introducing government by decree. None desired more passionately the welfare and happiness of the German people, yet he became known as the 'Hunger Chancellor', and was forced to impose the most crushing of burdens. It would have been difficult to find a greater German patriot, yet he was hounded from office and from his country for 'lack of patriotism'. Like Austen Chamberlain, 'he played the game according to the rules and always lost it', but to his less scrupulous successors was conceded all that he had sought to achieve and more. His vital weakness was that, being the soul of loyalty himself, he trusted blindly and without question those who had pledged their word to him and then had forsworn it.

VII

A sense of shock ran through the chancelleries of Europe at the news of Brüning's demission to be followed by a guffaw of incredulous laughter when the name of his successor as Reich Chancellor was announced. For the man whom Kurt von Schleicher had chosen to be his puppet in ruling the Reich – a role which Brüning had steadfastly refused to play – was none other than my old racing acquaintance Franz von Papen.

Indeed, had it not been for the critical and threatening situation, the whole thing would have been farcical. As it was it partook of tragi-comedy.

There may have been stupider politicians than von Papen but, if so, I have not encountered them. There were really very few virtues that one could attribute to him save the valour of ignorance and the imperturbability of supreme conceit. Frivolous, irresponsible and facetiously witty; unversed in politics, save for a spell in the extreme Right wing of the Centre Party in the Prussian Diet, Papen saw no difficulties in coping with the complicated and dangerous situation which confronted him and entertained no doubts as to his ability to outwit Hitler. He ignored completely the fact that he had no vestige of support in the Reichstag and that Hindenburg had just recently been re-elected by an outstanding majority of the Left and Centre. He was prepared to govern with or without parliament and depend for his authority on the bayonets of the Reichswehr if necessary. When I called upon him at his office soon after his appointment he reminded me of nothing so much as a cocky little housesparrow, and he assumed the frightening burdens of his office with all the disproportion of – to use a favourite phrase of my father's – 'a tom-tit on a round of beef'. He was not an evil man, like Hitler, nor even a bad man, like von Schleicher. He was simply 'clueless' as to how to control a predicament which would have defeated a far more experienced and able exponent of the political art.

'Now I can have a cabinet of my own friends,' had been Hindenburg's last muttered remark to Brüning, and this was exactly what Papen gave him. Among his nine ministers were five barons and one count, with General Kurt von Schleicher as Minister of Defence. For the first time in the history of the Republic organised labour was not represented.

If he had but known it, acceptance of ministerial office was von Schleicher's first major error. His forte was clandestine and crepuscular intrigue, protected and concealed from public life. Once, however, he accepted the responsibilities of cabinet rank, which entailed sitting on the ministerial bench in the Reichstag, he became an open target for his many enemies. As Brüning warned him, he was to became caught in his own intrigues.

But for the moment von Schleicher was riding high. Papen was appreciative of the General's influence in his appointment as Chancellor, and Hindenburg was delighted with his new chief minister who flattered him and made him laugh – no one could be funnier than Papen when he chose – and was generally very unlike Brüning who had always been reminding the Marshal of his duty. Hindenburg could refuse his 'Fränzchen' nothing, least of all a dissolution of the Reichstag and fresh elections, which he had refused to Brüning.

If I had been correct in my assessment of von Schleicher's character, I had been woefully in error in my judgement of Hindenburg. I had hitherto entertained a certain admiration for the veteran Field-Marshal, regarding him as the ideal type of single-minded patriot who had twice emerged from well-earned retirement to answer his country's call to further service, and having every claim to the title of *Vater des Volkes* and the more familiar and endearing designation *Der alte Herr*. Moreover, during this first term of office he had displayed a marked respect for the Constitution and his position as chief of state. He had supported successive chancellors even in unpopular actions once he was convinced that their policies were right and proper.

Englishmen are apt to be generous and magnanimous to a defeated enemy – one recalls the enthusiastic reception accorded by the London crowds to Marshal Soult at Queen Victoria's coronation – and to many in England the old Marshal was highly respected as a former enemy of considerable standing who had not infrequently beaten the Allies on two fronts but whom we had eventually succeeded in defeating.

I shared this view and, although I had for some years been collecting material for a book on Germany during the First World War and the Weimar Republic, the idea of writing this in the form of a biography of Hindenburg did not occur until this fateful summer of 1932. The occasion was a dinner party at the Wannsee Yacht Club on the evening of the day after it had been announced that there were to be new general elections (16 July). For once we were a naval rather than a military party, because our host was Gottfried Treviranus, who had been a minister in Brüning's cabinet and, in a sense, his 'floor manager' or chief whip in the Reichstag. 'Trevi' had begun his career as a naval officer and had been flag-lieutenant to Grand-Admiral von Tirpitz. He had fought at the Battle of Jutland – or, as the Germans call it, Skagerrak – in a battle-cruiser and had been awarded the Iron Cross (First Class). He was very much a 'funny man', but one of great political ability. Fanatically loyal to Brüning, he too had seen through von Schleicher at an early date.

Among his other guests was Captain von Müller, who had been commanding officer of the celebrated commerce raider *Emden*, which after a series of depredations on British shipping, had eventually been brought to book by the Australian light cruiser *Sydney*, in November 1914. Müller, after having fought a good fight, ran his ship, a blazing wreck, ashore on a coral reef. There was another distinguished veteran of the First War, I remember, an Admiral Ludwig von Schröder, who had commanded the Marine Corps on the Western Front, and, along with many decorations, had earned the nickname of the 'Lion of Flanders'.

The conversation turned on the most important news item of the day, which was that President von Hindenburg had given his personal guarantee that the forthcoming elections should be held with full freedom and liberty of the voters. It was felt by most of those among our company that this presidential pledge would allay in great measure the trepidation of those who had feared that the voting might have been held under the 'protection' of Reichswehr bayonets.

If the President had given his word everything would be all right. Such was the confidence reposed in him.

At length, however, a very different view was advanced by Admiral von Schröder. 'Hindenburg's record is a bad one,' he said. 'Ludendorff won his battles for him, and he betrayed Ludendorff; the Kaiser made him a Field-Marshal, and he betrayed the Kaiser; the Right elected him in 1925, and he has betrayed the Right; the Left has elected him in 1932, and he has betrayed the Left. I would not put too much faith in Hindenburg's promises.'

This, I remember, seemed to me little short of blasphemy and I left the party in a very puzzled frame of mind. On the one hand were my own previously held views of veneration for the Marshal; on the other a kind of nagging recollection of the way in which both Brüning and Gröner had been treated at their dismissals. There might be something to the admiral's strictures. Within that week I had taken two momentous personal decisions. One was to transform the original plan of my book into a biography of Hindenburg, in the course of which I would sift with greatest care all possible evidence for and against the admiral's censure; the other was to liquidate all my assets in Germany because I was now convinced that, unless something miraculous occurred, Hitler would be in power within a year. I was wrong by six months.

The process of liquidation came first and was a sad one. I terminated my lease at Fallingbostel, sold my beloved horses and my faithful Great Dane and paid off my stable hands. When all was completed and I had totted up my accounts for these three years I found I was twenty-five pounds to the good and had had a wonderful time into the bargain.

My other problem I took to Brüning, whom I used to visit regularly in his retreat at St Hedwiga's hospital, where he was doted upon by the good sisters, who kept his sparsely furnished cell-like room bright with flowers. I used to bring him Rhine wine, cigars and gossip, and when I told him of my decision to write a book on the Marshal he opened up in even greater detail than before. He told me all, or as much as he decently could, including the fact that, to add insult to injury, von Papen had offered him the post of Ambassador to London, an offer which he had peremptorily refused. Brüning urged me to go and see Gröner. This I was only too ready to do for I really admired him, and from him I learned of the circumstances of the Kaiser's departure from Spa and of Ebert's enquiry about accepting the peace terms and how on both of these occasions Hindenburg had 'passed the buck' to Gröner. He also told me that he had had indirect word

General Hans von Seeckt

General Wilhelm Gröner

Heinrich Brüning

General Kurt von Schleicher

General von Schleicher
and Franz von Papen
at the Grünewald Races

Benito Mussolini

To John Wheeler - Bennet
with cordial regards
Roma 25 febbraio 1935 - XIII -   Mus

from the Kaiser sympathising with him on his dismissal and saying that he too had suffered from Hindenburg's vacillating pusillanimity. And he told me, with remarkably little rancour, of the insults and calumnies he had suffered, even after his name had been cleared by a Court of Honour.

'But why', I asked him, 'didn't you do more to protect your name and reputation?'

'Because I believed that in the interests of the New Army the myth of Hindenburg should be preserved,' was his reply. 'It was necessary that one great German figure should emerge from the war free from all blame that was attached to the General Staff. That figure had to be Hindenburg.' Gröner was, as Brüning said of him, 'Ein fabelhafter Mann', decent through and through. Alas, I was to find that the admiral's views on Hindenburg were only too well founded.

Meantime von Papen was taking his fences in domestic politics at a perilous pace. The July elections resulted in the clearly expressed fact that, whatever the electorate *did* want, they very definitely did not want Franz von Papen and his reactionary 'Cabinet of Barons'. He was, however, completely undeterred by this and proceeded to further excesses with an assured equanimity, at which one stood fascinated if aghast.

He expelled the Prussian government by force and imposed a Commissioner, responsible to himself, in place of the Diet, and he made a *coup de main* against the Communist Party headquarters in the Karl Liebknecht House in the Bülowplatz. On the evening of this latter occasion Knick and I were dining together at Pelzer's (where they used to have the best prawn salad I have ever tasted) when the proprietor came over to our table. 'Have you heard that there is shooting in the Bülowplatz, gentlemen?'

It was enough. We were out of his restaurant and into my car as quickly as we could sign the bill and went tearing through the twilight. We soon found that it was a major police operation for which a number of young constables had been drafted in from the country districts. They were nervous 'rookies', as we were to find out. It appeared that there were three cordons of police, at the first of which we were required to abandon the car. Knick, of course, had his press credentials and I had a police pass which my old friend the Commandant of the Blue Police, a grand man and a perfect policeman, had given me as a favour. We produced these, were given the 'green light', and went forward. Suddenly, out of the darkness, there came a blinding beam of an electric torch and a somewhat uncertain young voice saying, 'Hands up!' We complied, saying that we had official passes. 'Show them.' said the young policeman. I put one hand down towards my breast-pocket, but at once felt a jab in the ribs from an automatic pistol – never a pleasant sensation. With infinite patience we explained to the young man, who had never been in Berlin before and was thoroughly unnerved by the whole operation, that we could either keep our hands up indefinitely or put them down for a sufficient time to produce our papers. Which would he prefer us to do? After deep thought he opted for seeing the papers, and having studied them closely but, I suspect, uncomprehendingly, he allowed us to pass through the second cordon unscathed.

We were now approaching the third cordon and the scene of action. The Bülowplatz, as I recall it, was (for I think it has now disappeared) about the size of Hanover Square, with one blank side and streets entering from each of the other three. On the left hand side of the square was a rather crummy little movie-theatre, which, it being Sunday, was closed and dark. We were walking up the street opposite the blank side of the square and as we entered it we found an extraordinarily well-organised military position. There were some half-dozen armoured cars, a number of searchlights – unlit at the moment – interspersed with riflemen prone on their bellies with their weapons cuddled against their cheeks. Out of the darkness came a police-lieutenant whom Knick knew personally and who was suitably impressed by my pass. He explained the situation to us.

'The Karl Liebknecht House is over there.' He pointed to the buildings opposite. 'The Commies are on the roof and are shooting at our chaps. So far we haven't opened up, but we've cut off all power and light around the whole square. We use the searchlights only every now and then because they make a target. So keep clear of them. In fact, if I were you, I'd go home.'

As he spoke one of the searchlights swept the opposite side with its white beam and a bullet struck the open surface of the square just in front of the riflemen – and us. If, as Knick has been kind enough to write in the passage which I have quoted at the end of my first chapter, I displayed 'imperturbability' at this moment, it was the best piece of acting I have ever done. I felt far from imperturbable. I had seen much street-fighting and rioting in various parts of the world, but this was the first time I had been directly under fire, I confess that I found it unpleasant but also exhilarating. I took cover behind an armoured car and from this comparatively safe position became an avid witness of what was first melodrama and later tragedy.

The scene was like something at the old Lyceum. It was bright moonlight and the stars shone clearly, but there was no other light.

One could see dark figures on the roofs opposite silhouetted against the summer night sky. They would take cover behind a chimney stack, fire at the police and then clamber quickly to another stack and repeat the process. One could see the flash of their rifles, then hear the sharp crack and then the thud of a bullet on the square. Every now and then the searchlights would play their long beams over the roofs and the police, with admirable restraint, would fire into the air. So far as I could see there had been no fatal casualties, though some police had been wounded by flying splinters. There was something unreal about the whole thing.

Then came shocking tragedy. In an attempt to end the affair peacefully, our police lieutenant went forward with great *sang-froid* and through a megaphone called on the Communists to surrender, as it was the intention of the police to occupy the Karl Liebknecht House by force if necessary. There was a silence from the roofs, but suddenly a rifle cracked from the ticket office of the cinema on our left, which was in complete darkness. The lieutenant fell with a bullet between the eyes. It was a remarkable shot, and the marksman must have been a former sniper with war experience. The young officer was killed instantly, and an N.C.O. who went out to bring him in met a similar fate. For a moment there was a deathly silence as the moon shone down on the two bodies lying in a widening pool of blood.

And then 'all hell broke loose'. Armoured cars went into action, machine-guns opened fire, and the riflemen fiercely replied to the shots from the roof. The front of the Karl Liebknecht House was pitted with bullets, and not a window remained unbroken; the façade of the cinema was shattered by machine-gun fire. It was a shambles from which I was glad to retreat. I never did know what the casualties were; but it was to such a pass that democracy had come in the final months of the Weimar Republic.

Franz von Papen, having failed to obtain any but the smallest support for his domestic policies, essayed to gain some increase in prestige in the field of foreign affairs. The moment was, in fact, propitious. The Hoover moratorium year was drawing to its close, and some agreement had to be reached as to what should succeed it. An international conference was therefore summoned at Lausanne, at which Ramsay MacDonald, Edouard Herriot and Franz von Papen forgathered, with representatives of other powers, to consider the future of reparation payments and inter-Allied debts. It was in effect a pretty dismal performance and produced little of material value. When the conference closed on 9 July, Germany had achieved little save an empty declaration that reparations were at an end – a fact which most Germans had known for some time past, and even this had only been won by conceding the principle of a final payment, though this again was tacitly understood to be a mere *façon de parler*.

What Germany did not gain were the much hoped for political concessions in the matters of 'war guilt' and disarmament and, although von Papen announced in the German press on 11 July that, since the reparation chapter of the Treaty of Versailles had been declared to have lapsed, the 'war guilt' clause, as an integral part of it, must be considered to have been erased with it, this was but a unilateral statement and found no echo either in the Final Act of the Lausanne Conference itself, nor subsequently in the other European capitals. Moreover the final Resolution which closed the first session of the Disarmament Conference on 23 July, gave no satisfaction to the claims which the German delegation had formally tabled for equality of status. It was, however, something more than had been accorded to Brüning in the field of reparations, and as Pope Pius XI acidly remarked: '*C'est peu, mais c'est toujours quelque chose.*'

Although my relations with von Papen were never on a warm and intimate footing as with Brüning, I still had access to the Reichskanzlei. Friends of mine at the Herrenklub were now among Papen's private secretaries and adjutants, and it was thus easy to get access to him. I dined with the Chancellor shortly after his return from Lausanne and was surprised to find him in his usual ebullient spirits. He insisted on regarding the outcome of the conference as a diplomatic coup for Germany and therefore a success for his own diplomacy. What, however, was inescapably funny were his imitations of his colleagues at Lausanne. As he mimicked them one could see Ramsay MacDonald's flowing locks and hear his Scottish burr uttering profound banalities; the long, depressing horseface of Neville Chamberlain; the cold and fishy eye of Sir John Simon and Edouard Herriot puffing his pipe with rotund good humour. Even von Papen himself was included, the Chancellor giving an exaggerated version of his own light frivolous humour.

It was a *tour de force* of which any music-hall or cabaret artist might well have been proud. I yelled with laughter, yet could not help thinking how different was this atmosphere of levity from the serious soul-searching conversations I had had in this same room with Brüning. But it was very funny.

Only once before have I known a 'turn' to equal this of Papen's, when some time in 1926 or so I was privileged to listen to as unlikely a performer as Sir Austen Chamberlain imitate, by speaking into an empty water-jug, the efforts of some of his political colleagues when broadcasting for the B.B.C.

There was also sheer farce mixed with the tragedy and comedy of these Berlin days. The July elections had resulted in a victory for the Nazis, who were returned as the largest party in the Reichstag with 230 seats. Papen's Government could rally only the 48 seats of the Nationalists and their allies. It was a ludicrous situation in itself but nothing compared with what was to follow.

The singularly unlovely building in the Königsplatz which housed the German Parliament for half a century had witnessed few more curious episodes than the session of the Reichstag which opened on 9 September and closed three days later. Through the kindness of my friends in the Chancellor's secretariat I was lucky enough to obtain an excellent seat in the equivalent of the Distinguished Strangers' Gallery for the only two meetings of this shortest of parliaments.

By the rules of procedure the oldest member in age, regardless of party, presided over the first meeting at which the permanent president was elected for the session. The Communists had taken advantage of this to stage a demonstration. Among their deputies – and there were 89 of them – was Clara Zetkin, a veteran octogenarian revolutionary who, since she had lived for years in Moscow, had been elected *in absentia*. This redoubtable old lady, to everyone's surprise, flew to Berlin and insisted on exercising her privilege to preside. There she sat in the Speaker's Chair, a grey wizened little figure, staring down at a House of which two-fifths wore the brown uniform of her inveterate enemies. Beside her stood Ernst Torgler, the parliamentary leader of the Communist Party, stooping every now and then to prompt her in the long discourse in defence of Marxism which quavered out in her weak old voice.

Whether in deference to the old lady's courage or whether held by the hopeless incongruity of the whole proceeding, Clara Zetkin was given an almost uninterrupted hearing, at the end of which she was lifted down from the platform swaddled in shawls like a mummy and returned to Moscow. It was at this point that the Reichstag resumed its usual appearance of a bear-garden. Amid tumult and uproar, Hermann Goering was elected to the Chair, and the House adjourned until 12 September.

With the full knowledge of the untenability of his position, but undeterred thereby, von Papen met the first business session with complete equanimity. By means best known to himself he had extracted from Hindenburg a decree of dissolution, which already bore the President's signature. Rarely can there have been another instance in history when a parliament's death warrant had been signed before it met.

The existence of the presidential decree had leaked – whether intentionally or not I do not know – with the result that the galleries of the House were packed at an early hour. In the diplomatic *loge* ambassadors and ministers jostled one another with little regard for protocol. The press gallery buzzed with rumours and conjecture. All expected drama but few were prepared for the farce which followed.

The Ministers filed on to their bench and the great bulk of Goering appeared in the President's chair. Serene and smiling, von Papen sat back, with all the appearance of having an ace up his sleeve. Ernst Torgler, on behalf of the Communists, moved a vote of censure on the Government. The Nazis, unwilling to vote in support of a Communist motion, yet anxious to embarrass the Government, moved for a half-hour delay in voting, and in a buzz of excitement the House adjourned.

The Chancellor called a meeting of the cabinet and announced his intention of dissolving parliament. Where, he asked, was the traditional Red Portfolio in which was the presidential decree? It was at once produced by the eager Erwin Planck, who had found no difficulty in transferring his allegiance from Brüning to von Papen. Now ensued anti-climax of the purest. As Planck told me shame-facedly afterwards, the Chancellor's jaw dropped when he opened the portfolio and for once he lost his vivacious equanimity; for it was empty. Consternation ensued; a search was instituted. The paper was clearly not in the Reichstag building. In an agony of apprehension Planck's car fled back through the Brandenburg Tor, and up the Wilhelmstrasse to the Chancellor's office. There he found the precious document on von Papen's writing table! He had forgotten to give it to Planck to put in the Red Portfolio. With but minutes to spare before the House was due to reassemble, the retrieved decree had received the Chancellor's counter-signature. The government was saved from humiliation if not from defeat.

Meantime in the chamber itself excitement had mounted. There was much visiting among the galleries and *loges* and great speculation. Again the cabinet filed into their places, von Papen bringing up the rear with his vulpine grin and waving the Red Portfolio with its precious contents at the diplomatic *loge*. The Chancellor at once demanded the word, but Goering chose to ignore him and announced that the Communists' vote of censure would be taken. The voting began and pandemonium broke loose. Von Papen remained standing; Goering continued to ignore him. White with anger, the Chancellor handed the Red Portfolio to Planck, who laid it on the President's desk, whence it slipped to the ground. Then he led his cabinet out of the House. The voting continued and the motion of censure was passed by 513 to 32. In the general uproar Goering could be heard declaring that the Government had been overthrown and the Reichstag then adjourned *sine die*. As we trooped out into the September sunshine most of us were wondering in some trepidation what would, or could, happen next.

'Fränzchen', however, was neither dismayed nor at a loss. He at once prepared for a new election campaign in which his government adopted the slogan of 'Support our ideas or we shall continue to govern alone until you do.' But the results of the polls on 6 November though they proved a considerable setback to the Nazis – whose seats fell from 230 to 196 – and a corresponding increase in the Communist votes from 89 to 100, were eloquent beyond measure or doubt that the German people would not support a Presidential Cabinet. It also became clear that this absurd and unrealistic state of things could not long continue. Bayonets are sometimes dangerous to use for other purposes than those for which they were originally intended. Poincaré found that you could not dig coal with them when he occupied the Ruhr, and even the pachydermous von Papen was now discovering that one cannot sit on them indefinitely with comfort. A *Putsch* of some sort from the extreme Right or the extreme Left seemed both imminent and inevitable unless some drastic change was wrought in the political situation. The general climate of ideas called for any kind of means, however unconventional, by which the Gadarene descent to the brink of disaster could be halted.

It seemed to me that even a government as invincibly lunatic as von Papen's was better than an ideological dictatorship, from which I felt we were only separated by a hair's breadth, and that therefore something should be done to improve its image. The only field in which this could be attained – Papen having won only an empty victory at Lausanne regarding reparations – was the reduction of armaments. The bureau of the Disarmament Conference was about to meet at Geneva to hear a statement from Sir John Simon, then Foreign Secretary, and this seemed a suitable opportunity for the German Government to make a *démarche*. I felt that something had to be done even if it were only a forlorn hope.

In a number of conversations with von Papen, his Foreign Minister, von Neurath, and State-Secretary von Bülow, I pointed out that Germany's attitude at the Disarmament Conference had so far been purely negative. They had rejected the draft Convention prepared by the Preparatory Disarmament Commission but had so far never stated what terms they would accept to satisfy their claim for equality. I urged with all the emphasis at my command that now was the moment to put all the cards on the table and to state openly what Germany wanted and what she was prepared to give in return. I also pointed out, which was not entirely popular with the inherently euphoric Chancellor, that time was running perilously short. As a basis for these proposals I suggested the draft terms Brüning had proposed at Geneva in April, which had been accepted by the British, Americans and Italians, and, though rejected by Tardieu had been approved by Herriot in June. After what seemed an interminable period of drafting and redrafting, a formula acceptable to the German Government was finally drawn up. It proposed no further concessions to Germany than those asked for by Brüning and offered not only the same guarantees on the part of Germany but some additional ones as well. I took the text with me to London, where I gave it to Vansittart.

My part in all this was, of course, unofficial and unauthorised, but it had the advantage in that the whole thing could thus be disavowed by the German Government if nothing came of it. Vansittart read the paper in silence and then drummed upon the table with his fingers. 'This will take a long time to be digested,' he remarked. 'We haven't got a long time to spare,' I answered, and I told him that I proposed to give publicity to the formula. Van did not attempt to dissuade me.

So on 15 November the following letter appeared in *The Times*:

Sir, – Before the public interest becomes completely absorbed in consideration of the French Disarmament Plan, and particularly in view of the Foreign Secretary's statement in the House of Commons on November 10, it is, I think, of great importance to emphasize the fact that the question of Germany's right to equality still remains unsettled, and that while this is so no advance can be made in the process of disarmament. May I, therefore, ask your assistance in putting forward the following formula as a means of solution of the problem of equality, and one which I have the best possible reason to believe would be acceptable to the German Government?

1. The new Convention to be drawn up by the Disarmament Conference, by general agreement, to supersede Part V. of the Treaty of Versailles.

2. The period of service in the Reichswehr to be partially reduced.

3. Germany to be able to create a volunteer Militia not to exceed

in numbers more than half the total number of the Reichswehr (i.e., according to present status, not to exceed 50,000 men).

4. Germany to be accorded the means of maintaining and supplying the Reichswehr and Reichsmarine on a more economic scale than that provided under the Treaty of Versailles, and under the same terms as other Powers.

5. Germany of her own free will to agree not to increase her fighting forces beyond the treaty limit for the period of the interval between the first and second Disarmament Conferences.

6. Germany to renounce immediately those aggressive weapons which the other nations agree to give up within a limited period of years.

7. Germany to have the right of 'token' equality in all categories of arms unlimited by the new Disarmament Convention.

8. Germany to undertake not to increase her normal average military budget despite the reorganisation outlined above.

It will be observed that the proposed concessions to Germany go no farther than those put forward by Dr Brüning to Mr MacDonald and Mr Stimson at Geneva in April of this year, of which the German aide mémoire of August 29 was merely a repetition. The Brüning proposals of April were 'sympathetically received' by Mr MacDonald and Mr Stimson. Certain of the guarantees were also proposed by Dr Brüning, and some have been added later.

I am, Sir, your obedient servant,

JOHN W. WHEELER-BENNETT.

The result of this, as far as I was concerned, was, as I had expected, an imperial wigging at the highest level. My head was washed first by Allen Leeper, on behalf of the Foreign Office, who, not unnaturally, bitterly resented the intervention of a non-professional on their preserves, and then by Malcolm MacDonald on the part of the Cabinet. Leeper was frankly furious and showed it; Malcolm was – and, I am happy to say, still is – an old friend of mine, and it was evident from his tone and manner that he was speaking to a brief with which he did not entirely sympathise.

What happened to me was, of course, of no consequence at all, but what was of interest, and of some small satisfaction to me, was that the von Papen formula, which was certainly the most constructive offer made by Germany in the whole course of the negotiations for equality, had been considered by Sir John Simon when he made his statement of policy at Geneva on 17 November. This was now accompanied by certain disarmament proposals by which it was hoped to effect a general reduction of armaments and went some way to meeting the German point of view. But, alas, by this time it was a case of 'too little and too late'.

There was a joke current in the political cabarets of Berlin at this time: 'General von Schleicher ought really to have been an admiral, because his military genius lies in shooting under water at his political friends.' No truer word was ever spoken, and to the long roll of victims of these 'torpedo attacks', which included Hans von Seeckt, Hermann Müller, Heinrich Brüning and Wilhelm Gröner, all of whom had given him trust and preferment, von Schleicher was about to add Franz von Papen. By devious means of his own he persuaded President von Hindenburg that 'Fränzchen' had shown himself incapable of dealing with the Nazis and he used once again the traditional formula that the Chancellor no longer enjoyed the confidence of the Army. With profound reluctance, for Hindenburg was fond of von Papen, who succeeded in making even the most serious problems seem amusing, he accepted Schleicher's arguments. The victory, however, was but pyrrhic, for Hindenburg's price for dismissing Papen was that Schleicher should assume the full burden of office himself. He insisted that the General became Chancellor.

The forty-five days of Kurt von Schleicher, which began on 3 December 1932, were an ever more complicated and shocking display of Byzantine duplicity, chicanery and betrayal. I have written of it in detail elsewhere and it is too intricate a story to repeat. Suffice it to say that the now thoroughly enraged von Papen was thirsty for revenge and was conspiring against his successor, with the powerful assistance of the President's son Oskar, to encompass his downfall at whatever price. Von Schleicher, for his part, was discovering the loneliness of the pinnacle of power, where he, who trusted nobody, was now trusted by none. Both sides were intriguing with the Nazis, under the impression that they could be brought into camp as hostages of a semi-military regime and the Nazis played with both of them and despised them both.

I did not see von Schleicher during his brief period of office, but I kept in touch with Erwin Planck who had now become the State-Secretary of the Chancellor's office (the equivalent of a Permanent Under-Secretary in Whitehall). From him I learned something of the steadily increasing isolation of the General and of his genuine bewilderment at the fact that the puppets who had for so long danced to his piping would now no longer respond to his manipulation. Indeed the strings which controlled them were in other hands.

The end came on 28 January 1933 when von Schleicher was summarily dismissed and von Papen was authorised to negotiate with Hitler on behalf of Hindenburg. On 30 January the Third Reich came into being.

It must in all fairness be recorded of Kurt von Schleicher – and how maddening it is to have to be fair to those whom one thoroughly dislikes and mistrusts! – that his first act as a private citizen was to call upon Brüning at St Hedwiga's hospital to make amends, to apologise and to ask forgiveness. 'You may think that your dismissal was rough,' he said, 'but, believe me, it was pleasant compared to mine.'

CHAPTER THREE

Brief Encounter with the Third Reich, 1933-4

I

IT is as well to remember that the Third Reich, that Thousand-Year Reich of Adolf Hitler's hopes and dreams, was not proclaimed as such when he took office as Chancellor on 30 January 1933. Indeed emphasis was laid on the fact that the new government was one of National Concentration based upon the parties of the Right. If Hitler was Chancellor, Franz von Papen was Vice-Chancellor, and remained at the head of the Prussian Government. The Nazis held but two portfolios in the Cabinet – Wilhelm Frick as Minister of the Interior and Hermann Goering as Minister with portfolio but also Minister of Interior in the Prussian Government under von Papen. The more perceptive observed that these two were key positions since between them Frick and Goering now controlled the greater part of the police forces of the Reich. Moreover, Alfred Hugenberg, the leader of the Nationalist Party, was included, and also Franz Seldte, the leader of the *Stahlhelm*, the Right-wing ex-servicemen's organisation which was more akin to the American Legion than the British Legion. It was also known that the new government had the unqualified backing of the Army, and that the new Minister of Defence, General Werner von Blomberg, enjoyed the complete confidence of both the President and von Papen, neither of whom seems to have known or suspected that he was at heart a crypto-Nazi. Above all the majestic figure of Marshal von Hindenburg gave a moral assurance to many waverers that all would now be well with Germany.

On paper, therefore, it seemed as if Franz von Papen had pulled off an amazing coup. He had made the National Socialist Party the hostage of the Right and of the Army. There were ample 'built-in' guarantees in the new political structure against a usurpation of power by Adolf Hitler and his followers. No wonder, when I saw him for the first time after the new government had been appointed, he was like a cock on a dunghill, crowing his own praises and demanding my congratulations on his superlative sagacity. I was reserved in my reply.

There were many, however, among one's friends and acquaintances, decent people of good family and upbringing, who for the moment were ready to give their support to the new government. It must be remembered that in the course of the fifteen years which separated that day from the Armistice of 1918, Germany had experienced governments of every kind of political combination and complexion, had suffered a terrifying national bankruptcy, had failed to obtain any major measure of treaty revision that was not already *de facto* and who genuinely believed that economic breakdown, a paralysing inflation and a Communist *Putsch* were both possible, probable and imminent. On these fears and memories Hitler had based his popular appeal. He had something for everyone in his bag of promises, and above all he offered an attractive – almost a romantic – prospect for youth. Where Brüning had called for sacrifices and had gained no concessions in return, Hitler offered pledges and made no concessions.

I offer these facts not in any way as an excuse for my friends' action but as an explanation. 'He's our last chance,' I heard over and over again in their houses when speaking of Hitler. 'We've got to let him have his opportunity. After all the Nazis are a minority in the government; the Old Man and 'Fränzchen' are sound at heart, and, if the worst comes to the worst, the Army can always turn the Nazis out.' It became a self-hypnotic chant which blinded and deafened many to what followed. The tragedy was that in their last argument they were right. The Army could have disposed of Hitler and the whole Nazi gang at any time during the next four years if they had had the leadership and the intestinal fortitude to do so.

For the Nazis, however, there was never any doubt as to the strength of their position. From my rooms in the Kaiserhof Hotel I watched the great torchlight procession which, on the night of 30 January 1933, wound its way through the city of Berlin, passing down the Wilhelmstrasse, where Hitler from the balcony of the Chancellery – almost opposite the Kaiserhof – took the first salute and, a little further along at the President's palace, Hindenburg also appeared to greet them. The *Stahlhelm* came first in their smart field-grey uniforms, marching with rigid military pace and bearing, and behind them the S.A. units, some having considerable drink taken and all bellowing the Party song, the *Horst Wessel Lied*, interspersed with mighty 'Heils' for the Führer.

Of this significant and not unterrifying sight, the political cabaret compères were soon to take advantage, and their victim was

Hindenburg not Hitler. As the Marshal watched the procession pass below him, the disciplined *Stahlhelm* and the shambling S.A., he was said to have muttered over his shoulder: 'Ludendorff, how well your men are marching and what a lot of prisoners they seem to have taken.'

On the night of 27 February Knick and I were again dining at Pelzer's and once again the manager gave us momentous news, which curtailed our meal. 'They say the Reichstag is burning, gentlemen.'

Hindenburg had granted Hitler a dissolution, and Germany had entered upon her third general election – the fifth if you count the two presidential election campaigns – within a twelvemonth. But the Nazi Party were not having it all their own way. The parties of the Centre and the Left were fighting gamely, and the Communists were campaigning with alarming success. For some days rumours were circulating in Berlin that some coup was in the making, for none doubted that Hitler intended to win at the polls by hook or by crook.

As Knick and I walked quickly towards the Reichstag we speculated on the method and meaning of the fire. The area was cordoned off but once again his press credentials and my police pass got us through and we found ourselves in a small lake of water in which fire-engines were hard at work, while hoses coiled and squirmed like great serpents. In a few minutes we saw a commotion at the entrance and down the ceremonial steps of the building came a dishevelled young man, stripped to the waist and hand-cuffed between two policemen. This was the semi-moronic Marinus van der Lubbe, who was later executed for his part in the proceedings. A short while later we also saw Goering throw a journalist – whom, it was later said, he had plucked bodily from a telephone-booth – down these same steps, at the foot of which he lay groaning.

Of the Reichstag fire much has been written and much more will doubtless be before the full truth is known – if it ever is. Of one thing there is no doubt, van der Lubbe was personally involved, but what his motives were or who prompted him to act in this criminal manner, and whether he was alone in his incendiary enterprise, is still disputed. Certainly contemporary opinion was in no doubt whatever. It was known that an underground passage connected the Reichstag President's residence with the Reichstag itself. It was at the same time alleged and widely believed that through this passage the matinée-idol leader of the Berlin–Brandenburg S.A., Karl Ernst, had led a fire-party into the building – it being remembered that Goering was President of the Reichstag at the time – to assist van der Lubbe in his work, which seemed a heavy job for one man. Within twenty-four hours the wags of Berlin had devised a riddle: 'Why did van der Lubbe take his shirt off?' 'Because', was the answer, 'it was a brown one.'

It is also of interest that, at a later date, Karl Ernst, and all those who had allegedly been implicated in carrying-out the fire were liquidated by firing squads, presumably, many thought, lest they might talk.

However, within a very short space of time, the responsibility for the Reichstag fire was pinned on the Communists; together with an added accusation that they had planned to poison the supply of drinking-water for Berlin and other acts of uncivilised and criminal nature. The Communist Party was proscribed.

The election campaign was the most bitter and brutal I have ever witnessed. Despite the pledge given publicly by both the President and the Chancellor that law and order should prevail, this did not prevent fifty-one opponents of the Government, by no means all of them Communists, from being killed during the campaign, and a far larger number from being badly beaten and manhandled. Opposition party meetings were broken up by S.A. men in uniform, and when Brüning went to speak at Kaiserslautern and I accompanied him, his audience found their interest in his discourse intermittently diverted by bursts of rifle-fire from the street-fighting outside.

Yet even with all these obstacles and disabilities, the Opposition parties made a good showing. The Communists lost only 20 seats, the Social Democrats only two, and the Centre actually gained three. However, the Government obtained between them 51 per cent of the total (the Nazis 49 per cent and the Nationalists 2 per cent), and in parliament, as Mr Churchill once remarked, 'one is sufficient.'

'How do you feel about things now,' I asked von Papen when we met after all the results were in, 'with the Nazis with 288 seats and your people only 52?' His complacency was utterly unruffled and he made the immortal reply: 'Nothing to worry about, my dear fellow; we can always outvote them in cabinet.'

Poor fool, with his incredible political ineptitude, his conceit and frivolity and his 'amateur riding' in politics; within a matter of weeks von Papen had been ousted by Goering as Prime Minister of Prussia and his influence reduced to the restricting limits of the office of Vice-Chancellor. Moreover, three additional Nazi Ministers, Goebbels, Hess and Röhm, had entered the Cabinet; Hugenberg had been dismissed, while Seldte and the *Stahlhelm* had cringed to the crack of the Nazi whip and had mounted the Swastika. Of all the 'built-in' guarantees, to which such emphasis had been given and in which so many had placed their foundering faith, only the Army remained, and the Army had neither the desire nor the courage to take action, though they knew that they had the power to do so. 'We shall tolerate this regime,' said Walther von Reichenau to me, 'just as long as it suits our interests to do so.'

A mounting wave of terror began to spread over Germany. As Prussian Minister of Interior Goering authorised the police who now wore swastika brassards, to shoot without fear of consequences and enlisted thousands of young Nazis as special constables to take what action they liked against Communists and Social Democrats. Frick, as Reich Minister of Interior, instituted the procedure of 'protective custody', meaning arrest without trial and confinement in concentration camps, wherein, said Frick, 'Marxists are trained to become useful citizens again.' Among those thus apprehended were a former President of the Reichstag and a former President of the Prussian Diet. In the 'Brown Houses' of the Nazi Party in Berlin and other cities Jews, Communists and Socialists – and even here and there a recalcitrant conservative – were beaten, tortured and often killed; political murders grew in number.

'How can you justify these outrages which are committed in the name of your government?' I asked von Papen at our next meeting. He was looking noticeably less assured, I noticed, and had difficulty in meeting my eyes. He simply shrugged his shoulders and gave what is perhaps the most despicable answer possible: 'You can't,' he said, 'make an omelette without breaking eggs.'

I put the same question to Count Lutz von Krosigk, the Minister of Finance. I had known him as a civil servant and found him always a kindly man of cultivated tastes, whom I would have classed as highly civilised; incidentally he was a former Rhodes scholar. How could he, I asked, remain a member of a government that not only countenanced but promoted such behaviour? His answer was at least honest, but to me it lacked nobility. 'Because I have a large family,' he said – an oblique reference to his pension on retirement. And stay he did, until the bitter end. Minister of Finance to von Papen, von Schleicher and Hitler, he ended his public career as Foreign Minister in the phantom government of Grand-Admiral Doenitz at Flensburg, where he made his one contribution to history when, in a broadcast to the German people on 2 May 1945, announcing their defeat, he used the term 'Iron Curtain' for the first time in the spoken word.[1] He too reappeared at Nuremberg.

It was not long before the Brown Terror, in the form of domestic espionage, began to infiltrate the lives of everyone. At first it was pretty amateurish. 'Bugging' – now a household word – was still in its comparative infancy forty years ago, and when one made a call from a telephone box one was aware of a pause and then a click as the monitoring record was turned on. This technique soon improved, however, and one dreaded the appearance of a telephone maintenance man who would suddenly arrive to rectify a fault which had never been reported. From then on it was assumed that a microphone had been inserted in the instrument not to record talks made on the telephone itself but conversation in the room in which the telephone was. It was not long before some inventive character discovered that a large tea-cosy placed over the telephone rendered it 'safe' and there was an immediate run on tea-cosies, but the enemy soon counter-attacked. The unwelcome visitor would now be an electrician to see about a short-circuit or some other defect in the lamps in several rooms, and once again the pall of uncertainty and fear would paralyse social life.

The technique of conducting a successful system of terror is to terrorise the maximum number of people with the minimum amount of effort. It is manifestly impossible to listen in to every telephone call or to overhear every conversation, but the art lies in the use of the spot-check, thereby letting people know when they were *not* being monitored. This itself was unnerving, but so was the increase in the spying by servants upon their employers – and even *vice versa*. One closed the door carefully and conducted conversations in a whisper. One looked over one's shoulder in a public place before speaking. One did not trust the mails. One chose with great care the rendezvous where one met one's friends. No one who has not experienced it can imagine the frighteningly oppressive atmosphere of a totalitarian régime.

Moreover it has its lasting effects. I assumed that the switchboard of the Kaiserhof 'tapped' all telephone conversations as a matter of course, and was increasingly discreet in consequence. I rarely wrote any letters, and those of the most innocuous. But the old fear of

---

[1] The story of the various original uses of the term 'iron curtain' is given in a book I wrote with Anthony Nicholls called *The Semblance of Peace* (London, 1972) p. 294.

being spied upon has never really left me. I am still, even after forty years, very careful on the telephone; I have a phobia against talking in a room with a door open; and a marked preference for sitting with my back to the wall in a restaurant. It is, I fear, irksome to my wife, but she is very understanding!

In these early days of the Revolution not even so distinguished a figure as Heinrich Brüning escaped harassment. At one moment he was being hunted from house to house, not daring to sleep two nights beneath the same roof. He made one exception to this rule, however, in which I was involved.

It was, I remember, a pleasant spring day, a Sunday, and I was spending it with Gottfried Treviranus out at his lakeside villa near Wannsee. Brüning turned up unexpectedly during luncheon and we were a very jolly party until a guarded telephone message informed us that the house in which Brüning had slept the night before had just been raided by the Gestapo.

The news put a damper on our gaiety, and we went into a council of war. After some discussion Brüning decided that, on the law of averages – which was as good a basis as any for taking a decision under these circumstances – having raided the place unsuccessfully the Gestapo would not return the following night. He therefore proposed to return to the same sleeping place. But how to get there? In a wild moment of irresponsibility I heard myself offering to drive him.

The shortest route entailed going across the heart of Berlin, which had its hazards, but, after all, what route didn't? We started off in my elderly but still quite powerful Packard, with Brüning in the back seat with the blinds pulled down. All went well until we reached the government quarter. Those who knew Berlin at that time – it is virtually unrecognisable now – will recall the Voss-strasse which skirted the Reich Chancellery. A traffic light controlled the crossing of the Wilhelmstrasse into the Wilhelmplatz, on which were situated both Goebbels' Ministry of Propaganda and my hotel, the Kaiserhof. The light was red as I drew up but I was at the head of the queue. The traffic was not heavy, for it was as yet too soon for the Sunday drivers to be returning from their country excursions. As I waited, to my horror, I heard the tramp, tramp of jackbooted feet. A squad of S.A. men drew up beside us. They also waited for the light.

Now I knew whom I had in the back of the car, but of course they didn't. I dared not look round and I could only pray that the fact that the blinds of the car were drawn would not arouse their suspicions. I confess I was scared stiff, and still the light didn't turn green. Cold sweat made my hands slippery on the steering wheel and I feared that I might not be able to grip it effectively. At last the green light appeared, and I have never got away from a traffic light so quickly, either before or since. I shot across the square and then slowed lest I should fall a victim to some over zealous traffic cop. Then by short cuts and side streets – for fortunately I knew that quarter of the city pretty well – I got the former Chancellor to his destination. When we did arrive he was as utterly composed as an old machine-gunner officer should be. As for me I bade him as warm a farewell as was compatible with my strong desire to 'get the hell out of there', and when I reached my hotel safely I had a couple of stiff brandies.

These early days of the Revolution were filled with tragedy and a growing terror and horror. The gaps in the ranks of one's friends seemed more frequent and the crowning agony was the sense that there was nothing one could do. That was the real anguish of the whole thing; one felt so hopelessly unable to help one's friends. It is true that, as a result of public outcry, both in England and elsewhere, certain distinguished persons, such as Kurt Holm, were released from custody, but these were very few and far between.

To me the most memorable and nightmarish of my experiences at this time was the session of the Reichstag which passed the Enabling Act. This was on 23 March 1933, and was a very different affair to that which I had last attended in the previous July. Here was no farce, no comedy, no grinning Chancellor, waving a Red Portfolio. What we saw was a grim set-faced Führer; a man bent upon power, ruthless and cruel. The very atmosphere of the place was one of death and destruction, for the Reichstag, the palladium of German parliamentary government, was being asked to do nothing other than commit suicide.

Hitler proposed to enact an emergency bill which would transfer for a period of four years the power of legislation from the Reichstag to the Cabinet who would even be empowered to change the Constitution if they saw fit in order to legalise such measures as might otherwise be held as unconstitutional. A nominal safeguard, one which appealed more to legalists than to apprehensive men of good will, provided that the rights and powers of the President should remain unimpaired. This, however, brought little comfort or security, partly because by this time all Germans knew that Hindenburg, both by reason of age and disposition, was a broken reed, and partly because a further provision of the bill vested in the Chancellor the principal presidential prerogative of ratifying legislation, in order, it was explained, 'to relieve the President of unnecessary work'.

Already the wits of Berlin were at work. 'Have you heard' a man would ask his friend, glancing over his shoulder to make sure he was not overheard, for such stories were now a penal offence, 'Hindenburg was at the Oranienburg Concentration Camp yesterday?' 'Oh, why?' 'He wanted to visit some of his electors.'

Hitler could count on a simple majority, but he desired a two-thirds majority to give his Enabling Bill full legal flavour and this he could not obtain without the 93 votes of the Centre and Bavarian Peoples Parties. Brüning had held his seat in the recent election and had been re-elected leader of the parliamentary group in the Reichstag, but the head of the Party itself was a wily cleric, Monsignor Ludwig Kaas, whose political fortitude was not equal to his intellectual ability. Brüning, as I subsequently learned from him, was opposed to voting for the Bill without a further written pledge that Hitler would respect the President's power of veto. He carried this point in the party caucus and a verbal assurance had been received from the Chancellery that a letter to this effect would reach Kaas before the Bill was voted on.

I shall never forget that spectacle. The Kroll Opera House, where the Reichstag met since its palace had been damaged by fire, was packed; nearly three hundred Nazi deputies, and half a hundred Nationalists; a marked absence of Communists and fewer Social Democrats than could have been present, because some were in hospital, the victims of electoral violence, some had fled the country and some were just too frightened to leave their homes – and who shall blame them. The Centre was a dark anxious group, unhappy and uncertain. Along the corridors of the building S.S. men, in their sinister black and silver uniforms, had been posted at intervals; their legs apart, their arms crossed, their eyes fixed and cruel, their faces otherwise expressionless, looking like messengers of doom. Outside a mob of S.A. chanted threatening slogans: 'Give us the Bill or else fire and murder.' Their clamour was clearly audible within the Chamber.

The session opened with Hitler introducing the Bill in a speech remarkable for its moderation and lack of colour, but from which, we had been told, various 'fiery particles' had been deleted at the suggestion of the Foreign Ministry. He was followed by Otto Wells, leader of the Social-Democrats, who, though he seemed to approach the rostrum on leaden feet, delivered a speech of such naked courage that one wanted to get up and cheer. The Government, he said, might take their lives, it could not destroy their souls. He gave his party's vote against the Bill. The effect on Hitler was demonic. So infuriated

76

was he that he gave us a second speech into which he put all the 'purple passages' which had been excised from the first, to the manifest embarrassment of von Papen and von Neurath, the Foreign Minister. His supporters were frenzied by his rhetoric; again and again they rose to him; only physical and emotional exhaustion brought the Führer to a close and his followers to order. In the silence which followed, Goering called Monsignor Kaas to the tribune.

In the party caucus, hastily summoned before the opening of the session, Kaas had had to admit that he had received no letter from Hitler. Brüning steadfastly and vehemently opposed support for the Bill without the letter, but Kaas had wavered and had carried the Right wing of the party with him. Now in almost breathless silence he gave the Centre Party's vote in favour of the Bill.

From my seat in the balcony I looked for Brüning and saw him refuse speech with Kaas on the latter's return to his seat. Then rising with great dignity, his head held high, he walked out of the Chamber and out of the public life of Germany.

II

I was not intimate with the Nazi hierarchy. Indeed the only members of the 'top brass' of the Party whom I ever met were Hitler, Goering, Goebbels and Röhm.

It was twice my doubtful privilege to be invited to the élite tea-time *Stammtisch* in the lounge of the Kaiserhof Hotel and on both occasions I was unimpressed by the high-flown loquacity of the Führer. There was, of course, no opportunity for conversation, an occasional question or the briefest of comments was all that was expected of one, but the monologues to which one was treated were delivered in so bombastic a style that it was almost humorous. The subject was always the same – Germany's wrongs and his means and intention of righting them. Once only did I see him lose his temper as a result of a remark of one of his henchmen and then he was for a moment diabolical, with saliva drooling from his lips, but otherwise he was a very dull companion. What struck one was his utter lack of humanity or humour. He gave the impression of a self-invented, self-inspired robot.

I never came under the personal spell of Hitler, but one cannot deny the almost mesmeric magnetism which he did exercise on others – both individually and in the mass. A great meeting in the Sportspalast, of which I attended several, was a spectacle never to be forgotten. Theatrical production at public assemblies of this kind was a strong point with the Nazis and they understood the technique of it very well. The Hall was always packed with men and women and youngsters, mostly in Party uniform, long before the advertised hour. Brass bands would play the *Horst Wessel Lied* and other Party songs and, thus accompanied, the audience would sing at the tops of their voices. 'Warming-up' speeches would be made by Party orators to create an atmosphere of excitement, and then suddenly the hall would be plunged in darkness except for one spotlight focused on Hitler as he made his way to the platform. He was greeted with cheers, of course, but the effect of his speech, whatever its subject – and it rarely varied except in detail – produced such fanatical enthusiasm as I have never seen elsewhere. That terrifying repetition of *'Sieg Heil'* and *'Ein Volk, ein Reich, ein Führer'* still haunt me and the idolisation reflected in the faces of the listeners, especially the young men and girls, was both poignant and frightening. There is no doubt that for twelve years Hitler held the souls of the majority of the German people under an evil and shameful spell.

If Hitler was black-hearted, Goebbels was evil personified, and by virtue of charm not mere magnetism. This miserable little shrimp of a man, twisted in mind and body, who deliberately perverted the soul of Germany which Hitler handed captive to him, was to me far more frightening than the Führer himself. For he did exercise charisma, and one felt that, while every hackle on one's neck was standing up on end, one had to fight hard against the magic of that Mephistophelean personality. He had almost irresistible attraction for women.

I can see him now, limping from behind his desk in his great room in the Ministry of Propaganda, and pausing to perch on the edge of it, swinging his club foot. His greeting was always genial, his smile that of Lucifer and the fine timbre of his voice could not be denied, but its quality was the spurious gold of Belial. Yet I found myself, with all my prejudice and aversion, having to resist the temporary effect of his spiritually persuasive influence. He was plausible, fluent, educated and amusing. One could readily understand how, shamefully and shamelessly, he 'brain-washed' the minds of the German people, who were at first, perhaps, all too willing victims of his inspiring oratory and, later, had become so mentally conditioned that they could not break the thrall of his witchery.

Per contra, Hermann Goering was at least a human being. Brutal, ruthless and cruel, he too, when one talked with him, could exercise his own particular kind of attraction. Alone of the upper ranks of the Nazis, he was 'a gentleman' in that he came of good family and of the officer class. His gallant war-record as a fighter-pilot and his cross

'*Pour le Mérite*' commended him to many and, in addition, he had a sort of animal charm. One has only to read Albert Speer's memoirs to realise the abysmal squalor of the majority of the Nazi leaders and their ambience. But there was nothing squalid about Goering. Vulgarity there was, as seen in his childish love of display and dressing-up. One never knew when he would appear in a new uniform of Ruritanian splendour or in a Roman toga with his toenails painted. This costume-complex became the butt of many of the jokes which circulated clandestinely in Berlin. It was said, for example, that Hitler, who was, of course, a Wagnerian fanatic, once attended a performance of *Lohengrim* and fell asleep during the interval; as was customary the leading singers came to the 'royal' box to pay their respects and to receive compliments, and the Führer suddenly awakened to find a figure in full armour standing beside him. Whereupon he exclaimed, still half-asleep: 'Really, Hermann, this is going too far!'

Unser Hermann, however, had the capacity of an aristocrat, which is denied to the bourgeoisie, of getting close to the working class and especially the farming community. His popularity was more genuine than Hitler's, who was too remote to communicate with the common man on any but the most Olympian level. Goering was essentially 'of the earth earthy' in both humour and relationship. One could talk with him in a man-to-man fashion though without trusting much that he said; he was hospitable and generally friendly and entertained in a somewhat grandiose manner. In many ways the German 'common man' found him understandable, if savage. Another story current at the time was one of Hitler and Goering motoring through the country-side, when outside a farm their car ran over a pig. Hitler was disturbed in a distant manner but Goering at once took the matter in hand and sought out the farm-wife in her house. Soon afterwards he emerged, followed by the woman calling blessings after him. His arms were full of farm produce, a goose under one arm and sausages were wreathed about his neck. He was in excellent humour as he climbed into the car. 'My dear Hermann,' said the Führer in surprise as they drove away, 'how did you manage it?' 'Easily,' was the reply. 'I only said "The swine is dead" and they were so delighted they gave me all these goodies.'

Yet with all his buffoonery and his clowning, with all his absurd and repulsive obesity, with all his ferocity and his truculent brutishness, I felt that Hermann Goering, when he was not under the influence of drugs, had the best brains of the lot and this was to be proved in the last act of the drama at Nuremberg where, in the course of his trial before the International Military Tribunal I saw him first confound and then rout, the Chief American Prosecutor, Mr Justice Jackson. He did, however, I am happy to say, himself fall a victim to the superior genius of David Maxwell Fyffe – but he had the last laugh after all.

To me, however, Ernst Röhm was the most malign and dangerous of all. This was not so much because he was a homosexual and a pretty promiscuous one at that – though his proclivities never reached the proportion of his subordinate Edmund Heines, the S.A. Leader in Breslau, who had a net-work of 'talent scouts' throughout Germany recruiting handsome boys for his harem – nor because of his quite manifest peculation and corruption, but because he was that hazardous amalgam: a dreamer, a revolutionary, a brave man and a man of action. His war record had been an excellent one, though not as spectacular as Goering's; and he had received the Iron Cross (First Class). But for him the war had never ended. Germany might have lost it, but she would win the next and he, Röhm, would win it for her. He dreamed of leading revolutionary armies, fired with the ideals of National Socialism, across a decadent Europe. He saw himself as the Carnot, 'The Organiser of Victory', of the Nazi Revolution and to this end he had transformed the S.A. into a private army, which, though acknowledging Hitler as the Supreme Leader, gave its personal loyalty to Röhm. Repulsive to look at, his fat cheeks criss-crossed with duelling scars, unimpressive at the outset yet with a certain compelling force, he was, in the early days of the Third Reich one of the most powerful individual influences in the régime.

I recall that in the winter of 1933, which was a hard one and there was actually suffering in Berlin, Hitler decreed a *Winterhilfe* fund whereby contributions might be made for the relief of the hungry by a street and house-to-house collection. As an example, he, Goering, Goebbels, Röhm and others of the Party Leaders, appeared on the streets for a short time, shaking their collecting-boxes under the noses of an apprehensive public who dared not respond except in the most generous manner. The whole operation was blackmail on a grand scale, for those who had the hardihood to be either hesitant or penurious in contributing when called to their front doors by fierce young S.A. men, had the alarming experience of seeing their names ostentatiously taken down. This happened to a number of my friends.

Not only was it blackmail but also a racket. Much of the money collected went into the pockets of Nazi bosses, and I can vividly recall the first and only time I experienced Röhm's hospitality. The wind was bitter. The chink of the collecting-boxes shaken menacingly by warmly overcoated S.A. men was the prevailing sound in the snow-covered streets, and yet in a private dining-room of the Adlon some twenty-five of us sat down to a flower-decked luncheon table, each place sporting a formidable array of cutlery and wine-glasses, betokening many courses (and of the richest) and behind each chair a handsome S.A. man, dragooned for the occasion into the service of a lackey. It was a revolting event, for the whole climate of ideas stank of moral and financial corruption, though the company was a distinguished one, including foreign diplomats, journalists, a member of a minor German royal family, bankers and senior civil servants. Representatives of the Reichswehr were notably absent. I never knew to what I owed my own invitation, but I had accepted out of curiosity. Once I had satisfied it, I was never again the recipient of Nazi hospitality.

It may be worth while to strike a comparison between the two outstanding dictators whom I have met. I should, I think, make it clear that I have no predilection for dictators or for authoritarian government, whether from the Right or the Left. I am a moderate Conservative inherently hostile to all forms of totalitarian régimes, yet it has been given me to spend a good deal of my early life in contact with them.

If one accepts the principle that everything is comparative, within these limits Mussolini was a 'nicer 'man than Hitler. The Duce had not the black heart of the Führer, or if he had it was of a lighter shade of black. Hitler was cold, humourless, fanatical and dedicated. He spoke no language but his own. Though he had written a book of historical importance, I doubt if he ever read for pleasure, except the works of Gobineau and Houston Stewart Chamberlain – an author whose works had the dubious distinction of being bedside books of both Kaiser Wilhelm II and Adolf Hitler. He had no forms of relaxation save music, and was therefore in his early days susceptible to my friend, Putzi Hanfstängl, who lulled him into relaxation with his quite exquisite piano-playing and whose clowning tongue could never resist a quip. It was he who christened Ribbentrop 'Brickendrop' during his ambassadorship in London and who nicknamed the Condor Legion, which Hitler sent to Franco's assistance, 'The Blond Moors'. I was to meet him for the last time under the strangest of circumstances during the Second World War.

Mussolini, on the other hand, had an essentially warm personality. He was a human being with all the failings and a few of the virtues thereof. He had at least read the novels of Gabriele D'Annunzio. He had edited a newspaper, he had been a working journalist, and in that capacity had not scrupled to accept a British subsidy during the First World War. He knew the practical working of parliament from having been a deputy. He had learned to drive a car, pilot an aeroplane and ride a horse with equal recklessness, but not ineptly. He spoke and read English, French and German with some fluency, and rather enjoyed doing so. He was a semi-sophisticated blackguard, but he did have a sense of humour, which I was to discover.

Through my friend Vittorio Cerrutti, whom I knew as an Italian Ambassador in Peking, Moscow, Berlin and Paris, together with his charming Hungarian wife, Elisabeth, who had been a glittering star of the Budapest stage, I obtained audience of the Duce; I wanted to talk to him about the deteriorating situation between Italy and Ethiopia. I stayed in Rome a week, and my appointment was maddeningly postponed from day to day. At last in exasperation I told his 'private office' that I was leaving that evening by the Rome–Paris Express and within an hour a firm date had been fixed. If I had been really bright I would have adopted this technique earlier, but Rome had been very pleasant and I had been given a good place from which to watch one of those magnificent public performances which the Fascists did so much more spectacularly and less rigidly than the Nazis, reminding one of *Aïda* rather than Tannhäuser. Mussolini had ridden up the newly completed Corso with the military attachés of every embassy in Rome riding behind him, all in full uniform. It was extremely impressive, and the Duce was riding a very fine bay mare, which reminded me of my 'Witch' in past days at Fallingbostel. She had just the same proud toss of the head.

At the appointed hour, which was about two hours before train time, I drove to the Palazzo Venezia, taking my luggage with me so that I could go straight to the station, being pretty sure that I should be kept waiting. Indeed I was, and I reminded the private secretary that I had a reservation on the Paris express. 'Do not worry,' he said. 'You will catch the train.'

At long length the moment came. I was ushered into what seemed to be the largest room in the world, at the far end of which was an equally colossal table. It seemed as if I were walking in treacle, yet the marble floor was also very slippery. I felt sure that I should either never arrive at all at the other end or should skid there in a sitting posture. At last, however, I reached my journey's end, and was received by a motionless Mussolini, who, having watched my discomfort quite imperturbably, greeted me with the sternness of a Roman and bade me be seated. He remained unsmiling during our conversation though he talked at length and told me some interesting things. Our conversation then became more general. He asked if I had enjoyed Rome; had I been there before? what had I seen? I replied that I had been a number of times before but what had especially impressed me during this visit was the triumphal procession which he had led up the Corso. 'What did you think of it?' he asked. I answered, perhaps on reflection not too diplomatically: 'I liked your horse immensely.' There was a pause, not entirely a comfortable one as far as I was concerned, and then he threw back his head and roared with Jovian laughter. 'You liked my horse, did you?' he said at length. 'Well, she's a very good horse. I'll give you a picture of her.' And reaching into a drawer of the enormous writing-table, he produced a large-sized photograph of his mare, with him on it, taken during the parade, and autographed it with a pleasing inscription. One cannot imagine similar behaviour on the part of the Führer.

Incidentally, by way of amusement for myself and bewilderment for my friends, I kept this photograph in my various offices throughout the war, along with autographed portraits of the Kaiser and von Seeckt. I can still see the look of quizzical puzzlement on the long unsmiling face of Lord Halifax when he came to inspect my mission in New York. 'I wonder which side you're really on,' he murmured.

Meantime, the Duce's private secretary entered and had a brief *sotto voce* conversation with his chief. Mussolini continued our conversation a moment or two longer, and then brought the audience to a courteous conclusion with a warm handshake. I found the 'long walk home' a good deal easier. When I was in the secretary's office I looked at my watch. It was already ten minutes to train time and we had to cross Rome at the peak of the evening homegoing traffic. The secretary said reassuringly: 'Everything has been arranged. You will catch your train.'

On reaching my car I found a particularly ferocious looking member of Mussolini's bodyguard, the Black Musketeers, seated beside the driver, and thus chaperoned we shot across Rome like 'a bat out of hell'. But when we arrived at the station it was already ten minutes past the time of departure. I was received magnificently by the station-master with the news that the train had been held by special order from the Palazzo Venezia. As I walked up the platform to me sleeper I was watched, as it seemed, by hundreds of unfriendly faces, inquisitive as to who had been responsible for their delayed departure. Somehow I was glad that the Black Musketeer had remained outside.

III

With the creeping paralysis of terror asserting itself in Germany, I found myself going there less frequently and for shorter periods. I was beginning to feel the strain of living under a totalitarian regime and of the increasing sadness amongst my friends. On entering the Reich one was at once conscious of an oppressive atmosphere, a superficial calm beneath which, it was very apparent, there lurked either a growing sense of fear or an inflated chauvinistic ego. Nothing seemed real, nothing was what it appeared to be. I felt myself to be in a kind of waking nightmare from which one only became free on crossing the frontier back into the Western world, where one literally and physically took great gulps of free air.

As the Brown Terror took actual form in the destruction of the trade unions and the confiscation of their funds, the dissolution of all political parties save the National Socialists, the disregard of protests from Catholic and Lutheran religious leaders and the ever-widening scope of Jewish and Socialist persecution, God-fearing, decent-minded Germans became appalled at the Frankenstein's Monster which the German people had helped to create. In the households of many of my friends there were sharp divisions between generations and within the same generation itself. Family life in Germany was already threatened and was later to be destroyed altogether.

A case in point were the Solfs. Dr Wilhelm Solf had been a distinguished public figure under both the imperial and republican regimes. He had been Wilhelm II's colonial minister for many years and also his last foreign minister. As ambassador to Japan he had served the republic both wisely and well. He and his charming wife Hanna gave the most agreeable parties in their house in the Alsenstrasse where one met intelligent people of all sorts and kinds, from experts in oriental ceramics – Solf himself having a very fine collection of Chinese porcelain – to university professors, representatives of the arts and former cabinet ministers. The conversation had always been frank and liberal, and even in these early days of the Third Reich was freer than was usual elsewhere. But the ranks were thinning; for one reason or another people were just not going out to parties as they had before.

After Wilhelm Solf died in the thirties, his wife carried on her opposition to the regime by means of the *Solf Kreis*, of which I have written elsewhere, describing her miraculous escape from death at the hands of the People's Court, but there was one courageous episode, among her many acts of courage and kindness, which bears repetition. When in May 1940 the British Ambassador in Brussels, Sir Laurence Oliphant, and his First Secretary, my friend Peter Scarlett, were both (though separately) caught 'off base' in France by the advancing German columns, they were interned at the spa of Bad Eilsen. Hanna Solf, staying in the same hotel, learned that they were there and persuaded the S.S. guards to allow her to visit them, bringing with her certain of the comforts and luxuries which they had long been denied in captivity. I feel that this act of Christian charity and personal gallantry should not go unrecorded.

To illustrate, however, how the issue of the day – loyalty to the principles and precepts of National Socialism – could divide a family, one has only to contrast the careers of the Solfs' two handsome sons. The eldest found no difficulty in assimilating the basic ethos of the new government. He entered the diplomatic service and, when von Ribbentrop became Foreign Minister, was chosen, I am informed, to 'model' the new Nazi diplomatic uniform before him. The younger son, Hermann, on the other hand, rejected National Socialism, refused to join the Hitler Jugend and was therefore penalised by being refused permission to accept a Rhodes Scholarship to which he had been appointed.

Another most gallant lady whom I used to meet at the Solfs', whom I greatly admired and who never for one moment 'bowed the knee in the house of Rimmon', was another Hanna – Hanna von Bredow (*née* Countess von Bismarck) – a grand-daughter of the Iron Chancellor. She had inherited the 'blood and iron' of her forebear and while two of her brothers (the third lived in Rome and remained there until his death) embraced National Socialism, though from different motives, she resolutely set her face against such pagan and brutal doctrines. Nor was she afraid to give vent to her opinions in the highest circles. When the Führer invited her to launch and christen the great new battleship *Bismarck*, she replied that she had already performed such an office for Kaiser Wilhelm II and saw no reason to repeat it. It was not surprising that such sustained frankness and courage should eventually bring about her arrest, and she suffered a long period of detention in a concentration camp, from which she emerged in a shocking condition at the end of the war. One of the happiest and kindest acts of my friend Kit (Sir Christopher) Steel, when he was Political Adviser to the British

Commander-in-Chief in Berlin in 1945, was to arrange for Hanna von Bismarck to be flown to Switzerland for rest and recuperation.

Nor were these all. I merely mention them as examples of the fact that brave people did exist in Germany at this time and continued to act bravely throughout the heyday of *Der Dritte Reich*. Later, when 'the going was less good' and it became ever more apparent to an increasing number that they had backed the wrong horse, the freshet of those who criticised Hitler became a spate. It is, however, those early opponents, that noble few who never wavered from the beginning, that one remembers with a warmth of admiration and esteem. I frequently find myself confronted with the thought, how should I have behaved under similar circumstances? One can never know the answer until one's courage and determination have been tested; one can only pray that this will never happen, but that, if it does, one could face it with the dignity of mien and gallantry of spirit of some of one's German friends.

In addition to the obvious fact that my visits to Germany were becoming more and more of a strain and a source of unhappiness, there was a further reason why I was absent for a considerable period. The Imperial Diplomatic Relations Conference opened in Toronto in September 1933. I was a member of the British delegation, which was led by Viscount Cecil of Chelwood. This was followed by prolonged journeying in Canada and the United States of which I shall write later.

IV

It was therefore not until the early spring of 1934 that I was again in Germany to find that the sequence of events had followed the course I had anticipated but at a swifter tempo. The position was now even more complicated than I had foreseen and a whole congeries of Gordian knots seemed so inextricably tied that only the use of the sword could sever them.

Reduced to its simplest forms the position was this: Hindenburg's life was ebbing away, slowly but certainly; he was already *compos mentis* for only a short period each day. While he lived, however, he still retained the unswerving loyalty of the Army and, if he could be persuaded to give the order, the Army would overthrow the regime. Hitler needed the support of the Army for two reasons; he was determined, by hook or by crook, to be Hindenburg's successor, and only the Army could guarantee him this; secondly, in order to hold the balance between the rising conflict of views held by the Right and the Left as to the future of the National Revolution; the Right demanding a period of retrenchment and reserve, with an easing of the atrocious policies towards enemies of the Party, the Left clamouring for a 'Second Revolution' with emphasis upon Socialism rather than Nationalism, and the elimination of the Right from formulation of policy.

In addition there was the ever-present problem of what to do with the two and a half million S.A. men who had pledged their loyalty to Röhm, and the personal and mutual enmity between Röhm and General von Blomberg which led to constant clashes in cabinet meetings. Moreover, the existence of so large a paramilitary force was a cause of constant anxiety in London and in Paris, in both of which capitals Hitler wished to make a good appearance at the moment.

If, therefore, he wished to inherit the position of Head of State and thereby retain the support of the Army, if he was to keep order in his own house and establish a modicum of confidence abroad, it was clear that Hitler must in some way reduce the size and influence of the S.A. It was this which accounted for the promises which he made to Anthony Eden in Berlin in February 1934 and which Ribbentrop secretly reiterated in London and Paris in April, that the S.A. should shortly be reduced by at least two-thirds and should never be an 'arms-carrying' organisation. The Führer was now placing his confidence more and more upon the loyalty of Himmler and his élite and fanatical S.S. troops.

As might have been expected so rich a confluence of muddy waters, so splendid an opportunity for the making of bad blood, was too great a temptation for Kurt von Schleicher, who now emerged from the boredom – but comparative safety – of his retirement to re-enter the arena of intrigue. In the houses which he frequented he openly criticised the government – and particularly von Papen – not realising that what was merely personal treachery before the establishment of the totalitarian state was now regarded as high treason. Nor did he seem to appreciate the fact that the control of the secret forces of espionage were in other hands than his and that he was completely discredited.

Very soon, however, he was indulging in his favourite pastime of Shadow Cabinet making, with a lack of discretion that was both incredible and alarming. One evening in the Adlon Bar, where it was a well-known fact that many of the waiters were Gestapo agents, there was handed round a list of a potential cabinet, with Hitler as Chancellor, von Schleicher as Vice-Chancellor, Röhm as Minister of Defence and – of all people – Brüning as Foreign Minister ! That this was the merest building of castles in Spain may be judged from the fact that when I mentioned it to Brüning at the St Hedwiga's hospital he not only swore that he had had no communication with von Schleicher after the latter's *amende honorable* following his dismissal, but that the idea of his serving under Hitler at all, let alone with Röhm as a colleague, was not only utterly impossible but would be farcical were it not so revolting.

Nevertheless, such indiscretions were highly dangerous, and it came as no surprise when both von Schleicher and Brüning soon received warning from their respective friends that their names now figured on another and more sinister list, that of those proscribed by Himmler. Characteristically von Schleicher retired to the shores of the Starnbergersee and then took a motor-tour with his wife to Spain. Brüning with greater prudence left the country by means of an 'Underground Railroad' organised by a group of Englishmen of whom I was one.

Even now I cannot give the full details of this escape route because others were involved in it besides myself and some of them are still alive. It is enough to say that it crossed the Netherlands frontier, where the services of a sympathetic and co-operative Dutch customs inspector had been enlisted, who overlooked the fact that Brüning had no passport. Having crossed the border he was driven to a famous religious house nearby where he was warmly welcomed. Shortly thereafter the Dutch customs official arrived to pay his respects and bringing a box of cigars which he begged the distinguished refugee to accept as a token of esteem. They were of the mild Dutch variety, and Brüning was accustomed to much stronger tobacco. His suspicions were aroused, therefore, when on lighting one of his gift cigars he began to feel extremely ill. He at once put it out and was sick. His host, a famous and practical prelate, insisted on sending the whole boxful to be analysed, and it was found that every one of them was poisoned. The possibility of the Dutch official's being a double agent had been overlooked.

Soon, however, Brüning was safe in London with friends and subsequently went to Lugano and America. But the Gestapo did not give up easily. There was at least one other attempt on his life while he was in Switzerland. He never returned to Germany until after the conclusion of the Second World War.

Meantime in Berlin the month of June had opened ominously. We now know that Hitler, Goering and Himmler had finally agreed to liquidate the high command of the S.A. and such other of the opponents of the regime as might be designated. There was to be mass murder, and it was to be on 16 June. Its postponement was due to the sudden and quite unexpected invitation from Mussolini to Hitler to meet him at Stra, outside Venice. In the course of their conversation the Duce, as I was afterwards told by his then ambassador in Berlin, Vittorio Cerrutti, urged his guest to 'set his house in order', little knowing, perhaps, that he was preaching to the converted or in what bloody form his advice might be taken.

These preparations for murder on a major scale were kept a grim secret. Von Papen was certainly unaware of them, but he was engaged on a project of his own, to which he made me privy. He proposed to gain the support of Marshal von Hindenburg for a speech which Papen should deliver opposing the idea of a 'Second Revolution' and urging the Führer to abandon the gangster tactics of the Left-wing Nazis and to liberalise the policy of the regime by permitting a free press, a cessation of persecution and the establishment of a sense of trust and willingness among the people to serve the state in freedom and without fear. Papen's idea was that the speech should be something in the nature of a veiled ultimatum and that, if Hitler refused to heed its warning, the Reichswehr would assert itself and compel him to do so.

On his return from Neudeck, the President's country estate in East Prussia, I received word from the Vice-Chancellor's office that 'Fränzchen' would like to see me. I found him completely restored in confidence and ebullience, and he gave me his version of what had happened at Neudeck. The President, he said, was in complete accord with his plans. He had approved the substance of what von Papen proposed to say and had promised to give his order to the Army to march if occasion demanded. Von Papen had, he said, made elaborate plans for what would now be called 'maximum media coverage' for his speech. It was also to be reprinted and distributed by his own Germania Press and also recorded on gramophone records. 'A new era is about to begin,' he said.

While not being over-optimistic as to the result of this adventure, I felt that anything which could cause 'alarm and despondency' in the ranks of the enemy – i.e. the Nazi Party – was to be encouraged. I was also encouraged myself when von Papen told me that he had entrusted the actual writing of the speech to a man whom I knew and respected, Edgar Jung, an intellectual of semi-Jewish antecedents and conservative principles.

Papen duly spoke before the University of Marburg on Sunday, 17 June 1934. It was a courageous speech. Jung had given his all to it, and the fact that von Papen had made it was justifiably adduced to his credit by his defence counsel when he came to stand his trial at Nuremberg some twelve years later. It had strong repercussions in Germany itself where it was hailed with immense relief by many of those who had originally voted for Hitler out of desperation and now bitterly regretted it, as the possible dawn of a new age of toleration. Fresh hope was kindled for the return of respect for the dignity of man and the freedom of the soul. Von Papen was suddenly a hero. When he appeared in the Jockey Club at Hamburg, a few days later on the occasion of the German Derby, he received a tremendous ovation.

Moreover the impact of the Marburg speech on the Nazi hierarchy was one of tumult and affright. It came as a bolt from the blue as they were gathered in the little town of Gera in Thuringia to hear the Führer's report on his conversations with Mussolini, and at first there were signs of near-panic, as rumours reached them that von Papen's warning and its barely concealed attack on Goebbels, had the backing of the Marshal and the Army. They soon rallied, however, and a counter-attack was swiftly mounted.

It now became apparent that von Papen had made two fundamental miscalculations, both based on ignorance of the facts. The first was that Hindenburg, surrounded as he was by a dedicated group of officials who kept him isolated from the world – Neudeck was already referred to as 'the smallest concentration camp' – was influenced by the last person with whom he talked, and the second was that, unknown to von Papen, the High Command of the Reichswehr had already pledged their support to Hitler as Hindenburg's successor in return for the liquidation of the S.A.

Thus, though the Marburg speech raised the hopes of many for a brief moment, there was no follow-through. No word of approbation came from Neudeck, and the Army received no order to march. Instead Goebbels opened a vicious campaign of vilification of the Nationalist Right on the radio and in the Party press. He also seized the Germania Press and destroyed almost all the printed copies of the speech and also the gramophone records.

I say 'almost all' because von Papen had given me several copies and I had sent them to England. I had done this by my own means and it gave me some mild satisfaction. One of the last kindnesses which Brüning had done me before leaving office was to give me a diplomatic *laissez-passer*. It was a large and formidable yellow document, printed in gothic type, and signed and countersigned with what to me were two completely illegible names, which were, in effect, those of Brüning and von Bülow. More important than this, however, was that it was stamped in two places with enormous

German eagles at the sight of which any well-trained lesser governmental official would kow-tow with the deepest respect. It rendered
both me and my luggage free from examination and an untrammelled
passage across the frontiers of the Reich. It was by use of this that I
had taken my copies of the Marburg speech across the border and
posted them.

I had, however, made a grievous error of my own which, knowing
von Papen as well as I did, was inexcusable. It had never occurred to
me that the Vice-Chancellor, with his knowledge of the police-state
technique, had not taken precautions against having his office
'bugged'. He had not, however, and the results were very nearly
disastrous for me.

I am not likely to forget those last two weeks of June 1934 in
Berlin. The atmosphere, both meteorologically and politically, was
stormy. Thunderstorms worked their way up and down the river Spree
without breaking but leaving a heavy pall of sweltering sunless
humidity. Equally oppression and apprehension beset all those who
knew anything at all of what was happening. Rumours flew about
the capital as was only possible in Berlin. Everyone seemed to feel that
a storm or a cataclysm was about to burst. I was deeply depressed
and not a little fearful. Yet I felt I must see the drama played out.

I received word through friends that Edgar Jung had gone into
hiding but would like to see me. Accordingly I was driven out in a
closed car to a wood near Döberitz, and there, sitting on a log, we
talked for hours. He knew that he would soon be killed; he said so.
He urged me not to waste time in conversation. 'You are writing a
book on Hindenburg,' he said. 'You must listen to me.' And then he
told me many things, of which I made brief notes on envelopes and
any scraps of paper I happened to have about me, and subsequently
used. When we parted I knew that I was saying goodbye to a man
already dead.

The days went on; the days of awful waiting. Would there be an
anti-climax? or when would Hitler strike? and against whom?
Late on the evening of the 28th two of von Papen's adjutants dined
with me on the terrace of the Kaiserhof. The heat, even at that hour,
was almost unbearable; even our well-iced champagne tasted warm.
Our conversation turned inevitably to the matter uppermost in the
minds of all of us. What, I asked them, did they think would
happen? Were they at all anxious about their own safety? To my
second question they answered with complete assurance; they felt in
no kind of danger. 'We are the Vice-Chancellor's men,' they asserted
with just a touch of arrogance.

In the course of our dinner I was called to the telephone. A close friend of mine Sir Neill Malcolm, whose daughter was seriously ill in Lausanne, asked me as a favour to come there at once; he was in grave affliction and needed support; I promised to leave next day. When I did so I little thought, as I waved my *laissez-passer* at the emigration officials, that I should not see Berlin again for some dozen years.

Thus it was in the safety of Switzerland that I read of the horrors of the Night of the Long Knives, the massacre of 30 June, 1934. I have written of this in detail elsewhere, and therefore will only say now that both my dinner guests were shot dead across their office tables, and that von Papen only escaped a similar fate through the personal intervention of President von Hindenburg. Edgar Jung too was murdered, and Kurt von Schleicher and his wife were gunned down in their own drawing-room.

How closely I myself escaped I only learned a little later. There had been in the receptionists' office at the Kaiserhof a young Englishman who was learning the hotel business and was doing his year's apprenticeship in Germany at this hotel. We had spoken occasionally and when I next went to Paris some time in July I found him doing his 'French year' at the Crillon. He asked to take me up to my room and there told me that on the morning of 30 June, the S.S. and Gestapo had ransacked and wrecked my rooms at the Kaiserhof and had been furious that I had escaped them. 'I hope,' he said, 'that you are not planning to return to Germany.'

Later still I asked a German friend of mine, who had left the Reich for good but had held an official position which enabled him to have seen my Gestapo file, what would have happened to me. After all, I said, I was a foreigner and not unknown in Berlin, or, for the matter of that, in London. 'Oh,' he said, 'they intended to kill you all right. They had recordings of all your talks with Papen. Then they'd have shot the boys who shot you. All an unfortunate mistake, you know. It would have been too easy.'

I need hardly say that I did not return to Germany until 1945 when I did so with the full force and authority of a representative of an Occupying Power.

CHAPTER FOUR

The Forgotten Peace

I

Of all the books I have written – and there are nearly twenty of them – I think that the one I most enjoyed writing (with one other outstanding exception) was the story of the Treaty of Brest-Litovsk, and for a variety of reasons. In the first place it was a nice tidy 'capsulated' historical event which had a beginning, a middle and an end. Then, though the event was of absorbing interest and great importance, it was not something in which one became deeply and emotionally involved. One was not troubled by 'goodies' and 'baddies'; indeed there was a predominance of 'baddies' on both sides. In addition, there was enough documentation and biographical material available; the distance of time between the events themselves and the moment at which I was writing was sufficient to make an historical perspective possible, yet there were a considerable number of the actors still living.

I first encountered the subject when I was doing research for my biography of Hindenburg in the early thirties – which included reading Winston Churchill's *The Unknown War*. I realised how very little was known of the war on the Eastern Front in the years 1914–18 until Mr Churchill had written about it and virtually nothing of the peace treaties which concluded it. I determined, therefore, that my next book should be on this subject, and to this end I followed my set custom of examining such documents as were available, reading the memoirs and studies, if any, which had already been written and finally seeking out and talking with those of the *dramatis personae* who still survived.

It would be difficult to over-emphasise the importance attaching to the Treaty of Brest-Litovsk in the history of the First World War – and indeed after. It was the high-water mark of stupidity on the part of German military-political diplomacy in disclosing the predatory nature of the terms of peace which they envisaged in the event of victory and thereby ensuring the wholehearted support of America for the Allied cause; it saved the Bolshevik Revolution from almost certain destruction; it robbed the German offensive of March 1918 of the last ounce of strength necessary for success; it set the ultimate pattern for Stalin's foreign policy and it greatly influenced the *Ostpolitik* of Adolf Hitler.

All these results and repercussions were revealed to me as I pursued my researches and particularly as I talked with the chief actors on both sides. In so far as the Central Powers were concerned, these persons included Freiherr Richard von Kühlmann and General Max Hoffmann for Imperial Germany and Count Ottokar Czernin for the Austro-Hungarian Empire. Of these three I rather liked von Kühlmann, I could not but admire Hoffmann as a brilliant but ruthless soldier – he was one of the two most outstanding staff officers in the German army during the First World War, the other being Hans von Seeckt – and my compassion was aroused by Czernin when I talked with him in a second-rate west-side hotel in New York.

Heinrich Brüning once said to me that one of the greatest failings of Berlin society during the Weimar Republic was that no one really knew how to give a dinner-party. This was largely true of this essentially bourgeois regime, but there were one or two exceptions, and Richard von Kühlmann was one of them. He owned a very attractive house in Tiergartenstrasse, built in the Schinckel period (roughly contemporary with our regency and the French Empire) and filled with furniture of a similar date. There he entertained in a most civilised and sophisticated manner, having a discerning appreciation for food, wine and women of the first order.

A Bavarian nobleman and a Catholic, he had been summoned in 1917 at the age of forty-four by Wilhelm II to be his foreign minister. Witty, cynical, a diplomat of the old school, with a slightly coarse face and a more than slightly coarse sense of humour, he had a fund of good stories, not the least funny of which was a description of an unforgettable morning in March 1905 when, green with sea-sickness and hampered by the full uniform of an officer of a Bavarian Uhlan regiment, he had scaled a heaving rope-ladder to greet his Kaiser as the imperial yacht was lying at anchor in the open roadstead of Tangier where he was then Consul-General. 'Never before or later did I approach my Sovereign on hands and knees and laying all at his Majesty's feet.'

But von Kühlmann could be serious too, and what he told me about Brest-Litovsk was fascinating to the listener and invaluable to the historian. He said that on his appointment as Foreign Minister he was appalled at the degree to which the control of policy, both external and domestic, had been usurped by the General Staff in the persons of Hindenburg and Ludendorff. Every person and every institution, from the Kaiser to the Chancellor and the party leaders in the Reichstag, from the tycoons of capital to the bosses of the trade unions, had surrendered the ultimate authority to these representatives of the military élite with the claret-coloured stripe of the General Staff on their field-grey breeches.

Von Kühlmann himself, when he assumed office, was already of the opinion that the chances of a 'victor's peace' had escaped Germany and that her best, if not her only, hope was to bring about a negotiated conclusion to the hostilities. This was the basis of his policy, and he proposed to utilise the peace proposals of the Russians to this end, to build up a position in the east with which to make possible concessions offsetting retention of territory in the west.

To his horror, however, he found that the policy of the General Staff at the coming negotiations with the Bolsheviks envisaged pure and naked annexation, the detachment of the Ukraine from Russia and its transformation into a satellite state, the restoration of a Polish kingdom under the protection of the German and Austrian Emperors, the imposition of a German prince as king of a semi-independent Finland and the incorporation of the Baltic provinces into the German Reich. The basic aim of this policy was the destruction and elimination of Russia as a political force in Europe, not particularly because she was a Communist state – few then knew what Bolshevism really meant – but because she represented a rival and an obstacle to the dominance of the Germanic Powers in *Mitteleuropa*.

This to von Kühlmann was madness, and he fought it to the best of his ability. I recall his description of a Crown Council at Spa, at which the Kaiser presided, when the preliminary directives for the forthcoming meeting with the Bolsheviks at Brest-Litovsk were to be discussed. Along one side of an oblong table were the Imperial Chancellor, the veteran and nearly senile Count von Hertling, together with his foreign policy advisers, headed by von Kühlmann; on the other were Hindenburg and Ludendorff, flanked by aides, staff-officers and experts of all kinds. At the head of the table, in a great chair of state, crouched William II, clearly unhappy at having to decide between his civilian and military chiefs, knowing in advance what that decision would be.

Hindenburg led off with a long memorandum, composed by Ludendorff and his staff, setting forth what were described as 'the minimum requirements' of the General Staff and ending with a demand for the Baltic States.

'But why', asked von Kühlmann in riposte, 'do you need to annex these territories? Why not continue to occupy them as at present and perhaps give them independence later?'

And back came the rumbling response from that gigantic uniformed torso: 'I need them for the manœuvring of my left wing in the next war.'

In face of this attitude which undoubtedly enjoyed the imperial endorsement, von Kühlmann retreated into silence, but when the negotiations actually began he did his best to prolong them to the utmost in the futile hope that they might eventually develop ino some basis for a broader agreement embracing other belligerents. These Fabian tactics, however, were in direct conflict with the views of the General Staff – who wished to transfer as many divisions as possible from the east to the west in preparation for their great March 1918 offensive – and with those of von Kühlmann's Austrian colleague, Count Czernin – whose chief anxiety was to get as much grain out of the Ukraine as quickly as possible in order to ease the food situation in the already starving cities of Vienna and Budapest.

Thus, von Kühlmann would say, 'My best efforts were defeated by my own allies.' At the end he was compelled to yield to the demands of General Hoffmann and Czernin to force the Russians to conclude peace or face the consequences, and they signed the treaty on 3 March 1918.

After the collapse of Germany, von Kühlmann retired from public life and afforded one of the few social oases in Berlin during the Republic. He had married the daughter of an industrial magnate, one of the Stumms, who managed to preserve her fortune throughout the financial turbulences of the Weimar period. They had two or three daughters and one son Kurt, who was the apple of his father's eye. He is now a member of the Bundestag in Bonn and figured somewhat prominently in the parliamentary dispute over the Ostpolitik of Chancellor Willy Brandt in 1973.

During the Third Reich, Richard von Kühlmann walked like Agag with great delicacy, but I always knew when he thought he might have temporarily antagonised the Nazi bosses because I would receive a telegram asking if I could arrange for him to give a lecture at Chatham House. For old times' sake I was usually able to do so. He was a frequent visitor at A14 Albany, and I recall that among my many hard-drinking acquaintances he could consume more neat whisky than I have ever known without showing the slightest effect. He died in 1949.

Neither Hindenburg nor Ludendorff was 'available for comment' on Brest-Litovsk when I saw them, for the simple reason that neither of them was fully *compos mentis* though, the Field-Marshal was *Reichspräsident* at the time. Oddly enough, when I visited him at Neudeck, he was clearer in his mind about current problems of a controversial nature than about what had happened in the past, which he seemed to have dismissed completely into limbo. Ludendorff, however, when I saw him in Munich, was completely irrational. He had made a second marriage to a lady whom local Munich gossip believed to be a practising witch. Certainly he had an altar to Thor in the back garden on which he was said to sacrifice a horse from time to time. He was utterly unreasonable, and our conversation – or I should say his monologue – consisted of a diatribe against a great international conspiracy in which the unlikely alliance of the Roman Catholic Church, World Jewry and the Grand Orient were combining to destroy civilisation.

I did, however, talk with Major-General Max Hoffmann, who, though the complete antithesis of von Kühlmann, confirmed much of what he had told me over the years. Almost a caricature of a Prussian military type – he was in fact a Hessian – Hoffmann, when I knew him, lived in a small and rather uncomfortable *Wohnung* in a Berlin suburb. He was a military genius of the first water, probably the most able of that combination HLH (Hindenburg, Ludendorff and Hoffmann) who brought victory to German arms on the Eastern Front, and certainly it was his original planning, completed before their arrival at G.H.Q., which enabled Hindenburg and Ludendorff to make their great coup at Tannenberg in 1914, which launched both of them on their notorious career.

But, apart from his outstanding military ability, Hoffmann was an unlikeable figure. Large and smooth, his hair (what there was of it) *en brosse*, his monocle firmly fixed in his eye and a bulging roll of fat at the back of his neck, he was a bully, and an impatient bully. His descriptions of the 'spiritual wrestling matches' in which von Kühlmann engaged with Trotsky during the conference were vivid and vitriolic. His contempt for the professional diplomats was only equalled by his loathing for his Bolshevik opposite numbers, whom he characterised as 'swine', 'barbarians' and 'savages'. He told me of his ever-growing sense of frustration, of Ludendorff's daily telephone calls from Spa demanding action and an end to discussion, and finally of that glorious day when he made up his mind to flout von Kühlmann. Taking the floor, he unrolled a map and with his thumbnail marked upon it the new boundaries between Russia, Germany, Poland and the Ukraine. The cat was out of the bag with a vengeance, to von Kühlmann's intense annoyance. The world now knew the nature of German demands upon a conquered foe. But Hoffmann was, he said, unrepentant. He had spoken to his brief; he had followed orders; he had done his duty.

The Bolshevik memoirs assert that his speech was punctuated with thumpings with his fist on the table and that at one point he went so far as to put his spurred boot upon it. This both von Kühlmann and Hoffmann denied, dismissing it as Bolshevik propaganda or alternatively as symbolism. 'What do you think happened?' I asked the scared and repressed Frau Hoffmann when her tyrannical spouse had left the room for a moment. Her answer was characteristic of the typical German *Hausfrau*. Looking carefully over her shoulder and adjusting a lace antimacassar on a horribly uncomfortable horsehair sofa, she said in a very low voice: 'All I can say is he never did it at home.'

Hoffmann returned to Berlin at the close of the war with a pathological hatred of Communism. He was largely instrumental in crushing the first Spartacist rising of 1918 and was forever bombarding Neill Malcolm, when head of the British Military Mission, with elaborate plans for a joint Anglo–French–German campaign against the Russians. He wrote one of the best books to come out of Germany after the war, entitled *The War of Lost Opportunities*.

Of all the surviving representatives of the Central Powers at Brest-Litovsk with whom I talked, my heart and sympathy were most deeply troubled by Count Ottokar von Czernin. Von Kühlmann had retained much of his position and his wife's wealth. Hoffmann had few regrets and lived in comparative comfort. But Czernin, Knight of the Golden Fleece, scion of one of the oldest Bohemian noble families of the Holy Roman Empire, not only lost everything, material as well as spiritual, but seemed haunted by ghosts of the past. Shabby and rather down at heel, he was on a lecturing tour in the United States and seemed to me to be wildly unsuited to such an enterprise.

It was clear from his conversation that he had suffered perhaps more than anyone else in those fantastic surroundings of Brest-Litovsk. More fastidious than the majority of his colleagues, he missed the amenities of ordinary civilisation more greatly than they did. The city had been burned in the fighting, and only the citadel remained intact. Here they were crowded together in cramped quarters and conditions of considerable restriction, with few distractions and little relaxation. The monotony was almost intolerable, and to break it they would drive out along tight-packed snowy roads and shoot with revolvers at the crows which perched on the telegraph wires He had brought a collection of memoirs of the French Revolution to beguile the time. He found his colleagues inimical and his opponents intolerable. All that he longed for was a separate peace with the Ukraine which would mean bread for Austria and for Hungary. Von Kühlmann's dialectical extravagances were as irksome to him as Hoffmann's military chauvinism. He had already seen the writing on the wall. If revolution were to be staved off in the Habsburg Empire food must be made available. For him the issue was as simple as that. He spoke with emotion and sadness, nostalgia battled with courage. It was most moving. As I left him I felt that I had seen the last of an ancient régime which was as dead as Thebes or Carthage.

II

But, of course, it was the Russians I really wanted to see. Interesting though it was to meet and discuss with the survivors of the former Central European imperial régimes, it was far more absorbing to me to encounter those Old Bolsheviks who had made the revolution in November 1917 and had at Brest-Litovsk confronted the representatives of traditional diplomacy with a new and unconventional technique which had baffled and enraged them. These were the men who destroyed the pitiful attempt at democratic constitutional government in Russia and had, by their very absence, strongly influenced some of the major decisions taken at the Peace Conference of Paris. Wrongheaded and tyrannical though they might be, they had made a determined attempt to turn the world, as we had known it, upside down – a process which had begun at Brest-Litovsk – and were therefore, I thought, well worth seeing.

I managed to see most of them, but I was only just in time. In the summer of 1935 the grim shadows of the Stalinist purges already loomed over Moscow, and within a very short space of time most of the men I had talked with were either dead or in labour camps.

I was fortunate in having two valuable allies, the then American Ambassador, William C. Bullitt and the Commissar for Foreign Affairs, Maxim Litvinov. Bill Bullitt was an old friend of mine, and I was one of the exceptions to his anti-British prejudice. 'He likes Englishmen but hates the English,' the British Ambassador in Washington, Sir Ronald Lindsay, once wrote of him He was one of the most remarkable people I have ever known, combining in one contradictory personality, great kindness with vitriolic hatred, amazing charm and ability with an almost irrational irresponsibility, wit and humour with depression and frustration, arrogance and a certain ruthlessness with naïveté and childish vanity. Amongst his virtues was his capacity to pick brilliant assistants, and the staff which he assembled when he became America's first ambassador to Soviet Russia was the cradle for that eminent school of Kremlinologists which included John Wylie, George Kennan, 'Chip' Bohlen, Charlie Thayer and Loy Henderson.

Maxim Litvinov I had met first at Geneva during the sessions of the Preparatory Disarmament Commission and had been much impressed by his subtlety in dealing with the capitalist powers and his remarkable sense of humour. He had a rather benign appearance suggestive of a large teddy-bear that had lost most of its cuddlesomeness. He was, however, in favour of an understanding with Britain and France against the menace of a resurgent German nationalism, and when this policy failed he fell with it to be replaced by the enigmatic, more sinister, more practically minded Molotov, who favoured an accommodation with Germany on the general basis of 'if you can't beat them, join them'.

In 1935, however, Litvinov was riding high, having brought the U.S.S.R. into membership of the League of Nations and signed treaties of mutual support with France and Czechoslovakia, and between them he and Bill Bullitt obtained for me access to all the essential documents I needed and arranged for me to meet most of the Brest-Litovsk survivors.

I am a historian who delights in the touch of original material, even as a devout medieval worshipper might derive inspiration from contact with pieces of the True Cross. The documents I needed were in the then Marx–Engels Institute and had all been photostated carefully but imperfectly, since this particular branch of science had not progressed very far at that time. Bill Bullitt had found a reliable translator for me. However I discovered that the originals, particularly the fugitive writings of Lenin, were stored in the vaults of the Institute and, after some pleading, I was eventually allowed to see them through Litvinov's intervention and under heavy guard.

I was greatly impressed by the technical method of preserving these relics. It must be remembered that much of Lenin's writings – and particularly those smuggled out of Finland during his exile there after the abortive Bolshevik rising of July 1917 and whence he directed the preparations for the November Revolution – were written on all sorts and conditions of paper – coarse war-time writing-paper, paper bags, even toilet paper, had been employed, all of them fragile and perishable. However, if the Soviet archivists were imperfect in the art of photostat, they were masters at conserving original documents. Each precious relic was sunk in silk and covered with a curtain of rice paper which could be rolled up for reading purposes. It was an extraordinary achievement of preservation.

It was through Bill Bullitt that I made contact with the Old Bolsheviks, and I succeeded in meeting virtually all of them who were still living. Joffe, who had led the original Soviet armistice delegation to Brest-Litovsk, had already committed suicide as early as 1924, and it is my lasting regret that death also cheated me of meeting Lenin, for without doubt he is the man who left his mark on the twentieth century more deeply and indelibly than any other.

But I saw many of the others, and what impressed me at once was how civilised and cultured they were. Hoffmann might speak of them as 'savages' and 'barbarians', but the fact remains that, because most of them had spent much of their lives outside of Russia in exile in Paris and Vienna and London and in Switzerland, they spoke three or four languages and had read widely in six or eight. They were infinitely more communicative than those Russians with whom I had subsequently to deal during the Second World War.

It was already suspected that Stalin was about to purge the Communist Party in a series of state trials, and the apprehension of the Old Bolsheviks was patent. Their reaction varied. I can see Bukharin clawing nervously at his little red beard and Borodin's cynical smile as we spoke of his activities in China nearly ten years earlier. Sokolnikov, Kamenev and Karakhan were fatalistic and apparently resigned; but they all were ready to talk about Brest-Litovsk because it seemed to be in most ways a non-controversial subject in which they had behaved well from a Party point of view and Russia had emerged as the injured victim.

The star turn, however, was Karl Radek, whom I visited at his *dacha* near Moscow. I went down by train to a wayside station and he met me on the platform with his little chin fringe of beard and his impish grin, which could change in a moment from humour to malignity. We walked for hours among the pinewoods, accompanied by his little dog Tchortik, of whom he was extremely fond.

I well recall his opening conversational gambit.

'Now, Mr Wheeler-Bennett,' he said in fluent English, 'You're an English Tory, aren't you?'

I admitted that I was.

'And wouldn't you like to cut my throat?' Radek asked.

'Oh no,' I replied. 'You know we Tories always employ others to do those jobs for us. You've always said so yourself.'

Radek laughed. 'Well, I see what you mean,' he said, 'but I'm a Bolshevik and I'd like to cut your throat; so let's start from there.'

And start we did on the most entertaining of conversations. Radek was in a sense diabolical. His humour was barbed and witty, and he was entirely uninhibited. He was a wonderfully good companion, and I found myself mentally allotting him a place among those with whom I would almost like to spend a wet week-end in Hull.

Radek's recollections of Brest-Litovsk were vivid and varied. His pet aversion was Hoffmann – a dislike which, as we have seen, was mutual – and at an early point in the proceedings he had discovered that the General was allergic, or at any rate had strong objections, to pipe-smoking, which he considered vulgar. Having established this fact Radek always chose a seat opposite Hoffmann and would puff smoke into his face across the conference table, with the result that he burst into shattering bouts of sneezing.

Radek was also an excellent mimic, and he would imitate Hoffmann's voice of outraged fury when Trotsky had produced his fantastic formula of 'No War – No Peace', with which he hoped to bring the Conference to an abortive conclusion.

'Hoffmann went first white, then purple,' said Radek, 'and the only word he could get out was one amazed: *"Unerhört"* ' (Unheard of).

Count Czernin was also made the butt of Bolshevik humour. Radek told of how on one occasion, at the end of a conference session, he had sidled up behind the Austrian Foreign Minister, who was struggling into his fur-coat, and gave him a hand with it, at the same time whispering in his ear in German, 'Ah, Your Excellency, I too have been a servant in my time.'

On our return to Radek's house an excellent meal awaited us, cooked, served and ultimately shared by an elderly and very silent lady. Whether she was Radek's wife or housekeeper or even mistress I cannot say, for I was never introduced to her and she remained mute throughout the meal. She reminded me of one of those characters in a Chekhov play, usually an aunt, who is merely a presence on the stage except for an occasional oracular utterance, such as 'The Little Father can do nothing', or 'We must all go to Moscow.' This lady, however, did not even say as much as that.

At the end of the meal, during which Radek talked incessantly like a machine-gun, both on Brest-Litovsk and on his experiences when held as a Prisoner of State in the Moabit Prison in Berlin after his arrest at the time of the Spartacist rising, we produced our pipes and this time it was my turn to suffer from his humour. He insisted that I should have a fill of what he called 'Red Army tobacco'. I did so without being aware that saltpetre was a major ingredient. The result was a minor pyrotechnic display. It was without doubt the vilest tobacco I have ever smoked, and I was devoutly thankful when I had finished my 'ration'.

I did, however, ask Radek whether, in return for his help and kindness, I could send him anything from London and he unhesitatingly asked for an English pipe. In due course I sent him one from Dunhill's. Whether it ever reached him or whether, if it did, it contributed to the cumulative suspicion directed against him, I shall never know for I received no acknowledgement.

Whatever one may think of Radek one cannot but admire his behaviour when, in the following year, he was arrested and placed on trial with other of the Old Bolsheviks on charges of 'Trotskyist deviation'. Most of his fellow-accused were persuaded into making abject confessions of guilt and sweeping recantations, which availed them nothing, for they were all liquidated. Not so Radek. He gave the notorious Public Prosecutor, Vyshinsky, as good as he got, refusing to recant and defending himself with deftness and ability. With Sokolnikov he escaped a death sentence and eked out an existence in a Soviet labour camp until about 1940, when, it was said, he was murdered – ironically enough – by a fellow-prisoner.

III

At the end of my researches in Russia I felt that I was sufficiently equipped to begin to write the book, and I settled down in Charlottesville, Virginia, adjacent to Mr Jefferson's University, to do so. I speedily found that I was completely wrong, that some grave lacunae existed in my information and that these could only be filled after a talk with Leon Trotsky. I therefore set about organising this not very easy project.

Trotsky was at that time (1937) living in exile in a villa lent him by the great muralist Diego Rivera in a suburb of Mexico City called Coyoyacan. Thither I flew from Washington, armed with a letter of introduction from an old friend of mine, Max Eastman, who from being an orthodox Communist had become a convert to Trotskyism and had translated many of Trotsky's voluminous works into English. I established myself in the neighbouring suburb of San Angel, made contact and was duly summoned to Coyoyacan. On arrival at the entrance of the villa I was first accosted by a Mexican military policeman, from the constabulary post which the government maintained day and night on the opposite side of the road. Having passed an initial scrutiny, I then approached the entrance which consisted of a solid steel gate set in a whitewashed adobe wall. There was a grilled wicket and in answer to my ring a face appeared. The grill was opened just wide enough to admit my letter of introduction and its 'coverer'. It was then slammed shut and I was left standing in the hot Mexican sunshine like Peri at the gate disconsolate.

After what seemed like an eternity, for there was no shade and the police post was inhospitable, the gate suddenly opened and I found myself faced by two young blond Ukrainians, whose sea-blue eyes were expressionless and seemingly unblinking, and both of whom held me covered by automatic pistols. I was beckoned inside and subjected to as thorough a 'frisking' as I think is possible. No article of my clothing, no part of my body was left unexamined, and in complete silence. I was then marched at pistol-point into a large sunlit room, through the windows of which, I remember, the branches of orange trees drooped inwards and there, seated behind a writing table, with a great wall of bookshelves behind him, was Trotsky.

We shook hands and his first remark, in German, was one of apology for the preceding ordeal. 'I have to be careful, you see,' he said, 'Stalin is always trying to murder me. Last month there was another attempt and he brought a letter of introduction, too – but not from Max, of course.'

His manner was not hostile. Indeed it was almost friendly. My first reaction was one of surprise that he looked exactly like his photographs; a large head with strong upstanding hair and a little moustache and goatee beard. My second discovery was that for the first and only time in my life I was in the presence of someone who was motivated largely by hatred. I have often felt myself to be in the presence of evil, but never before of abstract hatred which seemed to me to extend from society generally down to even inanimate objects. I felt that he positively loathed the ink-pot!

On the other hand, it did not seem that he included me in this general anathema. He appeared to be genuinely anxious to be helpful. In answer to my question in what language we should converse, saying that I thought I could probably follow him in German or French if he preferred these to English, he replied in a heavy accent:

'Ach nein, ve vill spik English and ven I cannot find de voids ve vill spik Goiman,' and I realised that he had learned his English on the East side of New York.

At the outset, he admitted that he had not thought about Brest-Litovsk for some time. Would I refresh his memory? I began to recount the story of the negotiations and it was like watching a machine gradually come to life. He came from behind his table and began to pace the floor; he plunged his hands into his abundant hair as if in search of inspiration, as if cudgelling his brain to remembrance, and then it happened. In the middle of a sentence of mine, the penny dropped in his mind and out came a torrent of reminiscence, justification, accusation and recrimination. He spoke in English, French, German, Russian and even Yiddish (the last two of which were incomprehensible to me) and it seemed as if I were submerged in a flood which had been dammed up for years awaiting release.

Desperately I sought to seize and salvage such items of historical flotsam and jetsam as were borne past me on the current. Gradually the first tide subsided and he threw himself into his chair in a state of exhaustion. Now was my chance to ask questions. Why, for instance, had he indulged in those 'spiritual wrestling matches' with von Kühlmann, which had ranged from Dan to Beersheba and from China to Peru, embracing such apparent irrelevancies as the degree of dependence of the Nizam of Hyderabad upon the British Crown and the scope and power of the Supreme Court of the United States of America?

That was easy to answer, said Trotsky. Both von Kühlmann and he wanted to drag out the negotiations but for different reasons. Von Kühlmann wished to delay as long as possible the moment when he must present an ultimatum, which he knew would damn Germany in the eyes of the civilised world; he hoped to arrive at a negotiated 'accommodation' with the Bolsheviks. Trotsky, on the other hand, though he had no intention of meeting von Kühlmann's terms voluntarily or to facilitate his task in any way, was under instruction from Lenin to gain as much time as possible for the consolidation of the revolution at home. Thus their prolix discussions served both their purposes. It was only the German General Staff and Czernin who wanted a quick peace, and it was only when Hoffmann virtually usurped the directive of negotiations from von Kühlmann that the ultimatum was presented.

I asked Trotsky whether he had really believed that his unorthodox formula of 'No War – No Peace' would prove practicable. He replied that at the time he had thought it a *coup de théâtre* which would confuse the Germans, put them more in the wrong than they had already placed themselves and perhaps cause a split between Germany and Austria-Hungary and between the German Imperial Government and the General Staff. He admitted, however, that he had been wrong and that Lenin had been right in forecasting that the terms which they would have finally to accept would be more severe, more Draconian, than those which Trotsky had refused to sign.

I had lunch with him and his wife and returned the next day – when I was again thoroughly and drastically searched – for a further session and we discussed many points of interest. I was not unnaturally anxious to get his reaction to Stalin, yet I wished to introduce the subject in not too naïve a manner. Eventually I asked what part Stalin had played in the peace negotiations – knowing that he had sided with Lenin against Trotsky in the final showdown. The effect was electric.

'Stalin,' almost screamed Trotsky. 'He is a terrible man. He has stolen my thunder. He has said that it is he, Stalin, who has created the Red Army. I tell you it was I, Trotsky, who created the Red Army. Where was Stalin at the battle of Kazan? Muddling in the Commissariat of National Minorities.' And there was much more. But I had got my money's worth.

Finally we parted, and I felt that he had enjoyed it almost as much as I had. I had talked with one of the single most destructive forces in the twentieth century and had learned a lot; he had released a lot of spleen and vitriol and adrenalin, long pent up within him, and felt all the better for it. As a parting gift he gave me a number of his own works including his History of the Russian Revolution, his book on the Brest-Litovsk negotiations (a very rare collectors' item) and a more recent, less valuable though nonetheless entertaining contribution entitled Stalin's Falsification of History. All these he autographed and inscribed, in his flowery hand, in not unfriendly terms – a Greek gift, if ever there was one, for when my aeroplane entered the United States at Brownsville, Texas, these volumes were found among my baggage by the U.S. Customs. I then spent a tedious hour explaining to the local, and not very intelligent, F.B.I. personnel that Trotsky hated Stalin as much as J. Edgar Hoover did, and that the books had in any case all been published in America already. Eventually I was allowed to proceed, bearing my trophies with me, though the authorities were still shaking their heads over the inscriptions. When I rejoined my fellow-travellers, who had been kept waiting in the broiling heat of a Texan summer day while I grappled with security, I found myself the most unpopular man alive.

My book was published in 1938 and two years later Stalin eventually 'got his man'. Despite Trotsky's stringent precautions a young man wormed his way into his confidence, and after living for some weeks in that beautiful little villa in Coyoyacan he killed Trotsky by driving an ice-pick into his brain. So strong was the victim's grip on his assassin's throat that it had literally to be broken after death. Trotsky died like a man.

The finale of this story is not uninteresting. My old and valued friend, Harold Caccia, later destined to hold such diverse and dignified offices as Ambassador to Washington, Permanent Under-Secretary at the Foreign Office, Provost of Eton, Lord Prior of the Order of St John of Jerusalem, President of the M.C.C., and to become a Life Peer, was, at the time that *Brest-Litovsk* was published in November 1938, a Second Secretary in the Private Office of the Foreign Secretary, Lord Halifax. He read the book over the Christmas holidays and was apparently favourably impressed by it, seeing a certain appropriateness in some of its contents in application to current events of the day.

On his return to the Office Harold wrote a minute to Lord Halifax (5 January 1939) commending the book, emphasising the possibility of Hitler's making an attack on the Ukraine, and expressing a belief that Stalin would be responsive to a British advance. He suggested that since a new Ambassador had been appointed to Moscow, in the person of Sir William Seeds, he should be empowered to have a very straight talk with Stalin, after discussion with the French.

'In such a talk', wrote Harold, 'I presume that we should start from two bases:

(1) That we could not undertake any defensive agreement with the U.S.S.R., just as we do not expect them to undertake in advance to give us military help if we were the first to be attacked.

(2) That we recalled that Lenin in 1918 had minuted "that Comrade Trotsky be authorized to accept the assistance of French imperialism against German brigands".'[1]

It was Harold Caccia's thought that similar circumstances might arise in which Stalin, in face of potential German aggression, would be prepared to adopt a similar line towards Britain and France. Should this be the case, it would be better to know what exactly the feelings of the Kremlin were before, and not after, the emergency arose. 'For us too', Caccia concluded, ' "Russian murderers" might in certain eventualities be a lesser danger than "German brigands." '

This was strong meat indeed, especially from an Assistant Private Secretary. What Harold was proposing was virtually a revolution in British foreign policy, which since the Munich Agreement had held

[1] *Brest-Litovsk*, p. 254.

Russia at arms length, and he had courageously and far-sightedly put this forward on the strength of reading *Brest-Litovsk*.[1]

In accordance with custom, the original Caccia minute went the rounds of the Office and elicited almost unanimous disagreement from his superiors. To some it was too daring, to others it was a waste of time, to others again it would merely excite the suspicions of the Russians, while yet others wished to restrict any negotiation with the U.S.S.R. to a commercial basis. The arguments adduced were all wise and carefully considered but they missed the essential point, which was that if we did *not* improve our relations with Russia she might herself make a complete *volte-face* in policy and make a deal with Germany.

Eventually, on 20 January, the paper reached Sir Robert Vansittart, then Chief Diplomatic Adviser to the Government, who at once grasped the essential purport of Harold Caccia's thinking. He deplored the unsatisfactory state of Anglo-Russian relations, which he termed 'not only regrettable but dangerous', and was anxious to repair them as soon as possible. 'Van', however, favoured action on an even greater scale; he dismissed the idea of sending Sir William Seeds to see Stalin. 'What the Russians need is a gesture by sending a Cabinet Minister to Russia. Cover is easily available in the shape of the hitch about the Anglo-Russian trade agreement. The President of the Board of Trade [Oliver Stanley] is the obvious person to go, and if he cannot, Mr Hudson [Head of the Department of Overseas Trade] might well do so. . . . The visit would then be a gesture of general good will and would be overtly connected with the trade agreement . . . it might and probably would have some deterrent effect on Germany, the aggressor of tomorrow. I hope that this suggestion will not only be seriously considered but acted on with the least possible delay.'

Alas, 'Van's' advice, though it was considered, was not acted upon with the urgency for which he pleaded. 'I should like to discuss' was Lord Halifax's final comment on his minute and there the record ends, though not the course of history. Two months later, on 16 March, Hitler tore up the Munich Pact and announced that 'Czechoslovakia had ceased to exist', thereby disclosing even to Mr Chamberlain the futility and mendacity of Nazi pledges. By the end of the month Britain had given her guarantee to Poland against Nazi aggression. On 17 April the Soviet Government proposed a triple pact of

---

[1] The original memorandum written by Mr Harold Caccia together with the subsequent minutes, ending with Sir Robert Vansittart's, are to be found in the Public Record Office. F.O.371 23677. 721.

mutual assistance between France, Great Britain and Russia, a military convention reinforcing such a pact, and a triple guarantee of all the border states from the Baltic to the Black Sea. From so starkly realistic a suggestion the Western Powers recoiled in alarm, with the result that on 3 May there occurred an event in Moscow which portended disaster; Maxim Litvinov was superseded by Molotov as Commissar for Foreign Affairs; a new phase of Soviet diplomatic policy had already begun.

Then and only then did Lord Halifax decide upon the advice tendered him by Sir Robert Vansittart nearly six months earlier, with a plea for action 'with the least possible delay'. Even then he did not grasp 'Van's' imaginative suggestion of sending a Cabinet Minister; in June he despatched to strengthen British representation in Moscow William Strang – whose chief recommendation to the Russians was certainly not the fact that he had accompanied Mr Chamberlain on his three visits to Hitler. Strang embarked upon a fruitless and foredoomed mission, which ended in August, shortly before the signing of the Nazi–Soviet Pact.

May one not wonder whether the possible adoption of the Vansittart–Caccia suggestion, in which *Brest-Litovsk* played its part, may not be numbered among the major 'Ifs' of history?

CHAPTER FIVE

Twilight in Vienna

I

There are few of us, I suppose, who have not indulged in a pet fantasy as to which period of history we would like to have lived in other than our own – and the choice is often revealing of our inner selves. There are, of course, certain ground rules. One may choose, on a long-term basis, a whole era in which to have enjoyed existence, and also a short-term period of perhaps a single year. Nor need these be of the same historical time-bracket. One might, for example, opt for a lifetime in Periclean Athens or an evening dining with Talleyrand, or both.

Personally, being of a romantic, hedonistic and, if the truth must be told, somewhat indolent turn of character, I have no doubt as to my long-term and short-term choices. If it were a matter of living one's life, I should have enjoyed doing this in the Commonwealth of Virginia before the American Civil War. Never has gracious living been more delightfully alive than in the ante-bellum South, and never was it lived in greater enlightenment than in Virginia, where the Jeffersonian tradition of the Universal Man was still paramount. Beautiful and spendidly appointed houses, many of them built to Jefferson's own design, abounded. Mr Jefferson's own University at Charlottesville and Christopher Wren's College of William and Mary at Williamsburg were centres of light and learning, producing good scholars and fine gentlemen. Men wrote and thought for their contemporaries and for posterity. For the romantic there were vivacious balls, flirtatious beaux and belles and 'tournaments of honour'; and for the sportsman fox-hunting, horse-racing and cock-fighting, there were fine wines and bourbon whisky and exquisite cuisine; swords and roses, jasmine and old lace, young loves and old. The climate, save for the humidity of high summer, was deliciously temperate. A hair-triggered chivalry made for a certain imbalance, but there was also much learning, sound argument and good conversation.

There were, however, two major counter-arguments, one physical, the other moral. It is true that medical science had not attained its present achievements, and therefore one was more susceptible to illness, infection and premature mortality. The answer to this, of course, is that one cannot have everything and that there were, in my opinion, many counter-balancing factors which amply compensated for a perhaps somewhat shortened span of life.

The moral factor was, of course, that the economic basis of life was what was euphemistically termed, the Institution – that is to say slavery, and while I do not wish to defend the system, it is only fair to say that, whatever may have been the case in the cotton states of the Deep South, in Virginia slavery was already diminishing in the years before the War; manumission had become so prevalent as to be a serious cause of unemployment and it was a growing custom for owners to include in their wills a provision freeing their slaves.

The ante-bellum South therefore had attained a degree of civilisation in its highest sense, a civilisation which has never again existed anywhere in the United States. Had it not been for the hot-headed Secessionists of the Deep South and the implacable Abolitionists of New England, this civilisation might have moulded the American way of life along very different lines from those it subsequently followed. But the Civil War destroyed it completely, for the highest of moralistic reasons, of course, but nevertheless irreparably and irrevocably. I am sure I should have enjoyed it very much, had I died comfortably – if prematurely ! – before 1860.

On the short-term basis I am equally definite in my choice; I should like to have spent the year 1867 visiting Paris, Budapest and Vienna. In that year of the International Exhibition Paris must have been entrancing. Never did the Second Empire seem more firmly established, just beginning its evolution from dictatorship to liberal government. Haussmann's transformation of the city had already borne fruit and great avenues and vistas had opened up where slums and mean houses had been. Offenbach was at the height of his career, pouring forth enchanting entertainment and every month a different monarch arrived to see the wonders of the Exhibition. The Tsar, the King of Prussia, the Prince of Wales, and a host of minor German royalties came to admire and exclaim and to accept the hospitality of a court which, fifteen years earlier, they had been satisfied to dismiss as *parvenu*. Even Bismarck, in attendance on his sovereign, had been moved by the sheer beauty of Paris and had momentarily disclosed the sentimentality which underlies the whole German character.

Much has been written in depreciation of the Second Empire, of the cynical duplicity and general slipperiness of Napoleon III and the fanatical, mystical, Catholic, monarchist influence of Eugénie. There is little doubt that tinsel was the predominant element in its make-up, but there was some high carat gold among the tinsel and both sovereigns knew how to conduct a court with the ease and comfortable relaxation of a great English country house. It would have been something to have attended a reception or a court-ball at the Tuileries; to have mounted the grand staircase with two motionless giants in the magnificent uniform of the Cent Garde on every step; to find at the entrance to the ballroom the Emperor and Empress receiving, he with his enigmatic smile and lazy, heavy-lidded glance that missed nothing, and she, as she has been immortalised by Winterhalter, in a crinolined creation of Worth's which set off both her beauty and her charm to perfection.

It would indeed have been something to remember, and, if one were lucky enough to be invited to dine and sleep at Compiègne or Fontainebleau – and numerous English visitors were so privileged – one could not but have enjoyed the variety of amusements provided, a ride in the forest, a mild and transient flirtation, a flutter at cards in the evening or impromptu charades or a programme of music by great artists from Paris.

One might also have been fortunate in being taken to Princess Mathilde's country seat at St Gratien, there to hear Dainte-Beuve and Prosper Merimée and others read their works or dispute, amicably or irascibly, on some intellectual subject.

Then on southwards to Budapest where the Hasburg Empire was in the throes of becoming the Dual Monarchy. One would have given a lot to have been present in St Matthew's Cathedral on 8 June to see Francis-Joseph assume the Iron Crown of St Stephen, a diadem now reposing in some secret vault in America under the trusteeship of the United States Government. The magnificence of the Magyar nobility in their feudal costumes, the excitement of this new adventure in government which was to hold the Habsburg dominions together for another half-century – this would have been worth seeing.

And Vienna itself – that most amazing of capitals, the centre of a polyglot, multiracial empire whose very existence was an achievement in itself. Nothing, it seemed could change the light-hearted irresponsibility of the Viennese, their *Schlamperei*, their love of pleasure, their amazing refusal to read or accept the portents of impending doom. Notwithstanding their humiliating defeat at the hands of the Prussians at Königgrätz only a year earlier, their summer cheerfulness in 1867 was as gay as ever, and one could not but have been infected by it. There would have been racing in the Prater, and one would have ridden there beside the carriage of some beauty and her chaperone; the cafés and restaurants under the trees would have been full of laughing crowds enjoying the *divertissements* of bands and comic entertainers. In the evening one would have swayed to the rhythm of Johann Strauss's latest waltz – or doing the 'one-two-three-hop' to his brother Joseph's newest polka. There would have been very cold champagne and golden Tokay

> Wine of the sun that will waft you along,
> Lifting you high on the wings of a song.

It was a highly enjoyable masquerade of gaiety which continued on its myopic way until the outbreak of the First World War.

A court-ball at Schönbrunn or the Hofburg would have been a stiffer and more formal affair than one would have known at the Tuileries but more brilliant. The Austrian Army, even if it never won a battle except against the Italians, had wonderfully decorative uniforms in all colours, but especially the speckless white of the general officers; their orders and decorations were more varied and dashing than the somewhat monotonous scarlet of the Legion of Honour, and though the women's dresses might have lacked the *chic* of Paris their jewels were unsurpassed.

I would have liked too to have seen the Emperor Francis-Joseph himself as a ramrod-straight-backed, handsome man of forty, rather than as the old, stooping, shadowy figure I can remember as a boy in the spring of 1914. In this year of destiny the procession of tragedy which darkened his later years, the violent deaths at Mayerling and Geneva and Sarajevo, were still in the future. His life had not been untrammelled, but he had surmounted his problems and misfortunes with obstinacy and courage and at this time he still enjoyed the matchless beauty of the Empress Elisabeth before her sad affliction came upon her. And it would have been worth seeing *her*.

Yes, the year 1867 would have been the year for me! But

> So much for idle wishing – how
> It steals the time! To business now.

II

It is odd, perhaps, that, though I was a boy of sixteen when the Austro-Hungarian Empire disintegrated at the close of the First World War, owing to centrifugal forces greatly aided by the short-sighted but effective influence of Allied propaganda, I have in my life experienced a number of contacts with it. Of these, the most dramatic was the murder of Austrian Prime Minister, Count von Stürgkh on 21 October 1916.

I had a friend, a Polish military attaché in a foreign capital, who once told me that on this date he and his parents were lunching in the restaurant of the M.u.S. (Meisl und Schadn) hotel in celebration of his receiving his commission as a subaltern in an Austrian cavalry regiment. He was about to leave for the Eastern Front, where, though the life expectancy of a subaltern was considerably longer than on the Western Front at this time, the war was still active and dangers many; it was therefore something of an *ave atque vale* occasion. The family group noticed the Prime Minister come in and take his usual table and then lost interest in him until they heard three muffled shots, saw von Stürgkh slumped in his chair and a posse of waiters surrounding the assassin, who later proved to be none other than the highly respectable Socialist leader, one Friedrich Adler, son of the leader of the Austrian Socialist movement, Viktor Adler, then still living at the age of sixty-six.

It was a matter of interest to me to have an eye-witness account of an assassination which had considerable historical repercussions in that hitherto the Emperor Francis-Joseph still believed that all was well in his empire and that victory was 'just around the corner', an illusion which was only dispelled by von Stürgkh's murder. This interest, however, paled beside my reaction when some years later during the Second World War, when I had a mission in New York, there came to my office none other than Dr Friedrich Adler himself. Arrested after the murder, he had been condemned to death; however the sentence was commuted to one of life imprisonment from which he had been released at the fall of the Monarchy in 1918 and had resumed his position in the leadership of the Social Democratic Party, becoming eventually Secretary-General of the Second International. He died in 1960. His record was one of great courage. At the time of the *Anschluss* in 1938 he escaped just in time to avoid arrest and perhaps death in a concentration camp, and now, after a catalogue of adventures – including further escapes from Prague and Paris – he had arrived in New York and had been advised to come and see me.

Over luncheon – the second I had had with a known murderer, the first being with Peter Rutenberg, who was credited with having 'disposed of' Father Gapon on behalf of the Russian Revolutionary movement, they having condemned him to death as a police *agent provocateur* after Bloody Sunday 1905 in Petersburg – I asked Adler about his motives for assassinating Stürgkh and how it felt to shoot a man in cold blood. His answers were simple and direct.

He was not, he said, a natural killer. The Socialist movement had never condoned political assassination, and he was essentially a respectable doctrinaire socialist, even a socialist of the Establishment. He had, however, reached the conclusion (I suspect very reluctantly) that an extreme demonstration must be made against the futility of the war and the shocking conditions of near-starvation under which the people of Vienna were living. Argument and protest in and out of parliament – which had in any case been prorogued for the greater part of the war – had proved useless, and he had become convinced that only the elimination of the Prime Minister could arouse the awareness of the higher Powers to the facts of life – in which deduction he was perfectly correct.

So much for motives; in performance Adler was almost engagingly naïve. Unfamiliar with such restaurants as the M.u.S., he felt himself to be out of his depth, but he was wearing a decent black suit and noticed that waiters were scurrying about with napkins over their arms. He possessed himself of one of these and approached Stürgkh's table. Then, like an actor who is about to muff his lines, he froze and stood for what seemed to him an eternity as if turned to stone. Meantime the Prime Minister continued to enjoy his lunch. Adler eventually came to and then found himself beset by feelings of conscience. Not that he had grown infirm of purpose, but he suddenly felt that he could not kill a man by surprise. He could not, as it were, 'shoot a sitting bird'. He salved his conscience and his unconscious sense of sportsmanship by saying in a loud voice 'Graf von Stürgkh' and then, as the Prime Minister turned towards him, he fired three shots at close range, got his man and waited quietly to be arrested.

Adler recounted this enthralling story with an extraordinary lack of emotion, almost as if he were speaking of someone else. It was one of my better luncheons.

III

I am glad that I did not see Vienna in that anguished period immediately after the First World War when she became *une ville sans âme*. Built and designed as the centre of a great empire, Vienna suddenly became, as a result of the Peace Settlement of Paris, the completely disproportionate capital of a minute Germanic state, whose natural desire to become part of the German Reich was forbidden under the Treaties of Versailles and St Germain. Hunger, misery, defeatism and a general ineptitude of government reduced the state of Austria to such depths of national bankruptcy that it was literally hawked around Europe to the highest bidder and, when none was available, was taken into receivership by the League of Nations, who effectively resuscitated it.

When I visited Vienna again in the middle twenties it was beginning to take on something of its old character but it was still *une ville sans âme*. Nevertheless I was fortunate enough in the comparatively short time I was there to meet four of the great ladies who had courageously survived the deluge and had resumed their lives adaptably under the new regime.

The first of these was Princess Stephanie Lonyay, the widow of the Archduke Rudolph. The daughter of that notorious old monarch King Leopold II of the Belgians, Princess Stephanie had been married in 1881 at the gawky age of sixteen to the Austrian Crown Prince, and those who had read her book, *I Was to Have Been Empress*, will know the trials and tribulations through which she passed before the tragedy of Mayerling in 1889. Twenty years later she married, *en secondes noces*, Count Elmer Lonyay, with whom she lived in great happiness, dying in 1945. This marriage, though it received the approval of the Emperor, caused the greatest displeasure to their Belgian majesties, who let it be known in no uncertain terms that they proposed to ignore it completely. There is no reason to believe that this greatly disturbed either of the principal parties concerned.

When I was presented to her she was in her middle sixties and had lost much of the shyness and lack of response which had characterised her on her arrival in Vienna half a century earlier. She was stately, but still somewhat withdrawn, with the frigidity of the Coburgs, untempered by the gaiety of her Habsburg mother. But she was gracious and charming, and she told one story of mild historical interest. Though her marriage to Count Lonyay was for love, she did not fully appreciate the significance of her change of status until after the ceremony. When she entered the church the guards presented arms to an imperial Archduchess, who still bore the title of Dowager Crown Princess; when she emerged with her husband she received no such honour, since she was now only the Countess Elmer Lonyay (he was in fact created a Prince in 1917), and this seemed to have impressed her deeply.

The second of my fascinating ladies was Princess Stephanie's daughter, the only child of the Archduke Rudolph. Born in 1883, she was christened Elisabeth and known as 'Erzi' in the family. Brought up under the shadow of her father's mysterious death, she had become the much loved grandchild of the Emperor who gave her the tenderest care and, shortly after her mother's second wedding, countenanced her own marriage to the young, dashing and dazzling Prince Otto

Windischgrätz. This, however, was not a very great success, and, though she did not divorce him until 1924, she reacted violently against the background and environment of her upbringing. She became indeed a wholly convinced, card-carrying member of the Austrian Socialist Party, in whose ranks she was affectionately known as *die rote Liesl* (Red Lizzy), a tribute both to the complexion of her politics and to her beautiful golden-auburn hair which she had inherited from her grandmother, the Empress Elisabeth.

When I visited her, however, the glory of the aureole had been somewhat dimmed. Shortly after her divorce from Prince Windisch-grätz she had married Herr Leopold Petznek, a leading light among the Socialist Party who had been a member of the Revolutionary Council which had assumed government after the collapse of the monarchy in November 1918 and had indeed released Friedrich Adler from prison. The Petzneks lived a comfortable bourgeois existence in one of those great blocks of flats (I think it was the Karl Marx Hof) built by the Socialist municipality of Vienna and later to become suspect as fortresses, bristling with rifles and side-arms. She was only thirty-five but looked older, and was neatly though not fashionably dressed, but it was her surroundings which interested me. Here relics of her past jostled with evidence of her present life. Revolutionary literature and an imperial snuff-box occupied adjoining shelves. Pictures of Francis-Joseph and Karl Marx adorned the walls. She herself was vivacious and talkative, but very little of what she said remains in my memory. Both she and her husband were said to have been involved in the armed resistance to the suppression of the Socialists by Dollfuss in February 1934. I have no idea, however, what happened to her and to her husband during the Nazi regime or whether they suffered acutely. Neither is it clear what, if any, part they played in Karl Renner's provisional government set up in 1946, but whatever adventures may have beset them, they – or at any rate she – survived until 1963 at the ripe age of eighty.

If these two relics of the old régime, if I may thus respectfully call them, were of true imperial vintage, there was another lady, still in good heart and fettle at the age of seventy-five, who had played an even more conspicuous role under the Empire than either of them. Katherina Kis von Ittebe, better known by her maiden name of Katherina Schratt, a star of the Burgtheater, had been introduced into the life of the Emperor Francis-Joseph by his wife Elisabeth, as a substitute or 'stand-in' for herself while she indulged in what virtually amounted to a mania for almost constant travel and sojourn abroad. The Empress chose someone from the theatre rather than the aristocracy because she realised the dangers of talk of a camarilla and well-knowing that the Emperor was adamant in rejecting even the merest suspicion of being influenced by unofficial persons. She selected Kathie Schratt as a *Seelenfreundin* (soul-mate) for her genuine kindness of heart and her cheerful disposition, and she never did her husband a greater or a more benign service.

What had the appearance of unconventionality developed into the most perfect 'Darby-and-Joan' relationship, which began in 1886 and continued without a breath of scandal until the murder of the Empress Elisabeth at Geneva in September 1898. During these years they saw one another constantly in Vienna and at Bad Ischl, and when separated from her Francis-Joseph wrote or telegraphed to her almost daily. Their affection was deep and mutual. They were cosy together, relaxed, happy and contented. This blissful existence ended with the Empress's death. Then Frau Schratt's traducers seized the opportunity to take advantage of her new vulnerability. Scandal began to circulate and, on her initiative, there was a formal and heart-rending farewell on the Emperor's seventieth birthday, 18 August 1900. When he needed her perhaps more acutely than ever before, he was deprived of her comfort; but his tenderness for her never waned, and their correspondence continued intermittently until his death some sixteen years later.

There was no mistaking the simple dignity of Frau Schratt. She was a great lady in her own right, and when I saw her, elderly, grey and dressed in the style of a passed age, I was deeply impressed by her presence and her sense of the fitness of things. Her drawing-room was even more reminiscent than those of the others. Her mementos went back into the obscure past. I recall a faded photograph of a somewhat dissipated face and signed 'Milan' and suddenly realised that this was the father of that King of Servia, Alexander Obrenovitch who, with his wife Draga, had been murdered by the Royal Guard in 1903. Now neither Obrenovitch or Karageorgevitch reigns in Belgra

Moreover, there was about Frau Schratt her *chic* of conduct. The letters of the Emperor to her have been published and provide a fruitful source to the historian,[1] but never a word, written or spoken, escaped Kathie either before or after his death. The representatives of newspaper proprietors, including the great William Randolph Hearst, grovelled before her for an interview; publishers offered her fabulous sums for her memoirs, either written by herself or 'ghosted'. All to no purpose. In loyalty to her *Seelenfreund* she cherished her

[1] Jean de Bourgoing, *The Incredible Friendship* (State University of New York Press, Albany, New York, 1966).

memories in silence, even when, in the years of the post-war collapse she must, like most other Viennese, have felt the pinch of hunger. 'You want to buy my memoirs?' was her answer to one importunate agent. 'There are no memoirs, and your public would be very much disappointed. I am neither a Pompadour nor a Maintenon.' She indeed had *panache*, and she retained it till her death in 1940.

If Frau Schratt was grand, Frau Sacher, the fourth of my 'great ladies', was magnificent. Surely one of the world's most famous *hôtelières*, she was wonderful in every respect. The food which her superb restaurant purveyed was unequalled; the comfort of her house was without peer; the whole ambience of 'Sacher's' was something to be savoured, cherished and remembered. Frau Sacher herself was in a way not unlike Rosa Lewis of the Cavendish. She was ripe, fruity and 'unflappable'. No emergency or crisis could disturb her equanimity or her sense of humour. She was the kindest and most welcoming of hostesses.

And she had courage. During that terrible post-war period when Vienna was 'cliff-hanging' on the edge of starvation and there were frequent hunger riots, the mobs, on one occasion, set out to wreck the luxury hotels and restaurants of the Ringstrasse district. They broke the windows of the Bristol and the Imperial and pillaged their food-stocks, and then they came to Sacher's behind the Opera. A trembling concierge sent word to the proprietress of their approach, and on their turbulent arrival they were received on the doorstep by Frau Sacher herself, smoking her habitual cigar. For ten minutes or so she addressed them in the Viennese equivalent of 'Billingsgate' and then, turning on her heel, said to her *maître d'hôtel*: 'Send them out a hot meal.' This was magnificence.

I was always deeply grateful to Frau Sacher for her never-failing kindness to me. After our first meeting I lunched and dined there whenever I was in Vienna, until her death in February 1930, and in the evenings she would talk with great freedom though never with positive malice or indiscretion. Her house had been a haunt for generations of the imperial Archdukes and of Austrian aristocracy – and they were a rum lot, many of them – and her fund of memories was inexhaustible. I have written earlier that I had been reared at Malvern on Coxe's *House of Austria* with its wealth of *contes scandaleuses*, some of which I would recount to her in order to stimulate reciprocation. Not that this was a difficult task. She was a wonderful source of anecdote. She told me, for instance, of one member of the House of Habsburg who had so bad a case of syphilis of the nose that he had to wear a casing of leather over the offending feature. And then she would chuckle reminiscently and add: 'And, my dear, there was that dear Archduke X – such a charming man and he used to come down that staircase naked, but *quite* naked. But he was such a gentleman, he always kept his sword on.' Yet despite her drolleries, she remained the staunchest and most loyal of monarchists.

I regretted the news of Frau Sacher's death as that of an old friend. I was thankful, however, that she did not see the swastika banner mounted over Vienna and that she was spared the shock of the stick of bombs which later demolished her terrace and also the rear of the Opera House. That she would have been undaunted I have no doubt, but it was better so.

IV

I have known few more controversially complex characters in my life than that minute Austrian statesman, Engelbert Dollfuss. To some his memory is that of a fiend incarnate, to others that of a hero and a martyr, to others again a curious schizophrenic amalgam of both. To me he was the tragic and almost predestined victim of a political dilemma virtually impossible of solution.

Born in Lower Austria of peasant stock, Dollfuss was well educated at the universities of Vienna and Berlin, and throughout the First World War he served with gallantry and distinction. After the war he entered politics as a member of the Christian Socialist Party, rose quickly in the cadre of leadership and in 1932, at the age of forty, was appointed Federal Chancellor. It was now that his problems became compounded. The Austrian state as created by the peace settlement of 1919 was politically impotent and economically unviable. As from the beginning of 1933, its northern neighbour, Germany came under the control of a régime dedicated to the annexation of Austria as a province of the Third Reich. Whereupon the Nazi Party in Austria opened a vicious campaign against the Federal Government. To the south, Fascist Italy, as yet unallied with Nazi Germany, offered support, but at a price. Austria was thus caught in a geopolitical quandary between two dictatorships.

Dollfuss therefore found himself walking precariously on a knife edge. He was intensely patriotic with a deep love of Austria – though with the peasant's distrust of Vienna. He had no intention of being absorbed into the Third Reich and was opposed to much of the Nazi programme. On the other hand he had an almost pathological hatred of the Social Democrats, whom he regarded as internationally

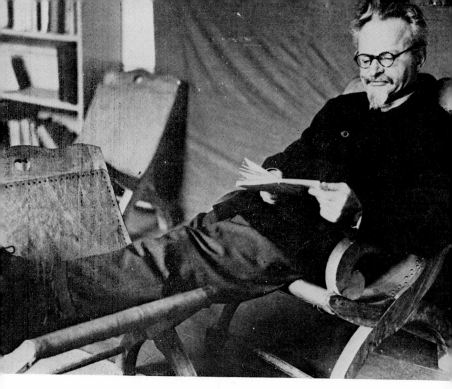

Trotsky in exile

Karl Radek

The minuscule statesman,
Engelbert Dollfuss

With Archduke Otto of Austria

oriented in loyalty and fallacious in their economic policies. Moreover he was developing a strong suspicion of parliamentary democracy. This rather odd blend of principles and prejudices inevitably inclined him towards Italy, where Mussolini offered support against Nazi aggression and whence he imbibed a predilection for the postulates of the Corporate State. The Duce also encouraged him 'to stand no nonsense' from the Social Democrats.

It was at the World Economic Conference held in London during the summer of 1933 that Dollfuss attained an international status. In an attempt to mobilise sympathy for Austria in her danger from Germany he made a courageous speech on 14 June, concluding with Schiller's warning that 'the best man cannot live in peace if his wicked neighbours do not leave him in peace', and from then on became not only an outstanding figure but something of a mascot of the conference.

It was during this time that I first met him at a luncheon party of old George Franckenstein's, that delightful diplomat who adorned the Austrian legation in Belgrave Square for so many years, and who, when Hitler eventually annexed Austria in 1938, became a British subject and was knighted by King George VI. I had listened to Dollfuss's speech in the Conference and had been deeply impressed by it, and I found him personally charming.

Exceedingly small, he was no midget. He was perfectly formed in a 'mini-size', and rejoiced in his nickname of the 'Milli-Metternich'. His wife, a very handsome woman of normal height, was also said by the Viennese cabaret artists to invite him 'to climb up and kiss me', and this too pleased him. Indeed he had something in common with Henry Ford who delighted in stories about his motor-cars and received enthusiastically a popular song which concluded:

> So they took four spools and an old tin can,
> And they christened it a Ford, and the damned thing ran.

Dollfuss's charm lay in his wit and his smile, his grace of mien and his undoubted sincerity. His small hands were eloquent, fluttering before him like little birds, and he would tell stories in a peasant dialect, which though they were incomprehensible to most of us, including myself, made us all laugh as he told them and then translated into *hoch Deutsch*. Altogether he was a great success socially and when I had a moment of conversation with him after lunch he asked me if I ever came to Vienna. I answered that indeed I did and went on to tell him of an ambition of mine so far unfulfilled. I was most anxious, I said, to see the room in the Ballhausplatz where the

Congress of Vienna had met and particularly to count the number of doors leading into it, because I had been told that, in order to solve a thorny problem of protocol, Metternich caused some extra doors to be cut into the conference room so that each of the great negotiating sovereigns might enter simultaneously, thereby avoiding difficulties of precedence. The Chancellor laughed and said that he too had heard this story, and if I would let him know when I was next in Vienna he would be delighted to show me the room.

I was not able to keep this rendezvous until the spring of 1934, by which time events had moved swiftly and significantly. In the nine months since our first meeting, Dollfuss had dissolved parliament, torn up the republican constitution, and introduced a statute of a corporate state; he had also outlawed the Austrian Nazi Party and after a few days of determined fighting had, in February 1934, ruthlessly suppressed the Socialists, after bombarding the working-class districts of Vienna with light artillery.

After this congeries of events it was not entirely surprising that there had been an attempt on his life and characteristically he made this his first subject of conversation when I went to see him. 'You know', he said, 'that someone tried to shoot me the other day. They tell me he was either a Nazi or a Socialist; but I have my own theory. I think he was a mad scientist trying to split the atom.'

After this endearing opening gambit we examined the conference chamber which in fact opened off his office – which had been Metternich's. The extra doors, he told me, had indeed been cut but had later been blocked up. Of the two leading out of his room one was real and one a dummy.

There is a terrible sequel to this story. I have been told that when, some few months later, on the morning of 25 July 1934, Nazi thugs broke into his office and gunned down an unarmed Dollfuss, he tried to escape into the next room but in doing so he ran to the *false* door, which we had examined together, and was shot as he struggled to open it. His murderers allowed him to bleed to death without the attention of a physician or the consolation of a priest.

It must be said of Dollfuss that he had great courage and never shirked what he regarded as a responsibility. But his position was really an impossible one, and he rendered it further untenable by his treatment of the Socialists. Gallant though their resistance was – they were the only Marxists, with the later exception of the Spanish Republican Government, to make armed opposition to the forces of totalitarianism – the Austrian Social Democrats never recovered from their defeat and the result of Dollfuss's action was to weaken those forces which were opposed – as he was – to a Nazi takeover. He bequeathed a *damnosa hereditas* to his successor, Kurt von Schuschnigg.

V

My last pre-war visit to Austria was in 1935 on my way to Moscow, it being impossible for me to take the more direct route through Germany. I found among the diplomatic corps two old friends, the British and American Ambassadors, Walford Selby, whom I had known in the Foreign Office, and George Messersmith, who had been Consul-General in Berlin for a number of years. There was also another former acquaintance who had become for me a *Pechvogel* (bird of ill-omen) – none other than Franz von Papen, who had been appointed German Minister to Vienna despite his 'near-miss' on the Night of the Long Knives, and who had, even more incredibly, accepted.

I did not call upon von Papen, considering it unwise to stray even on to the diplomatic territory of a German legation, but we met briefly socially and he had the grace to express concern at what might have happened to me on that bloody weekend of 30 June 1934, and gratification that it had not. But from both Selby and Messersmith and from other sources I learned that he was busily engaged in clandestine operations directed towards the infiltration of the Federal Cabinet by the introduction of Ministers who, if they were not openly declared Nazis, were certainly well disposed toward an *Anschluss* between Germany and Austria on a common basis of National Socialism. It was ironic to find that one of the chief obstacles to the progress of these manipulations was the independent and insubordinate attitude of the Austrian Nazi Party itself, which, scorning the ways of diplomacy, however tortuous and nefarious, favoured strong-arm tactics, blood-letting and a *coup d'état*. I was told that the Bundeskanzler, Kurt von Schuschnigg, was putting up a strenuous opposition to this German pressure and that so far Papen and his Austrian colleagues had made little progress.

Let it be said in passing that by far the nastiest Nazis were to be found in Austria, and of these the worst were in Vienna. Though there was bloody murder and bestial brutality throughout the Reich, in no other city have I found impeccable evidence that in March 1938 S.A. troopers, having deposited human excrement and other filth on the pavements, then supervised the cleaning of these same pavements by elderly Jews of both sexes and all classes on their knees, with obscene jokes at their obvious revulsion. Nor must it be forgotten that an end to this nauseating *corvée* was brought about by the courageous action of one man. The name of a former general of the Imperial army, of semi-Jewish stock and distinguished war record, who had been head of the Jewish ex-servicemen's association, had been omitted from the list of those to be rounded up for this loathsome purpose because of his great personal popularity. When, however, he learned what was afoot, this valorous old veteran put on his full-dress uniform and decorations, which were many, and thus attired, reported for 'scrubbing duty' to the considerable embarrassment of the Nazi authorities. After a hasty consultation, the operation was suspended.

I did not meet Dr von Schuschnigg during this visit in 1935, nor indeed until after the war. I was, however, fascinated to discover that, in addition to resisting the increasing threats and blandishments of von Papen, he was mounting a counter-offensive of his own in the shape of a revival of some of the pre-revolutionary aspects of Viennese life. It was almost like a minor monarchist renaissance.

For example, the federal army of 30,000 permitted to Austria under the Treaty of St Germain, had hitherto been clothed in rather sloppy ill-fitting field dress which did little for the morale of either officers or men. Now suddenly something very like the old smart imperial uniforms were restored. Officers blossomed forth in tunics of many colours, white, blue and scarlet, and Sacher's and other lesser cafés took on the appearance of gaiety which had been lacking for many years. It was as if one had suddenly stepped into a scene from *The Merry Widow* or *Bitter Sweet*, with a chorus of:

> We're officers and gentlemen,
> Reliable and true,
> Considerate and chivalrous
> In everything we do.

In addition, the House of Habsburg was once more brought into respect and even a certain prominence. For instance, it was an old established custom of Vienna to go after High Mass on Sunday moring to the Spanish Riding School at the Hofburg, there to watch in entranced amazement the incredible equestrian feats of the Lippizaner horses and their riders – if one was very privileged one was allowed to go into the stables after the performance and meet 'the cast' personally. Since 1918 the imperial box had been left vacant, though its gilt and maroon armchairs and fittings were kept in trim. Now, however, I was intrigued to see that the box was occupied by one of the most venerated and admired members of the royal house, the only brother of the Emperor Karl, the Archduke Eugen, a handsome man with a grey close-trimmed beard, who gravely acknowledged the applause which greeted his appearance.

It was a brave and typically Austrian conception of an alternative to National Socialism and for a brief moment hopes of a restoration of the monarchy were actually entertained in certain *milieux*. I was introduced into the close monarchist circle, the Iron Ring, headed by the Herzog Max von Hohenberg and his brother, the sons of the Archduke Franz-Ferdinand and his morganatic wife, Sophie Chotek, Duchess of Hohenberg, who had perished at Sarajevo. Here I found a state of euphoria which I felt to be wholly inconsistent with reality, but these fanatical royalists seemed convinced that 'when the crunch came' Chancellor von Schuschnigg would restore the monarchy rather than submit to a Nazi takeover. They were all prepared for it and seemed pleased that I was interested. Had I, they asked, met the Head of the House? As a matter of fact, I had.

A few years earlier, through Belgian friends of mine, I had been invited to call at the Château Steenockerzeel, near Malines, where dwelt the Empress Zita and her son, the Archduke Otto, heir to the Habsburg lands. It was the first of several visits but it was a somewhat trying experience. The Empress was magnificent in a Greek tragedy kind of way. One could see her cast as Clytemnestra. She had been Empress of Austria and the last crowned Queen of Hungary, had seen the structure of monarchy crumble and collapse around her, had taken part in two abortive attempts at restoration to the Hungarian throne, and finally had watched her husband, the most humane and progressive of men, die in an insignificant villa in the gardens of Reid's Hotel at Funchal.

All this was reflected in the tragic mask of her face, and it was not altogether surprising that she viewed foreign visitors with a certain suspicion. All her hopes, which seemed to have miraculously survived this catalogue of disasters, were now centred on her eldest son, about whom she cast an almost visible mantle of maternal and dynastic protection.

At this our first meeting she sat in regal state and he in subdued attention. To my various questions and conversational gambits it was the Empress who replied, 'My son thinks this,' 'My son thinks that.' He made little or no contribution. But I liked him at once, while she frankly overawed me. At the close of the audience I could appreciate Bismarck's comment on a conversation with Queen Victoria: 'She makes me schweat.' Not that Her Majesty was unkind or condescending. She was just an overwhelming personality, who radiated command and domination – an imperial tigress defending her royal whelp.

However, on my departure, the Empress did ask me to come back again, and I made shift to do so. On this second occasion she was indisposed, and I lunched with the Archduke Otto alone, except for a gentleman in attendance, who was I believe but am not certain, Edgar Czernin, nephew of the man I had seen in New York. My first impression was confirmed. The Archduke was charming, good-looking, witty and highly intelligent. We did not discuss the delicate matter of a potential restoration, but we did cover a wide range of topics bearing on the international situation and especially in Europe. He was highly knowledgeable on central European affairs and received his doctorate at the University of Malines on the strength of a thesis on the need and possibility of a Danubian Economic Confederation. This he wrote under the name of the Duc de Bar, a subsidiary Habsburg title which he had used for enrolment at the University, and he gave me an inscribed copy. It is a composition remarkable for its expertise and clarity of purpose in a young man of his age – he was then about twenty – even though his ancestors had ruled over the territory in question for the better part of a thousand years.

Our friendship continued over the years, and I was impressed by the Archduke's courageous if perhaps unrealistic conduct at the time of the *Anschluss* crisis of March 1938. For he reversed the roles which his followers in Vienna had forecast to me for himself and the Federal Chancellor, and at the peak of the crisis wrote to Dr von Schuschnigg calling upon him to hand over the chancellorship and the direction of national policy to him, the Archduke. I think he must have envisaged a demonstration of 'a man on horseback' which would rally all parties, except the Nazis of course, against German aggression, but it was a forlorn hope born to failure. Von Schuschnigg rejected the proposition and was himself forced eventually to capitulate. No one, however, can accuse the Head of the House of Habsburg with lack of courage, imagination or *panache*.

When the Nazi hordes drove across Belgium in May of 1940, the imperial household at Steenockerzeel fled just in time. The Archduke had been listed for arrest and imprisonment – a fate which had already overtaken his Hohenberg cousins in Vienna – because of his public criticism of the *Anschluss* in particular and National Socialism in general. He and his mother came first to Paris, then to London, then to New York. The Empress found asylum and consolation under the protection of the Cardinal-Archbishop of Quebec, but the Archduke went about his affairs in a most business-like manner. The Austrian refugees in New York were, like most of their kind, splintered and divided. Though all were anti-Nazi, there was one group which unexpectedly combined this with anti-Semitism, anti-Socialism and anti-monarchy; another was straightforwardly Socialist and a third, which was Otto's own, concentrated on being anti-Nazi and pro-monarchist. The difficulty lay in the interpretation of the word 'monarchy', which raised the hackles of the Czechs and the dreams of independence of the Hungarians. But the Archduke persevered and set up an organisation in London, New York and Lisbon, each headed by a brother, with himself in overall control. He had developed greatly since the 'My son thinks this' and 'My son thinks that' stage.

I saw him whenever he was in New York and on one occasion arranged a visit for him to the University of Virginia, where I gave a dinner-party for him at the country club at which Ruth Risher, who was later to become my wife, acted as my hostess. He addressed a couple of meetings, leaving a very good impression behind him.

Two of the bonds which bound me to Mr Churchill, apart from a profound admiration, were our common interest in the American Civil War and the potential restoration of the Habsburg Monarchy. We were both romantics and we both nursed a secret hope that, if the principle of partition of Germany were adopted, the Habsburgs might come again into their own. This accounted for a brief but not uninteresting incident.

The Archduke had submitted a number of memoranda of considerable interest to the American State Department, two of which were circulated to the first Quebec Conference of 1943. These concerned the Soviet ambitions and designs for Austria as a bridgehead in central Europe, to which end a Communist-dominated 'Free Austria' movement had been launched in Moscow, and also a not impractical solution for the problem of the Alto Adigo, which had been a festering sore in Austro-Italian relations since 1919. Mr Churchill was not unfavourably impressed by the views thus expressed and, as a result, I was called upon to submit what amounted to a personal sketch and character report on Otto. This I duly did and he did not suffer from my testimony.

Partition of Germany was in the air and a plan was put forward by the Americans for a south German state composed roughly of the existing territories of Bavaria and Austria. It was to be a Catholic monarchy and the question arose whether it would be the perquisite of the Wittelsbachs or the Habsburgs.

Mr Churchill was inclined to favour a Habsburg and the idea was mooted that Otto should go to Quebec for consultation. To this end the Prime Minister requested the Foreign Secretary to facilitate the Archduke's journey from Britain to Canada. Anthony Eden, however, being of a more practical turn of mind, and having already concluded that the further Balkanisation of central Europe would be disastrous, resisted this proposal and a spirited if not pungent exchange of telegrams ensued. Anthony Eden won the day, however – the forces of reactionary romance were defeated – and in due course the idea of partitioning Germany was discarded, but not before it had produced the lunacy of the Morgenthau Plan.

This was the end of any immediate dreams which Otto might have had for his return to his realm as a monarch but he fought a tireless battle after the war to reside within the new Austrian state as a private citizen. Litigation and prospective legislation were prolonged, and there were many setbacks and disappointments but in 1972 Dr Otto von Habsburg was permitted to enter Austrian territory. This was in great measure due to the preparatory negotiating tact and patience, the restraint and wisdom, of his cousin, Duke Max of Hohenberg, who, having behaved with great heroism in Dachau concentration camp, died prematurely in 1963, as a result of his sufferings there.

CHAPTER SIX

Tragedy in Prague, 1938

I

My original contacts with Czechoslovakia were tenuous and vicarious. My mother had a first cousin, Alexander Ross Hill, who was President of the University of Missouri and who during the First World War, became Vice-President of the American Red Cross in charge of foreign operations. He used to visit us at Ravensbourne when I was a boy, and I liked him very much. He was an exceedingly kind man, tall and good-looking and the epitome of the Victorian term 'a scholar and a gentleman'.

I never knew his first wife, but he married *en secondes noces* a charming woman whose forebears had homesteaded to the West in the eighteen sixties and became possessed of a large tract of land in the state of Kansas. This parcel of real estate did no harm to the family finances and my Cousin Ross's new wife was an extremely rich woman, which was nice for Cousin Ross. She was also a very nice woman and dedicated to the advancement of education, founding schools, endowing scholarships, and holding the office of national president of the American Association of University Women. She had, however, one skeleton in the family cupboard – or what she persisted in regarding as such – somewhere along the line she was related to Jesse James, the legendary American train-bandit and bank-robber of the seventies, who in his later years had become a pillar of the Baptist Church. It cannot be denied, however, that he died a violent death at the hands of an ex-accomplice.

Now, personally, I should not have suffered a qualm as to this eccentricity of heredity. After all, some of the former ruling houses of Europe began their careers as highway robbers on a big scale, for example the Hohenzollerns. Would one blench at discovering the genes of Robin Hood in one's pedigree? Not I. But there was a general conspiracy of the Hill family to ignore this intriguing historical connection, though I sometimes mischievously allowed the bones of the skeleton to rattle by sending my cousin some new biography of her distinguished ancestor!

I should add that, largely under his wife's influence, my cousin Ross took up political reform in Kansas politics and was sufficiently foolhardy to run as Mayor of Kansas City against a member of the local 'machine' of which the famous Mike Pendergast was boss. It was a rough-and-tumble campaign, and when the opposition had shot Cousin Ross's chauffeur's hat off his head, the Reform Candidate prudently withdrew from the mayoral race. I mentioned this incident once to President Truman, whose own early political career had been under the Pendergast banner, and he laughed very merrily. 'I liked your cousin a lot,' he said. 'He was one of the best of men. He just hadn't the temperament for politics.'

This was a prime example of the President's famous axiom which remains a basic principle of political life: 'If you don't like the heat keep out of the kitchen.' It is also a digression from my story.

In the course of the Great War Dr Thomas Garrigue Masaryk, who, more than any one individual, was the father of the Czechoslovak State, travelled extensively in the cause of the independence of his people. He formed the Czechoslovak Legions out of the Austrian prisoners of war taken by the Russians, travelled across Siberia and Japan and finally traversed the United States, visiting colonies of Czechs and Slovaks who had emigrated to America from the Austro-Hungarian Empire. Finally, on 30 June 1918, he signed the Pact of Pittsburg, which for the first time pledged Czechs and Slovaks to the establishment of a united independent state out of what had been the imperial provinces of Bohemia and Moravia and Slovakia.

During his wanderings in the United States Dr Masaryk stayed with my Cousin Ross at the University of Missouri and the two became friends. They were both scholars and philosophers, but if my cousin lacked 'the temperament for politics' Thomas Masaryk certainly possessed it. With Eduard Beneš he went on to found the Czechoslovak Republic, of which he became the first President, but he never forgot or lost touch with his friend in the Middle West of America and when I first went to Prague one winter in the nineteen thirties, I sent in advance a letter of introduction from my Cousin Ross Hill. In due course I received a charming reply, inviting me to stay at the Presidential country seat of Lany and to bring my riding kit. The President was himself a keen horseman and had somehow learned that I was also.

My arrival at Lany followed a heavy snowfall and a sharp frost. The forest roads were slippery, and though, if one took care, one could get along safely it was no time for an eighty-year-old chief of state to be in the saddle, and his doctors had forbidden it. President Masaryk was genuinely sorry that we could not ride together, but insisted that I should go with a mounted forester, and I greatly enjoyed it. I had a wonderful two days, with a choice of magnificent mounts and, in the evenings, alone with one of the wisest statesmen in the world at that time. I listened to him with fascination as he talked on a wide variety of subjects – of his youth in the home of his father, a great Bohemian nobleman's coachman, of his early battles as a deputy in the Austrian parliament, of his first-hand experiences of the Russian Revolution and of his memories of the Paris Peace Conference, where he had offered to reconstitute the traditional frontiers of Bohemia so as to cede to Germany those areas of the Sudetenland who were predominantly German in population. Had his wise and far-seeing proposal been accepted the whole Munich tragedy might have been avoided, but in 1919 the French had vetoed an addition to the people of the German Reich and insisted on the traditional front being maintained by the new Czechoslovak state. Twenty years later French statesmen were to regret this purblindness.

I parted from this wise old man with real regret and with a sense of having touched greatness. I was also saddened by the fact that winter had deprived him of the horseback exercise he loved so well. When I got back to London I made exhaustive enquiries as to what could be done about this. The Metropolitan Police, I found, 'roughed' their horses' hooves in winter, but this would not be suitable for my purpose because the snow would cake between the protruding nails and, freezing quickly, would make a glassy ball. At length I found that the Royal Canadian Mounted Police used a type of rubber galosh, which fitted over each hoof and which rendered them exceedingly secure. After some difficulty I obtained a set of these and sent them in the diplomatic bag to President Masaryk. I received a grateful letter in reply and I was told that he actually used them, but what particularly amused me was an announcement in the London financial press shortly thereafter of the floating of a Czechoslovak firm for the manufacture of equestrian rubber overshoes !

President Masaryk died in 1937, and one cannot but be glad that he was spared the agonies of the following year. I have, however, one very prized memento of him. He had become a friend and admirer of A. J. Balfour at the Paris Peace Conference and had sent to him a copy of his great work *The Making of a State*, which was published in 1927. Lord Balfour died in 1930, and this book, along with much of the rest of his library, was bequeathed to his beloved and adoring niece, 'Baffy' Dugdale, who was a great friend of mine. She gave it to me, together with all its inscriptions and her own, as a wedding present in 1946 and it remains among my treasured possessions.

II

It seemed but natural that I should know Jan Masaryk. I was commended to him by his father and brought into personal contact by my old friend Bruce Lockhart, to whom I was already greatly indebted for his help to me in the writing of my Brest-Litovsk book by lending me his Russian diaries of the period and by introducing me to Kerensky. I shall have much to say of Bruce hereafter.

Bruce and Jan had been 'bummeling' comrades in Prague after the war and from the thirties onwards we three were the closest of friends. Indeed, when, towards the end of the Second World War, there seemed a possibility that my wife and I might be married in London, they tossed up as to which should be my best man and Jan won; but, after all, we weren't married in London but in Virginia, and without either of them.

No one who did not know Jan well can really appreciate the depth of soul which lay behind that façade of what was too often and too easily dismissed as levity. He was never sufficiently credited with the deep and passionate feelings which he concealed all too well. It was truly an example of 'Laugh, clown, laugh'; and how often have I known that smiling face to hide a breaking heart! For basically, though the best company in the world, witty, accomplished, a superb pianist, an able diplomat and a courageous foreign minister, Jan Masaryk was a man of tragedy, almost of Greek tragedy, for looking back there seems to have been a fatal inevitability about his life and his end.

Jan's life, however, began in a prenatally romantic manner. His mother, a beautiful and gentle American girl, who had been a talented pupil of Liszt's, during a visit to Prague attracted the attention of young Thomas Masaryk, who took her on a water picnic on the Vltava. By some ill chance she fell into the fast-flowing river; the future President of Czechoslovakia dived to her rescue, plucked her from danger and married her forthwith. They had three children, of whom Jan was the youngest. His devotion to his father became a dominating factor in his life and from him Jan inherited his idealism, his liberal-socialist views, his great humanity, his capacity for warm and loyal friendship and his Western outlook.

Jan fought throughout the war on the Eastern Front in a Hungarian cavalry regiment but, as soon as the Czechoslovak Republic took legal form and established its diplomatic service, he was appointed to the Legation at Washington and there married the daughter of Charles Crane, the engineering tycoon who for years controlled the domestic plumbing industry of America. ('No house complete without us, my dear,' as one of the family once remarked to me.) There were close family ties between the Cranes and the Masaryks. Old Mr Crane was a great admirer of the President, to whom his youngest son, John, acted as private secretary for a period, and his eldest son Richard, who subsequently owned Westover, one of the loveliest of the James River houses in Virginia, was the first Minister from the United States to Czechoslovakia. Jan had worked in the Crane business before the war. His marriage to the daughter was both sad and childless and ended in divorce after five years.

It was in 1925 that Jan was sent to London as Minister and he remained there until the aftermath of Munich, thirteen years later. He was often at A14 Albany, and I at his little flat in Marsham Court, where he would cook succulent Czech peasant dishes and play with tremendous verve splendid barbaric yet haunting Slav melodies, which tore at the heart-strings and gave one an inkling of the impenetrability of the Slav mind to Western understanding. He was probably the most popular member of the *corps diplomatique*, for his parties were gay and amusing, informal but never undignified. yet never dull. His musical evenings were delightful, for he brought artists of the first order to entertain his guests.

Jan was a strange mixture of sudden changes of emotion. Rollicking fun would give place to bedevilling depression almost under one's eyes. He was one who had a host of admiring acquaintances who delighted in his company, but *au fond* had very few friends whom he trusted. I am very proud that I was one of them.

III

Eduard Beneš was a different cup of tea altogether. He neither evoked the veneration of Thomas Masaryk, nor had he the personal charm and diplomatic dexterity of Jan. He was a master operator, an indefatigable negotiator and he possessed unyielding courage and determination. Yet he was never really loved or indeed completely trusted in domestic politics by his own people, though he enjoyed an immensely high reputation outside his own country. He had much in common with General Smuts who, though recognised as a great statesman by the world at large, was still 'Slim Jannie' to his fellow politicians in South Africa. Beneš was a highly successful foreign minister, a not very good prime minister and a tragic though estimable president of the republic. The probable judgement of history will be that in the words which the late Lord Salisbury used on a memorable occasion, he was 'too clever by half'.

Beneš had few of the graces, though I happen to have liked and admired him. He was deadly serious and had little sense of humour. To many he was a bore, but never to me. I have never known anyone who talked as fast, as impressively or as continuously as he did while eating a meal. He seemed to absorb food through the pores, for his plate gradually emptied yet he never drew breath.

I first met Beneš in Geneva when, at the Assembly of the League of Nations in September 1924, he and his Greek opposite number, Nicholas Politis, took the high falutin, idealistic mishmash of Ramsay MacDonald and Edouard Herriot and moulded it into the Geneva Protocol which proved acceptable to the League membership, most of whom became signatories, though Czechoslovakia alone among them ratified it. It was a revelation to me to watch him produce formula after formula, first in the committee stage and later in plenary session until he had overcome the objections of most and the suspicions of many. It was a *tour de force* in negotiation.

Later thereafter, in Prague before Munich, in America during his exile, in England during the war and again in Prague after its conclusion, I got to know him better and better, and to admire his dogged courage in the face of adversity. In the course of many conversations he exhibited to me many secret pearls of history, much of which I found of the greatest value to me when I wrote my book *Munich, Prologue to Tragedy*.

I did not, by any means, agree with all his policies. I thought, for example, that he erred in placing so great a degree of confidence in French support as to make Czechoslovakia the virtual 'broker's man' of France in central Europe and by taking the lead in forming the Little Entente; I believed him to be mistaken in blocking any attempt to form a Danubian Federation or Customs Union; and I most certainly mistrusted his judgement after the Second World War in casting Czechoslovakia as the bridge between East and West, between the Free World and the Soviet Union and her satellites – a policy the unwisdom of which spelled disaster for himself and the independence of his country.

He had, however, one great virtue. He never resented disagreement from people he trusted and who were not among his own countrymen. We had many talks on the successes and failures of his policies which always ended amicably. He bore defeat, exile and disaster with immense dignity, and, as I have said, his courage was unflinching once he had made up his mind.

History had judged him sharply, but we owe it to him that the

Second World War did not begin in September 1938, when we were woefully unprepared for it, rather than a year later when we were in slightly better trim. For had he rejected the terms of the Munich Agreement and elected to oppose the German occupation of the Sudetenland with force, nothing could have prevented our eventual involvement.

IV

The year 1938 was one of greater tragedy for me than its successor. The humiliation of an enforced (if unavoidable) 'peace at any price' at Munich seemed infinitely more tragic than the acceptance of the challenge of war a year later. The first was mortifying, the second exhilarating. The first taught me that it was possible to be physically nauseated by shame, the second, though it smacked of anti-climax in the phoney war, at least showed that Britain stood once again foursquare in honour against aggression.

The year 1938 started on a note of foreboding. Anthony Eden resigned as Foreign Secretary on 20 February, no longer able to stomach Neville Chamberlain's policies of appeasement. His departure from the government came to me like a thunderous premonition of disaster and, like Mr Churchill, I was 'consumed by emotions of sorrow and fear'.

A month later came the second tragedy of that fateful year. Hitler's annexation of Austria and its bestial consequences, proclaimed his interpretation of the formula of 'peaceful change' and a further indication of the futility of international guarantees.

The Czech crisis, which culminated at Munich some six months later, began on the very morrow of the *Anschluss* with a barrage of assurances and reiterated pledges by Germany to Czechoslovakia that she had nothing to fear. Nor seemingly had she. Few countries indeed have appeared on paper to be more completely and impregnably protected against aggression. One the one hand she had a recognised line of very strong fortifications on which she had spent some £50 million, and on the other all the panoply and paraphernalia of international agreements. Very briefly these consisted of the overall guarantee of assistance provided by Article XVI of the Covenant of the League; both Czechoslovakia and Germany were ratified signatories of the Kellogg–Briand Pact renouncing war as 'an instrument of national policy' which Hitler had never bothered to repudiate, and the two countries were nominally bound by the treaty of arbitration of 1925. In addition, she had the promise of general support from her colleagues of the Little Entente, Yugoslavia and Romania.

More specifically, Czechoslovakia had a treaty of mutual assistance with France signed in 1925, and a similar treaty with the Soviet Union concluded in 1935 which assured her of Russian support as soon as the pact with France went into operation. Moreover France and Russia had signed a treaty of mutual assistance and guarantee in 1935 and Britain had pledged support to France in 1936 should the latter become a victim of unprovoked German aggression. What had never been made clear, however, was the position of Britain vis-à-vis France in the event of a German attack consequent upon a French implementation of her guarantee to Czechoslovakia.

Thus the Czech leaders seemed justified in a certain sense of optimism and security in the face of potential threats from Germany. They took immediate steps to protect the hitherto unfortified frontier with Austria and were at pains to remind their allies of the existence of their obligations. They by no means ignored the possibility of German threats and placed little faith in German promises, but they believed in their war potential to resist a German attack until France and Russia could send the aid which they were confident would come. They had a naïve belief in the good faith of their allies. As President Beneš said to me in Prague at the beginning of this momentous summer: 'I have France, and if I have France I have Russia, and you have given your pledge to France.'

In London Jan Masaryk was less euphoric but still confident that in the end Britain and France would stand by Czechoslovakia, but beneath his confidence one sensed a note of foreboding which he would not at first even admit to himself.

During that long summer of the Czechoslovak via dolorosa to Munich, I travelled frequently between London and Prague, and it was heartrending to witness the gradual disillusionment of the Czechs as the reluctance of their French allies to aid them became more and more apparent. In London Jan Masaryk battled with the obstructive inertia of Chamberlain and Halifax, and the baffling ignorance of those in high places of political geography. It was not infrequent to hear words such as 'Czechoslavia' and 'Czechoslovenia' across the floor of the House of Commons, and even a confusion between Budapest and Bucharest. As Jan once said to Bruce Lockhart: 'I spend most of my official time in the Foreign Office explaining that Czechoslovakia is a country and not a contagious disease.'

In Paris another friend of mine, Stefan Osusky, the Czech Minister, contended with the malevolent and mendacious hostility of

Georges Bonnet, the French Foreign Minister, and the more pathetic defeatism of Edouard Daladier, the Prime Minister. I saw Osusky on several occasions that summer and as time went on he did not scruple to tell me of his belief that even if Prague were bombed the French would not honour their obligations.

And in Prague, lonely and menaced, Beneš faced not only the direct threats of the German Reich but also the insidious propaganda and agitation of his native Sudetendeutsch. The optimism and assurance of the early summer had evaporated, and I found him saddened and morose, but still clinging to a pathetic if diminishing belief that in the final analysis the French would not desert him.

The old city of Prague is one of the finest examples of urban baroque architecture in Europe. The magnificent proportion of the Wenceslas Square dominated by its cathedral, the statued beauty of the St Charles bridge spanning the swiftly flowing Vltava, the stern severity of the Czernin Palace, now the Ministry of Foreign Affairs, and the majesty of the old royal palace, the Hradschin Castle, which had become the presidential residence, all seemed strangely peaceful in that terrible summer, dreaming in sunshine, while around and above them gathered the storm clouds of impending doom. The population still went calmly about their business, the opera and the ballet continued to perform, the cabarets and dance halls were crowded and sightseers gathered daily to watch the changing of the guard in the courtyard of what was popularly known as the 'Hrad'. This ceremony had a unique interest, since the troops involved wore the uniforms of the armies of France, Russia and Italy of which the Czechoslovak Legions had formed a part during the First World War, and it was therefore the last place in the world where one saw the uniform of the old Imperial Russian army on parade. It was a strangely unreal atmosphere yet one of gallantry and determination.

From my conversations that summer with Beneš, with his Prime Minister, Milan Hodza, and the Foreign Minister, Kamil Krofta, supplemented by what they subsequently told me in exile during the war, I pieced together their side of the crisis which ended at Munich. After the war Jan Masaryk opened the Czech archives to me, and with this singular privilege and my own information, together with the documentary material which became available at the Nuremberg Trials, I wrote my *Munich*.

In addition to the civilians I also had good relations with the Czech army leaders and more particularly with General Jan Syrovy, Inspector-General, the one-eyed, black-patched hero of the anabasis of the Czechoslovak Legions across Siberia, who subsequently became execrated as a collaborator with the Nazis. In July and August, however, he was full of courage and resistance, but guarded in his ideas of foreign aid. His wartime experiences with the Bolsheviks had left him with a deep sense of suspicion (very much a *timeo Danaos et dona ferentes* mentality), which ran counter to established Czech foreign policy. 'We will fight,' he said to me, 'either alone, or with you and the French, and we shall beat the Germans, but we want no Russian troops on Czech soil; we should never get them out.' I was to see him again that summer under less pleasant circumstances.

There was also another veteran of the anabasis, General Serjei Ingr, Director of Military Operations, who subsequently, in contrast to Syrovy, chose to leave his country after its annexation to the Reich and became War Minister in the Czechoslovak government-in-exile. He favoured resistance to Germany even to the extent of rejecting the terms of the Munich Agreement and precipitating the Second World War there and then, and he was prepared to stage a military coup to do so.

The information which these contacts of mine gave me, in addition to eyewitness accounts of such events as the arrival of the Runciman Mission at the Woodrow Wilson station of Prague – on which occasion I heard one of our group mutter a paraphrase of Wilde's 'Ballad of Reading Gaol'; 'The hangman with his little bag came creeping through the gloom' – brought me into confidential association with those circles in London who were desperately endeavouring to stiffen the attitude of the British government at least to the extent of giving definite guarantees of support to France. Indeed the one pleasant result for me from this terrible summer was the fact that I came to know Mr Winston Churchill more closely. I had first met him in 1936 when, after Hitler had reoccupied the Rhineland and torn up the pact of Locarno, he had embarked upon his noble but fruitless campaign to awaken England to an awareness of her own danger. Then he had been almost a lone figure crying in the wilderness and I only saw him to bring some piece of information; now, however, he was a recognised leader among the dissident Tories and others in the House of Commons, Anthony Eden, 'Bobbety' Cranbourne, Harold Macmillan, Dick Law, son of Bonar and now Lord Coleraine, Bob Boothby, Harold Nicolson and closest of all his followers, Brendan Bracken. In our deepening depression his great presence and indomitable courage restored sagging morale and on the occasions on which I saw him I always came away strengthened and heartened.

There was also a group of my more intimate friends, 'a ginger group' which sought to exercise influence behind the scenes. This included 'Baffy' Dugdale, Lewis Namier and Colin Coote who left *The Times* in protest against its editorial policy of appeasement and joined the *Daily Telegraph*, of which he subsequently became Editor. We used to dine and lunch together in each other's houses and clubs and in Soho restaurants and plan strategy which was relayed by various channels to the Cabinet and the Foreign Office, but all in vain.

These were dreadful days, and as the late summer slipped into autumn and it became more and more apparent that the Czechs were to be abandoned to their fate, one's heart was rung for Jan Masaryk. He became more and more haggard, great black circles formed beneath his eyes. It was like watching a man on the rack.

Yet his gallantry never abated, and he was wonderfully free from rancour, even when, after Chamberlain's visit to Berchtesgaden, the Anglo-French Plan for the surrender of the Sudetenland indicated the degree of Neville Chamberlain's surrender to Hitler. One remark of Chamberlain's, however, he never forgot or forgave. It was on the Prime Minister's return from his Godesberg meeting with Hitler. He communicated the results of their conversation to Jan, who expressed a certain dubiety as to the amount of trust which could be placed in Hitler's word. 'My dear Jan,' Mr Chamberlain replied, 'some people trust Dr Beneš; I prefer to trust Herr Hitler.' When Jan told me this there was still fury in his voice.

The last weeks of September 1938 in London will always remain with me as the lowest point to which my spirit has ever sunk. It was indeed, in the words of St John of the Cross, 'The dark night of the soul'. The British people were geared to war, the fleet was mobilised, trenches were dug in the parks, gas masks were issued. It was generally believed that Mr Chamberlain' peregrinations to and from Germany were for the purpose of making it clear to the Führer that there was a point beyond which Britain and France, even with the best will in the world, could not compel the Czechs to make further concessions.

I had evacuated my mother from Queen Anne's Mansions to Droitwich and as I returned to her flat after seeing her off, the telephone rang. A tired and somewhat ghoulish voice from a local authority enquired if I had any sheets to spare. I said I was sure that there were some in my mother's flat, but what, I asked, were they wanted for and to which hospital should I send them. 'They're not for beds,' came the macabre reply, 'they're for wrapping bodies in, we haven't enough coffins in London.' Heavy bombing was evidently expected.

'Black Wednesday', 28 September, dawned bright and clear. We woke with the eerie feeling that this was 'the last day' and that by tomorrow night London, Paris and Prague might be flaming ruins. I recall that while shaving that morning the hymnal injunction to 'live this day as if thy last' came into my head and remained with me much of the day.

Through the kindness of my old friend, Gerald Palmer, then Conservative Member for Winchester and who had been one of Stanley Baldwin's Political Private Secretaries, I had been given a seat under the clock in the House of Commons that afternoon to hear the Prime Minister's statement, which few doubted would conclude with some sort of ultimatum to Germany. I was therefore a witness of that famous scene which has been so frequently described, when the Prime Minister's P.P.S., Lord Dunglass (later Sir Alec Douglas-Home) passed a Foreign Office telegram to Sir John Simon who, after some difficulty, brought it to Mr Chamberlain's attention. It was the invitation to Munich. The ensuing example of mass hysteria was indescribable and unbelievable, but I was watching the Diplomatic Gallery where by a sardonic quirk of fate the German Ambassador, Herbert von Dirksen, was sitting cheek by jowl with Jan Masaryk. The former had a look of almost incredulous surprise on his face; Jan had the look of a man under sentence of death.

Later that week Jan told me of the meeting with Chamberlain and Halifax immediately afterwards at which he was told that neither Russia nor Czechoslovakia was to be represented at the coming conference. Jan said that he was so shocked that for a moment he was choked with emotion, then he said: 'If you have sacrificed my nation to preserve the peace of the world I will be the first to applaud you, but if not, gentlemen, God help your souls.' His voice broke as he retold the story.

Perhaps, in the days which followed, Jan performed his greatest act of filial piety and personal consideration for the feelings of others. The new government of collaboration, which General Syrovy formed in Prague after Munich, sent a circular telegram to all Czech diplomatic posts with instructions that the state portrait of President Masaryk which hung in every legation was to be removed. Jan would ask no member of his staff to undertake this task. With his own hands he removed his father's picture and the same day resigned his post.

V

Like 'Baffy' Dugdale, who has recorded the sentiment in her diary, I felt that 'honour had died at Munich' and, also like her, I was physically sick from the black shame of it. The Czech people had been sacrificed, the Czechoslovak democracy – one of the best things to come out of the Paris Peace Conference – had been destroyed, because the French had welshed on their promises and because Britain had been too ill-prepared in her armaments and too indigent in her defences to persuade the French to any other course of action. To save our skins we had acquiesced in the enslavement of a small people. As Jan Masaryk was to tell the San Francisco Conference which set up the United Nations in 1946, 'My country has been a concentration camp for the last eight years.' Moreover, shame upon shame, the Czech people had been compelled to drive into exile a man of the name of Masaryk, the son of the founder of their nation, who had been affectionately known throughout the country as 'Our Johnnie'.

Once again I felt impelled to *do* something about it. With vivid memories of what had happened in Germany and in Austria to those who, by reason of race, religion or political creed, had found themselves in opposition to the principles of the Third Reich, thousands of Czechs, as well as Jews and those Sudeten Germans who had been members of the Social Democratic and Communist Parties, had fled from their homes on the approach of the German occupying forces and were living behind the new Czech frontier in circumstances of great privation. It was, I thought, surely possible to relieve their sufferings in some way.

I therefore drafted a letter to *The Times* and took it along to Sir Neill Malcolm, who at this moment was League of Nations High Commissioner for Refugees, and we both signed it, together with Eric Duncannon (now Lord Bessborough), who was then Neill's assistant. It was a long letter, too long as a matter of fact, because into it had gone much of the passion which had been tormenting me, but it led the correspondence column on 4 October, and the pith of it was contained in the last three paragraphs:

> Finally, there remains the pressing question of the racial and political minorities in the Sudetenland. Was there no plea made for their protection during the conversations at Munich? Is it now too late to hope that an appeal might still be made to Herr Hitler on their behalf? With the example of Germany and Austria before them, few among those who, by reason of race, nationality, or political creed, have found themselves in opposition to the principles of the Third Reich will remain in the Sudeten territories if they can escape. Thousands of refugees have already fled and are living behind the new Czech frontier in circumstances of great privation, which may rapidly lead to the outbreak of epidemics.

We owe the Czechs a debt of peace and we have an opportunity to discharge it, at least in part. The Prime Minister has generously declined the proposal of a National Fund of Thanksgiving in his honour, but may we, the undersigned, suggest most urgently that a Mansion House Fund should be established for the relief of the refugees in Czechoslovakia?

Thousands of men and women in this country must feel moved to make some definite act of thanksgiving for the avoidance of war. Surely there could be no better expression of this desire than to contribute generously to the lessening of the load with which a small country has been suddenly burdened in the cause of peace, a country whose contribution of restraint and sacrifice went so far to make peace possible.

In response to this appeal the Lord Mayor of London, Sir Harry Twyford, opened a Fund for the relief of these unfortunate people, to which many men and women in Britain, moved to make a definite act of thanksgiving for their deliverance from war, contributed generously and gladly. In all the total amount subscribed was £318,000.

· The Lord Mayor wanted to superintend personally the setting up of a committee for the distribution and apportionment of these funds and, accompanied by Neill Malcolm and myself, he flew to Prague on 10 October. The journey was not uneventful. Because of the threat of war which had so recently overhung Europe, direct air communication between London and Prague had been suspended. We had therefore to fly in a Belgian air-liner to Brussels and change there into a Swedish aircraft to Prague. As we prepared to descend at the Prague airport I noticed that a very sizeable crowd, who seemed to be mainly press and photographers, had assembled to meet us. I whispered to Neill Malcolm: 'Even with the Lord Mayor of London aboard we don't rate this press coverage,' and it was not until we had disembarked that we discovered the reason.

We were at once surrounded by news-hungry press men who fired such questions at us as, 'What does it feel like to escape death by a hair's breadth?' and so on. At our obvious bewilderment they then told us that, just after our Swedish plane had taken off from Brussels, the original Belgian plane in which we had flown from Croydon had exploded, killing all passengers and crew immediately. On our return journey the head of the Belgian Security Police told us that his ballistics experts reported that a bomb had been secreted in the plane timed to go off before our arrival at Brussels. Fortunately for us the mechanism was faulty.

I can only conclude that, as both Neill Malcolm and I were on the Nazi Black List for our somewhat outspoken criticisms of German policies, this had been thought a good opportunity to eliminate both of us. But it would have been tough luck on the Lord Mayor.

To return to Prague after Munich was both humiliating and acutely unpleasant, and the fact that one's profound feeling of relief that war had been avoided was tempered by a deep sense of chagrin only added to our discomfiture. Gone were those calm and friendly faces which had so impressed me in the summer and in their place were sad and sullen countenances. We had an official car at our disposal which flew the Union Jack, and for the first time in my life I knew what it was to be publicly spat at. Yet the Czechs were not in general openly hostile, but they were, which was worse, demonstrably contemptuous. They did not hesitate to say that they had been betrayed, and who could blame them?

After some hard work, in the course of which we had to overcome considerable suspicion of our motives and intentions, we drew up a scheme, which, as I now look at it after thirty-five years, still seems to be practical and viable – if it had ever got off the ground. Having completed the preliminary labour the Lord Mayor returned to London, leaving Neill Malcolm and me to tie up the loose ends.

Scarcely had he left when we discovered an appalling state of affairs. The German Government had demanded that all those who were registered residents of the areas recently occupied and annexed to the Reich and who had since fled, were to be returned forthwith, and the collaborationist Czech government under General Syrovy was prepared to comply with this demand. As a result those refugees who had already arrived were being rounded up preparatory to forcible return and those arriving by rail and road were turned back immediately.

For many of those who had loyally supported the Beneš regime against the propaganda and menaces of the traitor Nazi stooge, Konrad Henlein, now the Reichskommissar for the newly annexed territories, the order to return to their homes was tantamount to a death warrant. Had not Henlein publicly announced that he would beat and imprison all political opponents 'until they were black'? Already the Sudeten Legion and the Henleinist Storm Troops were going from house to house with lists, arresting former political foes and working off old scores on the spot, and, as I had stood on the platforms of the Masaryk Railway Station watching the refugee trains come in – only to be turned back – I had seen heads swathed in bloody bandages, bruised and broken faces, arms in hastily manufactured splints and slings.

Neill Malcolm and I decided that the only possible chance of achieving delay in this heartless, ruthless compliance with the victor's orders was to make a personal appeal to General Syrovy, and we enlisted the aid of General Louis Faucher, a close friend of Syrovy's, who had been head of the French Military Mission with the Czech army, the termination of which had also been among Hitler's demands. The General, who had donned full uniform and all his decorations, French and Czech, for the occasion, was deeply moved. He was grateful to find in Neill Malcolm a fellow general who, moreover, spoke his language extremely well. As I sat beside the chauffeur on our drive to the Hradschin Castle, I could hear the conversation of the two old comrades-in-arms, which was every so often punctuated by Faucher's heart-broken exclamation: *'C'est pénible, très pénible,'* – and a murmured: 'The honour of France'.

Our interview with General Syrovy was as unpleasant as it was fruitless. He had changed since I had last seen him in the summer. He was now far from friendly and certainly not calm. His one eye glared at us balefully; his black patch looked more sinister than ever, and when he spoke his voice ran up into a high falsetto, which, as I knew, indicated extreme emotion. We urged him to grant a stay of only a fortnight in repatriating the refugees so that the plan which we had prepared could be put into operation and emergency refugee organisations abroad could take care of them.

It was like talking to a stone wall. He listened to our plea in icy silence; then he rejected it out of hand: 'Not fifteen days, not fifteen minutes. The Germans have asked for them, and back they go.' He addressed himself to me with venom in his voice: 'I told you in August that we were prepared to fight either alone or with Britain and France and that we should win, but you would not allow us to do either.' Then, rising to his feet and bringing the audience to an end, he said, more quietly but in tones full of meaning: 'In this affair, *messieurs*, we have been willing to fight on the side of the angels, now we shall hunt with the wolves.'

As we drove back to our hotel General Faucher was unashamedly weeping.

VI

In the twelve months that separated Munich from the outbreak of the Second World War, both Beneš and Jan Masaryk spent much of their time in the United States, pleading the cause of their country and warning their audiences against the Nazi menace. Jan operated in his own inimitable way; Beneš, more methodical in manner, followed the pattern of Thomas Masaryk during the First World War and systematically visited the many Czech and Slovak groups scattered across the country. Regretfully I did not see Jan at this time, but I did see Beneš.

In order to try to get the taste of Munich out of my mouth and indeed to recover from the emotional shock which I had experienced, I set up house in Charlottesville, Virginia. In doing so I was guided by two other factors. I was convinced that at most we had one year before a general European war broke out, and also, which was considerably more important to me personally, there lived in Charlottesville a girl with whom I was very much in love and still am, for I am happy to say that she became my wife.

The University of Virginia was kind enough to ask me to become a visiting lecturer in international law and relations in their Law School. Although my knowledge of the first of these subjects was sketchy in the extreme, I reckoned that I knew enough about international relations to get by; so I gratefully accepted, if with some diffidence, for I had no previous teaching experience.

It came about that President Beneš, having visited a colony of Czechs in Richmond, desired to place a wreath on the grave of Thomas Jefferson, for whom he had a deep admiration, on that great man's birthday, 13 April, and also to visit both Mr Jefferson's home, Monticello, and Mr Jefferson's University. Now, 13 April is celebrated by the University of Virginia, most appropriately, as Founder's Day. All classes are suspended, an academic procession in full regalia marches down the Lawn from the Rotunda to the Auditorium, there to listen to an address by some eminent public figure.

It would seem but natural to invite Beneš to take part in these celebrations as a spectator and a distinguished visitor, but it was not as easy as that. This was 13 April 1939. The United States government had just recognised, though with reluctance, Germany's Rape of Czechoslovakia and the establishment of the Protectorate of Bohemia and Moravia, and the speaker invited to give the Founder's Day address was none other than Mr Sumner Welles. The possibility of a confrontation between the American Under-Secretary of State and the exiled President of the Czechoslovak Republic was clearly something to be avoided at all costs, yet it was not desired to be in any way disrespectful or inhospitable to Dr Beneš.

Faced with this dilemma the President of the University – a delightful man but scarcely a cosmopolitan – sent for me. He had heard, he said, that I knew this Dr Beneš. Would I therefore take charge of him on behalf of the University and so arrange matters that a meeting between him and Sumner Welles could not possibly occur. Within those limits I had absolute discretion and freedom of action. We agreed that he would give a luncheon for the speaker of the day at his official residence and I would entertain Dr and Mme Beneš at a party at the country club, which incidentally as a private house had been designed by Mr Jefferson himself. As President John Lloyd Newcomb was an old and valued friend of mine – and indeed my boss at that time – I, as it were, saluted and asked permission to carry on. Besides it was the kind of challenge which rather intrigued me.

I was determined to use my plenary power to the utmost to give Beneš the reception which he merited and I received the warmest co-operation from all authorities. The Governor of Virginia promised a car and an *aide-de-camp*, and with my own car and driver I thought we could make a sufficiently impressive cavalcade. By great luck the train by which Beneš and his wife were travelling arrived at Charlottesville at an hour which, on my reckoning, would allow us to visit Monticello and Jefferson's grave and get back to the University just after the Founder's Day celebrations were over, and I could then show them round in peace and quiet.

All went well. The train arrived on time. I had discovered the one and only Czech child in Charlottesville to present a bouquet tied with the Czech national colours; the Governor's A.D.C. and I stood to attention as the train stopped, and behind stood a somewhat self-conscious state trooper carrying a large wreath which gave him the appearance of a not-very-well-trained circus horse.

The greetings over, I put Beneš and the A.D.C. into the Governor's car and took Mme Beneš and me in mine, and, escorted by a motor-cade of state police, we drove off to Monticello. It is a beautiful drive; the road winds up a rather steep and wooded mountain and the views over Albermarle county are superb. I pointed these out to Mme Beneš, whose mastery of the English language was a little imperfect, but she seemed to be enjoying it. Suddenly she turned and asked: 'Mr Vheeler-Bennett, vhere are all your vooden dogs?' My reason reeled.

'I beg your pardon, Madame,' I gulped, 'I don't think I quite understood.'

'Vooden dogs,' she reiterated very clearly. 'Everywhere they are telling me that the voods in Virginia are filled with vooden dogs.'

It still, I hate to confess, took a minute for the penny to drop, but at last mercifully it did. The lady meant 'dogwood', and I hastened to point out to her the qualities of these beautiful trees, whose drifts and tiers of white blossoms make Virginia such a paradise in springtime.

My eye on my watch, I shepherded my charges through the mansion and found them genuinely appreciative of its fine proportions and of Mr Jefferson's architectural eccentricities. The state trooper was disembarrassed of his wreath, which was placed, with due solemnity, on Mr Jefferson's tomb in the little graveyard below the house. As we began our drive back, I congratulated myself with relief on the thought that at that very moment the academic procession, with Sumner Welles in the rear, should be wending its way back to the Rotunda.

'The best laid plans of mice and men. . . .' I had not reckoned on the fact that the Under-Secretary of State would speak for longer than usual, and as we drove up to the University with a certain flourish, I observed with horror that the vanguard of the faculty were still milling about in the Rotunda and that President Newcomb and Sumner Welles were still coming up the Lawn. With the speed of light I whisked Dr and Mme Beneš behind an adjacent pillar and began a voluble, introductory and doubtless wholly inaccurate lecture on the architectural jewels of the University – which is undoubtedly the most beautiful man-made thing in the United States – and the loving genius which Thomas Jefferson had lavished upon it.

At last out of the corner of my eye, I saw the President accompany Welles into the portals of the Rotunda. At last the coast was clear and I happily conducted my party over the University and subsequently to luncheon. But it had been 'a damn close-run thing'.

Some years later, during the war, I told this story to Sumner Welles, whose usually solemn countenance dissolved into happy laughter; but I never quite dared to tell it to President Beneš. I had a feeling that he would not really have been amused.

VII

At the outbreak of the Second World War Beneš and Masaryk immediately formed the Czechoslovak National Committee in London, to which Bruce Lockhart was appointed as British Representative. Bruce has told eloquently in his *Comes the Reckoning* the story of his struggle to obtain official recognition of the viability of the National Committee as a fully fledged provisional government-in-exile. This he ultimately achieved in July 1941, but it was over a year later that he accomplished his second objective, the formal denunciation of the Munich Agreement by His Majesty's Government. The reason for this delay in taking what would seem to be the most logical, as well as the most obvious, of decisions was that appeasement died slowly in Whitehall and there lingered those in high places who, while they favoured the restoration of Czechoslovak independence, still toyed with the idea of the post-war retention by a non-Nazi Germany of the frontiers of Munich and even the *Anschluss* with Austria.

I was present at many discussions on this subject during the periods I was in London in the early part of the war, and I recall vividly the patience and yet the vigour of Bruce Lockhart and Jan Masaryk, now Foreign Minister, with members of the Foreign Office who were obstructive beyond belief.

At last, however, the final obstacle was overcome and I think that one of my happiest moments during the war was on the afternoon of 5 August 1942, when Bruce and I sat one each side of Jan Masaryk in the gallery of the House of Commons (which at that time was sitting in the chamber of the House of Lords, having been bombed out of its own premises) to hear Anthony Eden make the formal announcement that the Munich Agreement was no more. Eduard Raczynski, the courageous and delightful ambassador of Poland, was there with us too, and this was a further example of Jan's great magnanimity, for, though the Poles had behaved in a predatory manner at the time of Munich, both they and the Czechs were now victims of Nazi aggression and occupation, and, moreover, the Munich Agreement had altered the frontiers of Czechoslovakia with Poland as well as with Germany. After it was all over we toasted Jan in House of Commons sherry at a small party given by Anthony Eden in his room. It was the end of one unhappy chapter but, had we known it, it was the beginning of another even more tragic.

I kept in touch with Beneš during the war through the kindness of Bruce Lockhart, who even when he ceased to be British Representative with the Czechs and became Director-General of the Political Intelligence Department of the Foreign Office (a post in which I ultimately became his assistant) made weekly visits to the exiled President at the pseudo-Tudor imitation manor house at Aston Abbots in Buckinghamshire, which had been allotted to him by the British Government. Often he took me with him, and I felt increasingly that Beneš was becoming too much immersed in detail and certainly too trusting in his relations with Russia. Nor would he brook dissent. Bruce, after all, had had considerable experience of negotiating with the Bolsheviks in his time, but Beneš would often sweep aside his advice with an, 'Ah yes, perhaps so then, but it is different today.' Unfortunately this was just not so.

Throughout the war Jan Masaryk was magnificent. Combining the roles of Foreign Minister and chief of propaganda, he travelled the length of Britain and Northern Ireland and made annual visits to the United States. He spoke in city after city and never did he say one word of criticism or recrimination against the British Government. We were all allies now, united in one great struggle for freedom. There was no room for rancour. He spoke weekly on the B.B.C. to his own countrymen encouraging, reassuring, exhorting them to suffer the horrors of their persecution with hope for the future. 'His voice,' said a friend of mine in Prague after the war, 'Jan's voice brought us courage to go on, ghastly though our life was. He was so sure that in the end Germany would be defeated.'

I saw much of him in London and in New York during these years, and never do I remember his losing either his morale or his sense of humour, though occasionally it became rather wry. In the worst moments of the war – Dunkirk, the Blitz, disasters in Asia, defeats in Africa – he never lost heart. He trusted implicitly in Britain and, though loyal to the core to Beneš in every other respect, did not share his confidence in Russia. He was never happy about the treaty of alliance which Beneš signed with Stalin in 1944 and deplored – as did many of us – the fact that Czechoslovakia was ultimately liberated by Soviet rather than American armies.

Jan's love for his motherland also never wavered, although he would refer to it as 'my poor funny little country', and the wryness of his wit may be judged from his christening the playing by the B.B.C. each Sunday evening of the allied national anthems as 'The Beggar's Opera'.

He was in many ways broader in his views of the future than Beneš. He had favoured the idea of a federation with Poland when this was first mooted and it was not his fault that the hopes of this evaporated. He was also convinced that only by some form of Danubian Confederation could central Europe become economically viable. When we were discussing this in New York on one occasion I mentioned that Jan's views were broadly shared by Otto of Habsburg and asked if he had ever met him. Jan answered 'no' but that he would very much like to, but that it would have to be kept deadly secret because his colleagues would at once suspect him of treason if they heard about it. He would tell Beneš and I could tell Bruce but otherwise it was to be between ourselves.

The Archduke was in New York at the time, and I arranged a

very hush-hush' luncheon *à trois* at the house on East 70th Street, which I was then sharing with Aubrey Morgan, a close friend of mine, who combined tremendous British patriotism with being the brother-in-law of Charles Lindbergh. On the appointed day, I could almost have laughed aloud. For the best of reasons the two principals were really terrified of the fact of their becoming known and they each arrived practically wearing false noses and blue glasses. Conversation was a little sticky at first, but a couple of very dry martinis apiece helped a lot and very soon a thaw set in. Soon they were talking in complete amity, and I could not help but be fascinated at the idea of the heir to the Habsburg lands discussing the future of Central Europe with the son of one of the greatest rebels of his time against the Austro-Hungarian monarchy. They talked, I remember, until four o'clock in the afternoon and separated with expressions of mutual respect and pleasure at having met. Jan's subsequent comment was typical: 'Too bad that nothing will ever come of that talk, but it was worth it.' This was Jan the romantic going in double-harness with Jan the realist.

Shortly after this episode, in the high summer of 1943, to be precise, Jan Masaryk and I flew back from America to Britain together. In those days there was a transatlantic service of flying-boats which were most efficiently run. One started from Baltimore at about two in the morning, flew to Gander in Newfoundland, where we breakfasted and the aircraft refuelled, and then set off on the long flight, fetching up eventually, with luck, at Poole. The only drawback was that one left Baltimore in a teeming humid heat with clothes sticking to one's body, and arrived at Gander to find it very much colder. The wary traveller learned to take a thicker suit in his flying-bag at the sacrifice of practically anything else. It was slower and a good deal more comfortable than air-travel today and the acme of luxury compared with the unfinished bombers in which one flew from Montreal in the earlier stages of the war.

Jan was, of course, staying at his legation in Washington, but Ronnie Tree, who was also travelling with us, and I were put up by David Bruce (subsequently American Ambassador in Paris, Bonn and London, but then among the top brass of O.S.S.) in Georgetown. There was, alas, a jinx on this flight from the start. For two successive mornings we arrived blearily at the point of departure, only to be told that one of our four engines had developed some acute mechanical complaint and that we should not be flying that day. Never have I admired anything more than David Bruce's calm patience and never-failing kindness at this time. He did not seem even resigned in his welcome to us on our return at four o'clock two mornings running; he appeared genuinely glad to see us and offered a warmth of hospitality which suggested that we hadn't met for years. This is only one of David's many great gifts; he is a pearl among men.

Eventually on the third morning we finally got airborne and actually reached Gander, taking off for Poole a few hours later. I was sitting next to Jan and almost immediately went to sleep. When I awoke I was at once aware of two things, the noise of our engines had greatly diminished and, according to the sun, we were flying in diametrically the wrong direction to what we should have been. We were, in fact, headed not for Britain but America.

Jan grinned. 'I was wondering when you were going to wake up,' he said. 'Three of our engines have conked out and we're heading back.'

Several hours passed and we seemed to me to be going slower and slower, and lower and lower. To add to our troubles when we were off Nantucket we saw a U-boat surface beneath us. We were out of range, of course, but the query arose in my mind, as to how long we should remain so, and indeed what would happen then.

Now we were quite a distinguished company, for, beside the Foreign Minister of Czechoslovakia, we had aboard the British Ambassador and Lady Halifax, the Head of the British Shipping Mission in Washington, Sir Arthur Salter, the Parliamentary Private Secretary to the Minister of Information (Ronnie), and the Head of the New York Office of the British Political Warfare Mission (me). This in itself was a fairly succulent morsel for any enemy submarine to swallow, but there was also among us a military man of some importance who had been on a visit to Washington to confer with Joint Staff Mission and the Combined Chiefs of Staff. I regret to say that, when the U-boat made its appearance, the general was the only one among us who was demonstrably agitated. We were none of us very happy about the situation, but we kept quiet about it, whereas he was positively petulant – and out loud. He told us all that because of the information he carried he must not be captured by the enemy; he demanded that the plane should head at once for the nearest shore. I almost expected him to declare that he was too young to die – which he certainly wasn't – but he did stop short of that.

The captain of the aircraft, however, was a man of steel. He assured us that he could get us back to Baltimore in safety and would not consider even putting down at La Guardia, New York, where there were landing facilities for seaplanes. Baltimore was his base and to

Baltimore he would return, be the opposition from the most exalted of quarters.

To pass the time Jan and I played a private and somewhat macabre game. Supposing that we were brought down by gunfire from the U-boat, what would be our respective receptions? The Halifaxes, we agreed would be welcomed aboard and made much of on the basis of Munich, strongly supported by Dorothy's charm. Arthur Salter would be so minatory that he would compel respectful treatment as from peccant schoolboys. Ronnie would be well treated because the Commander could recognise in him an example of a perfect English country gentleman, whom the Germans have always admired – even Engels did – and still do. Jan and I, we agreed, would be put over the side immediately, as the submarine submerged. We also agreed that we didn't mind what happened to the general. It was an agreeable pastime and, with embroidery and elaboration, it lasted us pretty well into Baltimore, where we eventually arrived safely.

When the flying boat left again at two o'clock the following morning Jan and I and Ronnie were the only members of our original group to travel in her.

At the close of the war the Provisional Government returned to Prague in May, and at once the Soviet presence was felt to be in the ascendant. Czech airmen who had fought side by side with the Royal Air Force were denied repatriation. General Ludwig Svoboda (the present President of the Soviet-satellite republic), who had fought with the Red Army, was compulsorily substituted for General Ingr as Minister for War, and Jan Masaryk, who did not get back to Prague until July, after the close of the San Francisco Conference, found that in his absence his Communist second-in-command, M. Clementis, had filled the key positions in the Foreign Ministry with 'fellow travellers' of the most incarnadine.

Jan was deeply disturbed by this Soviet influence, but placed his faith in the good sense of his fellow-countrymen not to be in the final analysis deceived by the blatant blandishments of Communism. Beneš still believed in himself and had confidence in his ability to be the bridge between East and West, to keep two balls precariously in the air without dropping either of them.

My last visit to Prague was in April 1946 when I stayed with our Ambassador, Philip Nichols, an old Foreign Office friend. I dined with Jan in his small flat in the magnificent Czernin Palace on the Loreta Place with a wonderful view over the old city, and we talked of many things, more especially of the increasing menace of Soviet Russia to the stability of Europe and the peace of the world. It was then

T. G. Masaryk

Jan Masaryk

Eduard Beneš

Kaiser Wilhelm II
with his youngest grandchild

too that he made it possible for me to consult the Czech archives for my forthcoming book, *Munich*. I said that President Beneš had asked me to drive up next day to his private country house at Sezam Usti in the Moravian mountains for lunch. 'I hope you'll find him well,' Jan said. 'He hasn't seemed too good lately.' As a matter of fact the President seemed in good health (though he suffered his first stroke not long after) and talked as ever vivaciously and ceaselessly. I noticed that he spoke entirely of the past, and I used this to my own advantage, for in the course of our talk (which lasted for hours) he spoke more freely than ever before of the part played by Russia in the very last stage of the Munich drama.

Throughout the month of September 1938, he said, the Soviet Minister, Alexandrovsky, had brought repeated assurances from Stalin in Moscow and from Litvinov in Geneva, that the U.S.S.R. would stand by its pledges to Czechoslovakia. Gradually the tone of their messages had increased in warmth. Beginning with a mere reiteration of Soviet intention to implement Russia's treaty obligations, which, it will be remembered, depended on France's honouring hers, the word from Moscow and Geneva reached a point where, on that unforgettably terrible morning of 30 September when the terms of the Munich Agreement, already signed, were made known to Beneš, Alexandrovsky again appeared with a telephone message which he had just received from the Kremlin to the effect that, if Czechoslovakia chose to reject or ignore the terms of the Agreement and to resist the Nazi invasion, she could count on the military support of the Soviet Union, *whether the French fulfilled their treaty pledges or not.*

'Imagine my dilemma,' said Beneš. 'I could have fought with Russian support at once, and if I had done so I have no doubt that in due course you and the French would have joined us. But I should have fought with a divided country. The Agrarians would have opened the frontiers to Germany rather than accept the sole support of Russia, and Syrovy was so anti-Russian that I could not have complete confidence in the Army. I had to accept the terms.'

I did not quote this revelation in its entirety in *Munich*, but I tell it now with the same note of query which it has always raised in my mind. What were the motives of the Russians in this matter? They were not doing it just for the *beaux-yeux* of Eduard Beneš, and there is no particular reason why he should have invented the story for my benefit. Was it possible that they wished to precipitate the Second World War at that moment because Germany was not yet entirely prepared, because she would have been occupied on two fronts, the western and the southern, leaving Russia a free hand to advance into

F

Poland, who, it must be remembered would at that moment have been Germany's ally? We shall, of course, never know the answers to these questions because no official word has ever come out of Moscow on the subject of Munich. This, in itself, provokes further speculation. Why, when on the record, as we know it today, the U.S.S.R. comes very well out of the Munich affair, have they never published the documents which could historically confirm what has been widely stated? What have they gained by not doing so? Or what have they to hide?

Finally, is it not possible that the confidence which Beneš placed in the Soviet Union during and after the war might stem in some kind of misplaced gratitude for the gesture made by Moscow in September 1938 when all Czechoslovakia's other allies had deserted her?

I saw Jan again later in 1946 at the Peace Conference in Paris, and he seemed more depressed than ever, though superficially he was still the same delightful and amusing companion. When we said goodbye it was for the last time.

In June 1947 came the superb American gesture of the Marshall Plan, and the free world in Europe was invited to a conference in Paris to put it into operation. Czechoslovaks had been included in the invitation, and Jan had accepted unreservedly. Five days later he was summoned to Moscow and directly forbidden by Stalin to partake in the Conference. It was the final humiliation and the final warning. 'I went to Moscow as the Foreign Minister of an independent sovereign state; I returned as a lackey of the Soviet Government,' he said bitterly on his return to Phil Nichols.

Seven months later (February 1948) the long expected *coup d'état* in Prague heralded the establishment of a Communist regime, and Czechoslovakia passed finally behind the Iron Curtain. Jan, on the urgent plea of Beneš, remained in the new government out of loyalty. He was much criticised. But it was not for long. On 8 March, Bruce Lockhart and I both received by devious channels word from him that he contemplated coming to London very soon. On the 10th, the world knew that he had been found dead that morning on the pavement of the Loreta Place beneath his flat in the Czernin Palace.

In all the controversy of Jan's death – murder versus suicide – I have not the slightest hesitation as to where I stand. I am convinced that he was murdered – in the traditional Czech manner of defenestration – by Czech Communists who had learned of his plans for escape and feared that, if successful, he would establish a rallying point in London or in America for the enemies of the new régime. There is only one valid argument in favour of suicide. Jan had a dread of pain, and if he had thought that he would be tortured he might have taken his own life, but he would have used a different method. I know that flat and that bathroom in the Czernin Palace. The window is not one through which one can climb with ease, and Jan had put on a good deal of weight in recent years. Nor does a man who intends to throw himself out of the window first wreck his own bathroom, and all the officially published evidence agrees that it was a shambles of smashed glass tables, toilet flasks and medicine bottles, all pointing to a struggle. For me there is no doubt.

As I write there lie before me two slim volumes. The first is the bound collection of Jan Masaryk's wartime broadcasts to his native land, with a *dédicace* in his flowing hand: 'To my dear friend Jack in all modesty, Jan Masaryk. At almost the end of the War.' The other is a specially bound copy of Bruce's memoir of Jan, with an inscription in his neat meticulous calligraphy: 'For Jack Wheeler-Bennett, who loved Jan and was loved by him, In memoriam. R. H. Bruce Lockhart.'

I am the only survivor of this triumvirate of friendship.

CHAPTER SEVEN

La Sale Epoque: France, 1938

I

WHENEVER I re-read A *Sentimental Journey* – which, I confess, is not all that often – I am persistently perplexed by the opening sentence. What could Laurence Sterne have meant by saying: 'They order this matter better in France'? All my sympathy is with his companion, who, 'with the most civil triumph in the world', turns quickly upon him with the very natural enquiry: 'You have been in France?', and, of course, he hadn't.

Leaving Sterne's epoch of the eighteenth century aside, I can recall no period in my lifetime when his statement could be applied with historical accuracy to contemporary France. Indeed, I am prepared to subscribe to the view that the *dégringolade* of France as a great power dates from Waterloo (as the similar decline of Britain began at the Modder River at the hands of the Boers) and the actual historical moment of time was when the horrified, incredulous groan of 'La Garde recule!', followed by the panic-stricken cry of 'Sauve qui peut!', echoed over the stricken plain of Mont St Jean.

There were, of course, still flashes of genius and moments of greatness, but they were fleeting. The Second Empire? Perhaps, but it perished in blood and ignominy at Sedan. *La Belle Epoque?* Again perhaps, but it never survived the Panama Scandal and the fissures of the Dreyfus Affair. The magnificent fighting qualities of the *poilus* in the First World War? But the thrust of offensive disappeared with the mutinies which followed the débâcle and appalling casualties of the Nivelle offensive, and only the indomitable and courageous personality of Clemenceau held the Republic together during the dark and fateful spring of 1918. And twenty years later there was descent into the Avernus of Vichy. Between Napoleon I and Charles de Gaulle there were no French giants, with the single exception of Georges Clemenceau.

At the close of the First World War and of the Peace Conference which followed, Clemenceau left France in what was apparently a position of great power, and his own reputation was so exalted that the National Assembly rejected him as President of the Republic (as the British electorate rejected Mr Churchill in 1945). Instead they elected a political and neurotic non-entity, Paul Déschanel, who having been found standing in his pyjamas in a duck-pond and subsequently roosting in the trees of the Elysée Palace, resigned after eight months of office. The authority of government soon passed into the hands of Raymond Poincaré, who had been President throughout the war.

This then was the French situation which I knew in the inter-war years, and nowhere was it more clearly illustrated than in Paris itself. Opinion was divided between those who believed in a strict and rigid enforcement of the Treaty of Versailles and those who were prepared to envisage a gradual and progressive revision of the treaty terms as and when signs of a return to grace might manifest themselves on the far side of the Rhine. Feeling between the disciples of these two schools ran very high. The disputes among the early Christian Fathers as to whether the Blessing should be given with two fingers or three were as nothing compared with those between the rival factions of 'Enforcement' and 'Revisionism', and one had to walk warily amongst one's friends in discussing this explosive subject – and it was practically the only subject discussed. Moreover Britain's retreat from Europe into a new phase of isolation was a further cause of friction and embarrassment. 'L'Albion perfide' was apt to enter any discussion without warning. It was 'war to the knife and fork', for one never knew when what started out as a perfectly civilised luncheon or dinner-party might degenerate into a passionate and uninhibited display of rancour and recrimination.

Yet Paris in my early manhood was very lovely, although I rank it third to London and New York in my affections. I stayed first at the Hôtel Wagram in the rue de Rivoli and later at the Crillon, where I remained a steady client until my last visit to Paris before the war in the spring of 1939. I was also elected to the Union Interalliée, almost next door to the British embassy in the rue St Honoré, where in summer one can lunch alfresco in one of the most beautiful gardens in Paris.

There was a glamour about Paris which enchanted me, and I delighted in the theatre, from the Comédie Française to the Folies-Bergères, and in the Russian Ballet which was then attracting great audiences as it did in London. To walk the streets and wander through the gardens of the Tuileries and the Luxembourg, to repeople them with figures of the past – for history is more present to me in Paris than anywhere else – was a joy in itself, and the bookstalls along the quais yielded many treasures. There were the restaurants too (so many of which, like Foyot's and Larue's have now disappeared); the famous ones and the little ones where, after a short while as a 'regular', you were adopted into the family. One likes to remember those pleasant days, especially when contemporary Parisians seem to be so unwelcoming.

Nor am I likely to forget an early journey of mine to Paris. The first time was in 1920, and then I travelled conventionally by train and channel packet, but a year later I was more venturesome; I decided to fly. I had never done so before and very nearly never did so again. It was a bitterly cold winter; because of engine trouble we were compelled to make a forced landing in a ploughed field near Amiens and the frozen furrows played havoc with our undercarriage. We made a tardy and rather ignominious arrival in Paris by train at the Gare du Nord.

Ever thereafter, unless greatly pressed for time, I travelled in that acme of luxury the Golden Arrow, on which the comfort was superb and the cuisine delicious. How much I deplore its demise. I have a horrid feeling that the 'Chunnel' will provide no worthy successor.

But, being a political animal and ever hot upon the trail of information, I found other attractions in Paris than merely the aesthetic or the gastronomic. If history was being made in Berlin it was certainly also being made in Paris, and I was a frequent visitor between the two capitals keeping contacts in both. I had a number of friends in various walks of life. There was Ralph Wigram, then first Secretary at the British embassy, who knew more about the general European situation than anyone of his age and experience and to whose wisdom and sound counsel such glowing tributes were paid at the time of his untimely death in 1936. Among members of the French Foreign Ministry there were René Massigli and Pierre Comert, and on a few occasions I was allowed to see the almost legendary Alexis Léger. There was also Roland de Margerie, whose father had been ambassador in Berlin and who remained a good friend of mine, both at the Quai d'Orsay and at the French embassy in London.

There were admirable British and American correspondents too, although nothing comparable to the Taverne in Berlin, and there were great French political journalists whose names became household words. Men such as Vladimir d'Ormesson of the *Figaro* and Bertrand de Jouvenel of *L'Europe Nouvelle* and Louis Joxe. Chief among them in my memory however is Geneviève Tabouis, niece of that famous Ambassador in London Jules Cambon, who was one of the French architects of the Entente Cordiale. Mme Tabouis who, I am happy to say, though of an advanced age, still lives in Paris, was politically an adherent of Edouard Herriot, from whom she gleaned much invaluable information in the exercise of the technique of the 'official leak', in which the French are such past-masters. She would ask me to lunch with Herriot at Chez Marius, that famous restaurant in the Place Bourgogne, just behind the Chambre, where many deputies lunched and dined. There the great man – great in every sense, in girth and in moral stature – sat with his napkin around his neck, consuming an inordinately large number of the delicious *moules*, for which Chez Marius is famous, talking the while on the political situation in France and in Europe generally and occasionally listening to what I had to say about what was happening in Germany. Though I think that Herriot's socialist ideals led him to a certain degree of muddled thinking (as when he became co-sponsor with Ramsay MacDonald of the Geneva Protocol in 1924), he was definitely on the side of the angels, and both as Mayor of Lyons, an office which he held for thirty years, and as President of the Chamber of Deputies, he steadfastly withstood both the German occupation authorities and the Vichy régime until deported to the Reich.

Geneviève Tabouis was *petite*, attractive, gallant and indefatigable. She never seemed to rest, and she seemed to be everywhere at once, Geneva, Paris, London, or wherever there was a story to be had. Her book, *They Called me Cassandra* describes perfectly her percipience and her clear thinking. She cried 'woe, woe,' among the earliest, and they would not listen. She escaped at the eleventh hour from Bordeaux in 1940, and I was glad to be of some assistance to her on her arrival in New York. I can still see her coming into my office with her inimitable charm and *chic* and saying 'Well, *mon cher ami*, and what are the news?' for though she spoke English perfectly she could not master the fact that 'news' is not plural (like Rudyard Kipling's American in 'An Error in the Fourth Dimension' who spoke English so perfectly that he *would* ask for the 'Worcestershire' sauce).

A different type altogether but no less impressive was 'Pertinax' who wrote under this pseudonym and was thus universally known (I am not sure if I ever knew his real name but if I did I have certainly forgotten it). Further to the Right politically than Mme Tabouis, he was nevertheless at one with her in his courageous opposition to the policy of appeasement in the later thirties, and his admirable work *The Grave-Diggers of France* is one of the most blistering indictments of French political leadership during that period. With him one lunched at Foyot's and met Louis Marin and Charles de Kérilis (though not together), those two dauntless figures on the Conservative benches who denounced the policies of Daladier and Bonnet, for the forces of the Right were *Munichois* ('All that is best in France' as one British diplomat unguardedly described them) almost to a man.

Among other great French politicians, good and bad, whom one was privileged to meet were Poincaré, Briand, Barthou and Laval, a very mixed bag. I only met Poincaré once, but I heard him speak in the Chamber on a number of occasions, and a colder fish I have never encountered. A Lorrainer by birth and a lawyer by profession, he was the personification of the policy of 'Enforcement'. As President Coolidge remarked of the repayment of the inter-Allied debts, 'They *hired* the money, didn't they?' So might Poincaré say of the Germans and the reparations wrangle, 'They lost the war, didn't they?' It was this uncompromising attitude which finally led France into the morass of the occupation of the Ruhr from which she had to be rescued by Edouard Herriot and Aristide Briand.

II

Of all the French political rhetoricians I have listened to, and there have been many of them, only two have stirred me to the depths. René Viviani, known as the 'Silver-Tongued Orator' of his day, was decidedly *passé* by the time I heard him, and the two men to whom I refer were Charles de Gaulle and Aristide Briand. They were very different as speakers, different in content, style and delivery. De Gaulle was cold, classical, clear and clinical; he made few gestures; his voice, magnificent in its detachment, compelled attention by the very mastery of the language which he spoke. In the historic broadcast of 27 June 1940, which changed the destiny of France, one could sense the call to arms, the appeal for endurance, the promise of victory. There was a regality about him which could not be denied but it was an Olympian regality.

Aristide Briand was almost completely the antithesis. There was the warmth of Brittany in his voice, a golden quality which struck to the heart of every man and woman within earshot. I have watched that speech-weary, word-calloused audience, the Assembly of the League of Nations, thrill again and again to his passionate appeals for peace and understanding, which momentarily, at least, evoked responsive echoes in the hearts of all of us, even if we cynically realised on the morrow that the chances of fulfilment were as slim and as dim as ever. Briand was a spellbinder, not so much in the Lloyd George tradition – for despite the immediate effect of the Welsh Wizard one felt, even as he spoke, that he lacked sincerity – but in an inimitable fashion of his own, which clutched at the heart and summoned forth devotion.

I remember very well when I first heard the name of Briand. It was in 1910, when as a small boy, I recall my father holding forth in admiration of the political strategy of the French Prime Minister, who, faced with a general strike of railwaymen, declared a partial state of martial law and summoned them to the colours, where they found themselves required to work the railways! It was an original idea and typical of Briand. But though he won the battle he lost the war because his Minister of Labour (who happened to be Viviani) was so appalled by this *folie de succès*, that he resigned and brought down the government with him – such being the nature of French politics under the Third Republic. The story, however, captured my imagination, and from then onwards M. Briand became something of a hero of mine.

He had had rather a chequered career in the war, and Clemenceau had little use for him, but with the peace he came into his own and became one of that little band of statesmen, which included Austen Chamberlain and Gustav Stresemann, who gave to many of us a brief period of hope – which proved alas to be but a false dawn.

Briand had a pretty turn of wit, and the story I like most about him was when, at the time of the Cannes Conference in 1922, he met Lloyd George with a view to concluding an agreement for British assistance to France in the event of German aggression. Briand's majority in the Chamber was uncertain, but before leaving for Cannes he had entered into a pact with his principal opponent, Louis Barthou, that his ministry should not be brought down at any rate until after the conference.

The two prime ministers got on famously, so well indeed that Lloyd George insisted on trying to initiate Briand into the mysteries of golf and Briand was misguided enough to co-operate. A photographer caught a picture of the two on the links and it appeared widely in the French press next morning. The effect was disastrous. This smacked of levity and frivolity and to many Anglophobes it suggested that the British Prime Minister was in some subtle manner attempting to seduce his French colleague from the primary interests of France. Warnings reached Briand that a crisis had broken. He rushed back to Paris to arrive just as his ministry suffered a vote of no confidence; but he was an old hand at the game and knew well how to roll with the punches. Meeting Barthou in the *coulisses* of the Chamber, he asked with a coldish smile: 'Ah, my friend, and what is the exchange rate of thirty pieces of silver this morning?'

I met Briand at a party given by the French delegation at Geneva and he was very pleasant to me. His appearance was that of a friendly lion with a mane of dark hair and a heavy moustache. A cigarette always seemed to depend from his lips, but it never appeared to be lighted; gradually, as he dribbled into it, it became sodden and turned brown, and was then replaced by another. His eyes were sleepy and heavy-lidded. He had a most infectious smile and a jovial laugh. Behind a pleasing and agreeable exterior there was a certain inscrutability.

At the end of our talk Briand asked me to call upon him in Paris 'whenever I am in office; I come and go, you know' (as a matter of fact he was Prime Minister more often than any other parliamentarian in the French Republic and Foreign Minister in many successive governments). This I did, and he always seemed to have time to talk. His desk never had a paper on it, but there was a rumour that he had had a false top made for it which when pulled into place covered the document-covered surface beneath! He was always interested in what was going on in Germany and he formed a genuine admiration for both Stresemann and Brüning, in whom he recognised fellow-believers in a European settlement. He visited Brüning in Berlin in the dubious company of Pierre Laval, and it must not be forgotten that in 1930 he launched a plan for a European Union which was well in advance of the present Common Market. It failed of success for a variety of reasons but was remarkable for evoking a Soviet proposal for the outlawing of economic aggression. Not a bad idea !

The apogee of Briand's greatness was of course the Locarno Agreement of 1925, and it is a thousand pities that his informal understanding reached with Stresemann at Thoiry very soon thereafter was never pursued. There was, however, a curious repercussion of the general spirit of euphoria which characterised this brief period of false hopes. I suppose we shall never know the full motives which prompted the somewhat fantastic proposal which Briand made to the United States in the spring of 1927, but one can be pretty sure that when he made it he had no idea of its ultimate consequences. It was indeed the only occasion that I can remember in which he fell rather heavily over his own feet.

On 6 April of that year, the tenth anniversary of the entry of the United States into the First World War and near enough to the hundred and fiftieth anniversary of the original treaty between France and Britain's rebellious American colonies to make it significant, M. Briand proposed to the government of the United States that France and America should publicly subscribe to a mutual engagement to outlaw war as between their two countries.

On the face of it, this appeared a perfectly harmless and feasible proposal. The chances of a war between France and America were inconsiderable; there was therefore nothing to be lost and perhaps something to be gained by their entering into such a bilateral engagement, which would indicate the general pacific desires of France, which had been somewhat suspect over the postwar years and could do with a little refurbishing.

But it didn't turn out quite that way. The policies of the United States, and specially of the Republican Party, had also come in for some pretty severe criticism since the war on the grounds of their rejection of the League of Nations, and, although they had taken the initiative in calling the Washington Conference of 1922 and had made valuable contributions in the field of reparations and disarmament, it seemed to President Calvin Coolidge and to Secretary of State Frank Kellogg that Briand's proposal offered a God-given opportunity for the further rehabilitation of America's world image.

The reply to the French proposal, therefore, was that this wonderful idea of M. Briand's was altogether too grand and splendid to be restricted to two countries but should be expanded to include 'all the principal powers' under the joint invitation of the United States and France.

This was not at all what Briand had either expected or desired. At once the fat was in the fire, and the cat among the pigeons. To outlaw all war between the major powers under all circumstances would negate not only the Locarno Agreement but also the bilateral pledges which France had given to Belgium, Poland, Czechoslovakia, Romania and Yugoslavia for their mutual protection. Across the Channel the British Government was also apprehensive of this new outbreak of idealism. Britain had obligations not only to Germany, France and Belgium under Locarno, but also to her Dominions beyond the Seas, her Colonial Empire, India, Egypt, Iraq and Palestine. These could not be left protected only by the shadowy shield of a renunciation of war. And what of Russia with whom the United States had no diplomatic relations but who played an important part in European affairs?

Aristide Briand found that he had indeed stirred up a hornet's nest where he had meant to establish a resting place for doves. As one French journal very honestly put it:

Lorsque M. Briand avait parlé en avril dernier de la guerre considérée comme instrument de politique nationale, il s'agissait d'un pacte bilatéral entre deux nations qui n'avait aucune raison *de se combattree avec un pact; plusilatéral, les données du problème ne sont plus les mêmes.*

At once reservations began to pour into Washington explaining the 'peculiar circumstances' of Britain and France and other major powers which must be taken into consideration and safeguarded before adherence to such a sweeping statement of principle could be accepted. With a certain wiliness the American State Department sought to meet these objections with placating reassurances that they should indeed be met by inclusion in the preamble to the treaty rather than in the body of the text.

It was at this moment that I played my tiny part in the history of the Briand–Kellogg Pact. Mr Kellogg had shortly before this made a speech before the Council of Foreign Relations in New York in which he had made an important statement of policy. For once the unusually strict measures of the Council to avoid publicity had broken down and the text of Mr Kellogg's remarks had reached the press. I had read them with interest and had noticed what I thought to be a not insignificant point. I consulted the Foreign Office and the French embassy and then wrote a letter to *The Times* which they published on 26 June 1928:

> Sir, – The American concession to the French reservations is embodied in the third paragraph of the revised Preamble to the Draft Treaty for the Renunciation of War, in the following words:
>
> > Convinced that all changes in their relations with one another should be sought only by pacific means, and be the result of a peaceful and orderly process, and that any signatory Power which shall hereafter seek to promote its national interests by resort to war should be denied the benefits furnished by this Treaty.
>
> Mr Kellogg in the course of a speech before the Council on Foreign Relations in New York on March 15, 1928, committed himself to the definite statement that 'a Preamble is not a binding part of a treaty.' I believe this point to be of the greatest importance in connexion with the relation of the proposed Treaty for the renunciation of war to the Covenant of the League of Nations and the Locarno Agreement.
>
> > I am, Sir, yours, &c.,
> > JOHN W. WHEELER-BENNETT.

I am not suggesting that the legal luminaries of the Foreign Office and the Quai d'Orsay would not have reached this same conclusion without my assistance, but the outcome was a personal letter of thanks from M. Briand and, what was even more welcome, an official invitation in due course, to the ceremony of signature in Paris.

Thus on the afternoon of Monday, 27 August 1928, I was present at one of the most fantastic episodes of modern diplomatic history. It was held in the Salle de l'Horloge of the Quai d'Orsay in which, ten years before, the Covenant of the League of Nations had been officially adopted. Great arc lights had been installed and at the head of the delegates' table a microphone and broadcasting apparatus had been installed; for Mr Kellogg had no intention that this thing 'should be done in a corner'. It was to have the maximum media coverage, greater than any which had previously been given on a similar occasion, and for this reason representatives of the press jostled Cabinet Ministers and diplomats in competition for the small and uncomfortable gold chairs supplied for the audience.

The affair had many undertones not readily apparent. In the course of the negotiations Briand's government had fallen and, though he remained as Foreign Minister, his successor was Raymond Poincaré, whose political orientation was scarcely in consonance with the *mores* of that day. However, there they sat side by side, Poincaré glum and glowering, Briand bland and mildly derisive. I have always thought that he realised that his original suggestion had got out of hand but he was resigned to the enjoyment of the result.

Stresemann was there, looking so grey and ill that his personal physician was in attendance behind him and when I saw him later that evening I wondered whether he would live out the year – he just did, dying in October 1929. His presence had a special significance, for it was the first time since Bismarck's visit in 1867 that a German Foreign Minister had been officially received at the Quai d'Orsay.

Beneš was to have spoken on behalf of the minor states, for by this time all France's allies and Britain's Dominions had been included, bringing the total of the original signatories up to fifteen. He had intended to make a eulogy of Woodrow Wilson, but as this did not commend itself to a Republican administration, he remained silent. There was, indeed, no speech-making save for an eloquent and beautifully worded address such as Aristide Briand could always be counted on to make on such an occasion.

Perhaps the most ironic aspect was that, owing to Sir Austen Chamberlain's having gone on a cruise for his health, Britain was represented by Lord Cushendun (formerly Ronnie MacNeil). His real claim to fame, though he had risen to the position of Under-Secretary for Foreign Affairs, was that in the course of those turbulent parliamentary debates before the First World War, he had thrown a book across the floor of the House of Commons striking Winston Churchill, then a Liberal Minister. Lord Cushendun was an uncompromising Ulster Unionist and his presence at this ceremony was about as incongruous as that of M. Poincaré. For good measure he had to sign the document twice, on behalf of both Britain and the Government of India.

The only man who seemed completely happy and at the same time deeply moved by the occasion was Mr Frank Kellogg himself. He was probably alone among his fellow signatories in believing heart and soul in the potential power of the Pact of Paris to bring about a war-less world. Tears of pure faith and emotion ran down his cheeks and spotted the original document, much to the embarrassment of the *chef de protocol*, whose duty it was to blot the various signatures and not to deal with lachrymose inundations.

The actual ceremony of signature was performed with a gold pen which had been presented to Mr Kellogg on his arrival in France by the Mayor of Havre. It was encrusted with laurel wreaths and bore the legend: '*Si vis pacem, para pacem*'. In the course of his remarks on accepting it, the Secretary of State uttered at least one incontrovertible truth: 'It is impossible,' he said, 'to say today what the American Senate will do tomorrow.'

I suppose there may have been in history greater monuments of cynical futility than the Kellogg–Briand Pact but, if so, they would be hard to find. Scarcely were the ink and Mr Kellogg's tears dry upon the text when the world entered upon a period of the most naked aggression ever known, beginning with the Japanese invasion of Manchuria and ending with the outbreak of the Second World War. The only value of the Pact – and certainly its greatest irony – was some seventeen years later when it formed one of the bases of Counts One and Two of the Indictment of the major Nazi War Criminals in the preparation of that document for the International Military Tribunal at Nuremberg.

But at the time of its signature the Pact of Paris aroused many hopes, which proved, of course, to be based on the flimsiest of wishful thinking. I wrote a book on it myself[1], to which Philip Kerr (later Marquess of Lothian) contributed an introduction and in which I blush to say that, in the idealism and wisdom of my twenty-six years, I described it as 'the greatest step towards peace since the Covenant of the League of Nations'. This was, in point of fact, perfectly true –

---

[1] *The Renunciation of War* (London, 1928).

but not in the way I meant it. I can, however, say with Sir Winston Churchill, that 'I have at various times had to eat my own words and have always found them a very palatable diet.'

Briand continued as Foreign Minister until the moment when, as in the case of Georges Clemenceau a decade earlier, the National Assembly, partly out of jealousy and partly from fear of a president of outstanding character, rejected his election to the highest office of the Republic in favour of an undistinguished candidate, Paul Doumer, who a little over a year later was assassinated at a book fair by a White Russian fanatic, dying, it is said, with the immortal words 'Oo, là-la' upon his lips.

III

Louis Barthou was the last of the great statesmen of the Third Republic. He was a hard character, who had spent most of his life in the hurly-burly of French politics. Born in the country of the Pyrenees he had the toughness of the mountaineer about him, and, moreover, he had been twelve years old, an impressionable age, at the time of the humiliation of France at the hands of Prussia in 1870. His bristling clipped beard and steady grey eyes gave him a forbidding appearance, and he believed, with Poincaré and with Clemenceau, that the terms of the Treaty of Versailles were infinitely too lenient for the security of France, the peace of the world and the punishment of Germany. From this view he never deviated, and in the course of time he won his abiding niche in history as the last French statesman who endeavoured to organise Europe against the threatening policies of the Third Reich.

He was feared by his enemies and had few friends, and he gloried in his reputation as a maker and breaker of cabinets. He was indeed a wrecker in both domestic and international affairs. Government after government fell to his hatchet, and he was largely responsible for blighting the Cannes Conference of 1922 and the Geneva Conference which followed it in the same year. Though never himself prime minister, Barthou was content to be the power behind the throne of many who were, and he staunchly supported the efforts of Poincaré to re-establish the franc in 1926.

It was during these frenzied days in Paris, when the currency was approaching zero and, I regret to say, Americans and British were lighting their cigars with thousand-franc notes in public and getting their faces slapped for it, that I met Barthou and I found him a frightening man. Together he and Poincaré were two of the most fearsome and coldest men I have ever encountered, and their joint frigidity constituted something only comparable to that heroine of a popular song of my youth called 'Hard-hearted Hannah', of whom that great lady Sophie Tucker used to sing that:

> Making love to Hannah in a big armchair
> Was like strolling through Alaska in your underwear.

But they were courageous, and between them they saved the franc, and, a while later, Louis Barthou made a brave but unavailing attempt to save France.

The year 1934 was a crucial one for the French Republic, for during these twelve months its fundamental weakness and disunion were revealed. The Stavisky scandal of the previous December had laid bare the state of corruption within the nation. Public attention was drawn to the fact that not only could a common swindler successfully evade the law and avoid imprisonment but that he could actually acquire accomplices in high places. The respectability, the probity and the credibility of the Republic were called in question; the integrity of democratic parliamentary government came under grave suspicion and disrepute. The revolutionary forces of the Right, encouraged by the success of Hitler's disposal of the Weimar System, were well aware of the opportunity now presented and on 6 February 1934 what were collectively called 'Les Ligues', composed of royalist, fascist and militant ex-service elements, marched upon the Chamber of Deputies with the intention of overthrowing the Republic.

I was in Paris at the time staying at the Crillon, and I well remember that grey and gloomy afternoon when the future of republican France hung in the balance. I had indeed a ringside seat, for the whole incident began with a rally of the Rightist forces in the Place de la Concorde, immediately outside my hotel. The general call had gone out for an *assaut dans les rues*; some thousands had assembled and were prepared to force the passage of the Pont de la Concorde and storm the Chamber. They were in an ugly mood, exemplified by the use of hat-pins with which the mob stabbed the horses of the mounted police, and of marbles thrown on the streets to make the horses lose their footing. For good measure a number of newspaper kiosks were set on fire and, after one or two shops in the rue de Rivoli had had their windows broken, there was a general lowering of the steel shutters.

From the balcony of that large room of the Crillon, in which the Committee of the Peace Conference appointed to draft the Covenant of the League of Nations had held its sessions, I could watch the drama beneath. The demonstrators were in deadly earnest. They made several attempts to cross the bridge and, had they gained an entry into the Palais Bourbon, it would have gone hard with the Representatives of the People. The police, foot and mounted, behaved extremely well, but were outnumbered and were slowly being pushed back to the *Rive Gauche*. The Cabinet of Camille Chautemps, which had been in session all day, resigned in panic and, with commendable courage, Edouard Daladier formed a *very* emergency government. He ordered a cordon of troops to be thrown across the entrance to the Chamber between it and the bridge. By this time the situation had become so critical that he had no alternative but to warn the mob that, if they did not withdraw, he would give the order to fire and to make good his threat if it went unheeded. It did. I, however, had circumspectly left my coign of vantage when the warning was given and did not actually see the carnage which followed, though the sound of rifle-fire was perfectly audible in the hall of the hotel. Sixteen persons were killed at the first volley, among them a maid standing at a window of the Crillon, of which the façade was spattered with bullet marks, showing that in some degree the troops had fired high. There was a danger of open street fighting, but *Les Ligues* retreated, threatening to return next day with arms in their hands. Faced with this possible renewed defiance of authority Daladier's courage evaporated. He too resigned next day. 'I could not shed the blood of the *petits poilus* of France,' he excused himself.

When I spoke to the manager of the hotel on duty in condolence for the death of the maid, I was assured, with a certain detached satisfaction amounting almost to indifference, that she was employed by a guest and was not a member of the Crillon staff. This seemed to dispose of *her*.

February 6, 1934 was a climacteric in French history. Though the *Sale Epoque* had really begun a year or two earlier, it was only after this *descente dans les rues* that the lines became clearly drawn. In the salons and clubs and restaurants one noticed the difference. The desirability of an accommodation with Hitler now became openly canvassed whereas before it had been only whispered, and the interesting thing was that it was now advocated by those who, only a few short years before, had been the strongest supporters of *constrainte à outrance* of the Treaty of Versailles. The voices which a couple of years later were speaking of 'Better Hitler than Blum', and later still of 'Better Hitler than Stalin', were already to be heard in a sinister murmur. From then on the parties of the Left were regarded by an increasing number of people as constituting a greater menace to the 'good life' than Nazi Germany. The thesis of 'if you can't beat 'em join 'em' was becoming an act of faith, with Pierre Laval as its chief disciple and champion. The road to Munich, to Bordeaux and to Vichy began in the Place de la Concorde on that bleak and bloody February day.

But before the Gadarene descent really got under way there was a burst of energetic statesmanship, a display of diplomatic virility, which recalled the robust policies of Georges Clemenceau. Louis Barthou became Foreign Minister in that Cabinet of National Concentration which Gaston Doumergue formed to re-establish equilibrium and public respect within the Republic. Barthou believed – as I did – that Hitler was committed, nay dedicated, to a programme of unilateral revision of the Treaty of Versailles but that in executing it he did not want a war 'just for the hell of it'. If he could get what he wanted by 'peaceful means', that is to say without armed opposition from the Great Powers or armed resistance on the part of his various victims, he would prefer this to a war, but, in the final analysis, he did not rule out war from his planning. Moreover, Hitler did not want war at that moment. He was in no way ready for it. There was yet time for Europe to prepare. It therefore behoved the Continent to look to its armaments and defences. Then, if and when the time came, as it surely would, for a confrontation with Germany eager for expansion, the Versailles Powers could meet the challenge with a united front and speak from strength rather than from weakness. (I had said this at a lecture at the Royal Institute of International Affairs as early as March 1933 and had been somewhat severely criticised for my views.)

On the other hand, Barthou had no sympathy with proposals such as those put forward by Marshal Pilsudski a year earlier for a 'preventive war' against Germany, for which Poland was prepared to provide a *casus belli*. Alluring though such a prospect might be, Barthou, who was a sternly practical politician, knew well that there was no hope of gaining popular support for it in France or in Britain. He had but limited confidence in the British, except for Anthony Eden, and one is somehow grateful for his reference to Sir John Simon as 'my respected colleague and almost friend.'

Barthou himself was fluent in German and read it with ease. He was one of the few in France who had read *Mein Kampf* in the original (a formidable achievement in itself) and was always prepared to discuss the changing attitudes in Germany, with which he kept fully abreast. He still confidently believed that if France set her own house in order, had faith in her own strength and confirmed her obligations under her system of central, eastern and south-eastern alliances, she could meet the German threat with calm assurance. He did not believe in making concessions which could only lead to further concessions; he was convinced that to break such a sequence was as well-nigh impossible as to wrest oneself from the talons of a blackmailer.

For the next ten months Louis Barthou, with great vigour and courage considering his seventy-two years, devoted himself to this line of action. He travelled indefatigably throughout Europe, mending his fences. He renewed France's pledges to the Little Entente and to Belgium and welcomed his hitherto inveterate enemy Soviet Russia into the League of Nations. Everywhere he was received rapturously as a harbinger of the renewed vitality of France. Only in Warsaw was he greeted coldly. Marshal Pilsudski, having been rebuffed in his proposals for a preventive war, had already taken out his insurance with Hitler and would not budge from it. Nevertheless, when Barthou returned to Paris at the end of June, he could say, 'I think I have checked him [Hitler] in eastern Europe, but it will require hard work to keep him in check.'

That the Führer did not underestimate the danger to his plans for expansion of the new courage which Barthou had infused into France's European allies may be judged from the fact that the French Foreign Minister's train was unsuccessfully bombed by the Nazis on 19 June, during his journey across Austria. But Hitler had not long to wait. On 9 October 1934, Barthou and King Alexander of Yugoslavia, one of his staunchest allies, were murdered at Marseilles on a state visit. Two of the leading opponents of Nazi expansion had been eliminated at one stroke. The last spark of French resistance expired with the death of Louis Barthou. 'These were the first shots of the Second World War,' wrote Anthony Eden.

There are many details about this assassination which are still unknown, and mystery surrounds much of the inadequacy of the security arrangements. One poignant aspect of it was told to me years later by King Peter of Yugoslavia. His father had apparently received warnings of a possible attempt on his life in the course of his visit to France and had taken the precaution of providing himself with a bullet-proof vest of the finest steel link-mesh. It was his intention to land on the soil of France wearing the uniform of a French admiral, but unfortunately he had not previously tried on the dress coat over the steel vest, and when he did so it would not button across his chest. An immediate decision was necessary and, alas, unwisely, he discarded his protective armour. By such small incidents is the course of history changed.

CHAPTER EIGHT

Doorn, August 1939

I

WHEN I was a small boy of nine, I remember, I listened with some awe to my father, who, speaking with the full authority of an English autocrat at his own breakfast table, pronounced the German Emperor to be 'a howling cad'. I was given to understand that what later became known as the Agadir crisis was at its height, that Europe was on the brink of war and that my father's additional complaint was that, at great inconvenience to himself, he was preparing to go out to Germany to bring back my sister Irene, (then at a finishing school at Dresden) before hostilities actually broke out.

As it happened he never had to do this because the crisis was dissipated largely as a result of an historic speech at the Mansion House by Mr Lloyd George, which even my father described as 'statesmanlike'. It must have cost him a lot – and is a considerable tribute to his fairness of mind – to speak in any but the most pejorative terms of a member of the Liberal Government. I had frequently heard him refer to Mr Lloyd George as 'a howling yahoo'. 'Howling' was rather a favourite word of his, and his use of it always rather confused me as I had only heard it applied at any other time to hyenas.

I can clearly trace the beginning of my interest in Wilhelm II to this incident, and I can well recall the three occasions on which I saw him before the First World War. The first was at King Edward VII's funeral procession in 1910, for which my father took a stand in the Edgware Road to watch the cortège *en route* to Paddington. On this occasion the Emperor marched with the new King, George V, and his only surviving uncle, the Duke of Connaught, all resplendent in the uniform of British field-marshals. Although what impressed me most deeply at the time was the sight of Caesar, the late King's wire-haired terrier, being led by a royal groom behind the charger with boots reversed in the stirrups, I do remember these three figures in scarlet with plumed helmets and thinking that the one with the upturned moustaches was the most regal-looking of all. The second time was some two years later at the unveiling of Queen Victoria's statue in front of Buckingham Palace (of which he subsequently spoke to me as *Grossmutterdenkmal*) when he wore the uniform of a British admiral, and the third, was, as I have already described, in the spring of 1914, when in the full glory of an *Adlerhaube*, he took the salute of his guards at Tempelhof.

I cannot deny that the Emperor seemed immensely impressive to me on these three occasions. He fulfilled my idea of how an emperor should look, and I conceived a youthful admiration for him, which I carefully concealed from my father. But I remember having a fight at my preparatory school before the war in defending him against what I regarded as calumnies by the son of a Liberal Cabinet Minister. Thereafter, however, in common with everyone else in Britain, I came under the influence of British wartime propaganda regarding the German Emperor, with the result that I became convinced that in principle, if not in fact, he wore horns and a tail and was personally responsible for all the atrocities which were luridly depicted for us, especially the Belgian children whose hands were said to have been cut off.

> Tramp, tramp, tramp, along the road to *Ber*-lin,
> (we had carolled with gusto in the Malvern O.T.C.)
> Singing, cheering, seeking all the way
> A wild cat whose moustaches want uncurling,
> A man-eating tiger brought at last to bay.

But, in the course of my historical reading and research my interest in the Kaiser never waned, and, though my judgements grew to be more balanced as my reasoning became more mature, I remained fascinated by this extraordinary figure, whom one of his biographers has justly termed *The Fabulous Monster*. Later still, as I became more and more absorbed by the problems of the enigma of personality in history, my attention became the more riveted by this almost legendary personality who had dominated Europe, albeit for ill rather than for good, for thirty years; the man who had 'dropped the pilot' and who had coined the phrases 'shining armour', 'the rattling sabre' and 'Attila and his Huns'; the last monarch to believe – and quite genuinely – that he ruled by Divine Right; the man in whose arms Queen Victoria had died – 'She was so little and so light,' he said to me of this occasion – the man who had given the blank cheque to Austria-Hungary in July 1914 and, consequently, became the first man in modern times to be indicted as a Major War Criminal. Whatever one's opinion of him might be one could not deny his historical significance, nor the obvious psychological complexities which accounted for his erratic and sometimes almost frivolous behaviour in statecraft.

I decided that in the course of time I would write a biography of him and I think that what clinched my decision was when a sizeable segment of the Holstein Papers were entrusted to me for safe-keeping, pending the suitable time for their publication. In accordance with my established beliefs in personal contacts I felt it was absolutely necessary to meet him.[1] I took this decision, or rather I acted upon it, rather late in the day. It was not until the summer of 1939, when the shadows of war were again darkening the summer skies of Europe, that I set the wheels in motion by applying to my friend Bruce Lockhart for an introduction to the Kaiser.

Bruce had been several times to Doorn in the course of his journalistic career during the inter-war years. He had earned the gratitude of the Kaiser in connection with the publication in German of the correspondence between the Empress Frederick and her mother, Queen Victoria, the abstraction of which from Potsdam by Sir Frederick Ponsonby on behalf of King Edward VII, at the time of the Empress's death, had created such a furore. Bruce was agreeable – as he always was – and we both wrote polite letters to the Marshal of the Court seeking an audience.

This was in June, and by July no response had been made. The storm-cones were flying over all the capitals of Europe, and I became desperately aware that if I didn't see the Emperor, who was already eighty, that summer I probably never should, and in any case a European war would more than occupy one's time. Then I had a stroke of good fortune. Walking down St James's Street I met Prince Friedrich of Prussia, the youngest son of the Crown Prince, whom I knew well and I hauled him in to Brooks's for lunch. Did he, I asked, ever see his grandfather? Yes, he was in fact going to spend next weekend with him at Doorn. Would he, I begged, try to find out what had become of Bruce's and my letters and what had gone wrong about them? He would indeed.

On the following Tuesday we again lunched together at Brooks's, and he had an odd story to tell. His grandfather had never seen our letters, which had apparently been deliberately kept from him by the gentlemen of his *Umgebung* (Household), the majority of whom were pro-Nazi and were opposed to His Majesty's receiving two persons who were well known to be hostile to Hitler and all his works. To be quite fair, it should also be stated that under the German exchange restrictions, the Kaiser was the sole non-resident to have an 'unblocked mark' account and his entourage may have been anxious lest news

---

[1] I never did write this book because the Second World War intervened and afterwards I wrote *Munich* and *The Nemesis of Power* instead, but I have given certain impressions of the Kaiser in *Hindenburg, Brest-Litovsk, A Wreath to Clio* and *History Makers of the Twentieth Century* (London, 1973).

of our presence at Doorn should jeopardise this very privileged position. At any rate, the Emperor had been furious and had berated his courtiers. ('Grandpapa was very, very angry,' said Fritzi.) He was anxious to see us and would send an official invitation very soon.

This was a great relief, and the invitation duly arrived to come and stay at Doorn in the middle of August. I felt this to be running it pretty fine, but one could not look a gift invitation in the mouth, and we gladly accepted.

Before our departure, however, an entertaining incident occurred. I was staying for a weekend with Sir Courtauld Thomson, a somewhat mysterious but kind and pleasant man, who lived with his rather forbidding – but really very nice – sister Winifred, at an extremely comfortable Queen Anne house near Burnham Beeches called Dorney Wood. This he subsequently presented to the nation as a country retreat for the Foreign Secretary in the manner of Chequers.

'Scorts' loved royalty, and among his house-party was Princess Helena Victoria, the daughter of Princess Helena and Prince Christian of Schleswig-Holstein, and a granddaughter of Queen Victoria. She was a very amusing old lady, and I remember, during a previous visit two years earlier, she had arrived late for lunch because of a rehearsal at Westminster Abbey for the Coronation of King George VI and Queen Elizabeth. She was in wonderful form despite the rigours of her recent experience. 'My dears,' she addressed the table at large, 'the seating arrangements in the Abbey are terrible – but terrible. Those poor peeresses, those poor peeresses! They have only twenty-four inches to sit on. Thank God I am a Serene Highness and get thirty-two.'

During this same summer she had been at a luncheon party given by Edouard Raczynski at the Polish embassy in Portman Place. I was there too. It was an odd sort of party considering the political climate of ideas in Europe, for the wife of the German Ambassador was also present. Frau von Dirksen was at pains to indicate that there was really no problem at all to disturb the peace of Europe, and exhorted us all to remain calm and to ignore any wild talk of war. Whereupon Princess Helena Victoria remarked with some asperity: 'I find it difficult to ignore or be calm when they are digging a dugout in my garden.' This rather 'put paid' to the Ambassadress's further conversational contribution.

On this particular July day at Dorney Wood I told the Princess that, after considerable difficulties, I had at last arranged to go to see the Kaiser at Doorn in the following month. She was at once all attention. She plied me with questions and delighted me with her own recollections of Wilhelm II. She said that her 'Uncle Arthur', the Duke of Connaught, who was also, of course, the Kaiser's only surviving English uncle, would enjoy hearing about it.

A few days later a very affable invitation arrived asking me to go down to lunch at Bagshot, the Duke's country house in Surrey. I accepted with alacrity and, having borrowed my mother's car and chauffeur, presented myself at the appointed day and hour. The house itself was not by any stretch of imagination beautiful (it is now the headquarters of the Corps of Military Chaplains or some similar title) but it was full of good solid Edwardian comfort and, naturally, of family relics of great interest. I waited for a moment or two in a pleasant morning room with french windows opening on to the garden, and then a very small (I had not realised he was so small), very pink-and-white military figure, remarkably straight and militarily dapper for all his ninety-odd years, came into the room on the arm of an equerry. It became immediately clear to me that the Duke of Connaught had at that particular moment no vestige of a clue as to who I was or what I had come about, but with that great courtesy which always characterised him he appeared to be at no loss at all and said in a rather quavering voice: 'It's very good of you, my dear boy, to come all this way to see me, and which campaign was it we were together in?' As he was old enough to be my grandfather this was rather a daunting question, and I parried it by saying that it was indeed a long time since I had seen him and how grateful I was for the pleasure of doing so now. As he was almost entirely deaf this proved as good an answer as any other.

We then went in to lunch and I found that besides the members of the Duke's household, there were also his daughter, Princess Patricia Lady Ramsay and also Princess Helena Victoria. The presence of the latter gave me courage and confidence, but I was still at a complete loss as to how the object of my visit was to be introduced. So, it seemed, were the royal ladies between whom I sat. They discussed the matter across me and eventually one of them raised her voice to a well-developed shout and announced: 'Uncle Arthur, Mr Wheeler-Bennett's going to Doorn.' The Duke, who was concentrating on his luncheon, gave no indication at all of having heard. The two ladies then repeated the remark together and *fortissimo*. The Duke looked up with a flash of interest. 'Who's going round the Horn?' he enquired amiably. 'DOORN!' the ladies bellowed in chorus. I dreaded to think of the injuries being inflicted on their larynxes but I was too much occupied in keeping a straight face and a grip on my sanity.

Clearly we were getting nowhere, and a sense of despair began to settle over the luncheon table. At the end of the meal, however, a kind of field telephone was wheeled in, having the appearance of a miniature garden hose on a roller, with head-phones attached. These were adjusted to the Duke's ears, he tossing his head the while like an irritated pony. The remark, the same fateful remark, was then repeated and immediately had a galvanic effect. Suddenly the whole position became clear in my host's mind, and he rose from the table and, grasping me by the arm, proceeded at a surprising rate of knots down a dark passage, which reminded me of the White Rabbit and *Alice in Wonderland*.

At last we reached our goal – a large sunny room, lined with drawers and in the centre of which was a model of the Taj Mahal in sandalwood. The Duke was now fully aware of what he wanted. He went without hesitation to a certain drawer and began to burrow in it like a terrier at a rabbit-hole. Masonic aprons, foreign orders and other relics of his past were thrown over his shoulder and then at last he found what he sought. From the bottom of the drawer he produced and waved a blue velvet, gold-encrusted baton which he shook at me triumphantly, saying in a stronger voice than he had so far used : 'I may be an old man, but you tell my nephew Wilhelm that I'm still proud of being a Prussian Field-Marshal !'

He then retired, and I took my leave with such grace as still remained within me.

II

Bruce Lockhart and I flew from Croydon to Amsterdam on 15 August 1939. We motored to Utrecht and, having spent the night there, reported to Doorn on the following day. During our journey I thought upon the ironies and peculiarities of our circumstances. A Second World War was not only brewing but on the very edge of eruption, and here were we on our way to see the man, who a quarter of a century earlier, had unlocked the avalanche of the First World War. Yet never had the Dutch countryside looked more calm and peaceful than on that sunny, lazy summer afternoon. But we were not without our omens. On our way to Utrecht we passed the results of a motor-accident. Two cars had collided and a body, covered by a white dust-coat, lay by the roadside. Bruce has recorded that, 'Jack, always superstitious, predicted the worst. We should, he said, certainly be caught in Holland by the war.'[1] We might easily

[1] Bruce Lockhart wrote his account of our visit to Doorn in *Comes the Reckoning* (London, 1947).

have done so. The Danzig boil, which had been nascent since June, was now coming to a head, and the lancing of it was very near.

I had, however, other things on which to speculate. I had taken some soundings and done some specific research in preparation for our mission. In addition to my father's original views of thirty years before that the Kaiser was a 'howling cad', I had gleaned from a former Imperial Russian Ambassador in Berlin the opinion that 'he was the rudest man I have ever met'. I had read in the memoirs of Prince Chlodwig von Hohenlohe, one of his Imperial Chancellors, that he had an unpleasant habit which he sometimes exercised, doubtless caused by a desire to compensate for the deformity of his left hand, of turning his many rings with their jewels and signets inwards, thus causing excruciating pain to those with whom he shook hands. I had been told, moreover of a further act of boisterous barrack room humour of his taking any opportunity of slapping an unsuspecting person hard on the buttocks and of the historic effect of one of these indulgences.

When, it is said, after the First Balkan War, Tsar Ferdinand of Bulgaria came to Germany for a family gathering of the Coburgs, he brought with him a pocketful of armament contracts. In the course of the celebrations the Tsar was wearing a uniform which comprised, among other items, very tight breeches. At a reception he was leaning out of a window, when the Kaiser noiselessly approached and dealt him a stinging blow. So incensed was the Bulgarian sovereign at this assault upon both his dignity and his person that he left the ceremonies forthwith, taking with him his contracts which he had originally intended to give to Krupps of Essen and delivering them to the French armament firm of Schneiders of Crevzot. Given the then existing state of the interlocking interests of the armaments trade, it is probable that the contracts went into one pocket rather than another of the same pair of trousers, but it must have given some balm to Tsar Ferdinand's wounded ego.

What then, I asked myself, with, I confess, a shadow of trepidation, would be the nature of our host and what kind of a reception could we expect? I need have had no apprehension. Whatever adverse impression I had formed was completely dissipated on our arrival at Haus Doorn. Undoubtedly in the heyday of his arrogant manhood, Wilhelm II had lacked the finer niceties of behaviour; admittedly his handshake, though warm, was painful because he had turned his rings inwards, but I hung on and just managed not to wince. Old age and twenty years of exile had mellowed him, and he appeared before us as a charming, humorous, courteous old gentleman —

though full of guile – and a highly considerate host. He greeted Bruce as an old friend and me as a new one. He apologised anew for the delay in our communications and said frankly that his gentlemen had been at fault. 'Sometimes they are very naughty,' he told us confidentially, 'and do you know how I punish them? I read P. G. Wodehouse to them – in English.'

General von Dommes, the Hofmarschall, was instructed to take us to our apartments which were in the *Torgebäude* or gatehouse, a picturesque German-style lodge which the Emperor had built to house his guests. Indeed the property and capacity of Haus Doorn were meagre. When he had first arrived in Holland in November 1918, he had billeted himself on Count Bentinck at the Castle of Ameron-gen, his involuntary host having been assured by the Dutch Court that the Emperor would only be his guest for some six weeks or so, while he looked around for more permanent quarters. In fact he stayed at Amerongen for nearly six years, owing in part to the view of that grand and courageous lady, Queen Wilhelmina, that his original ideas for a permanent residence were altogether too grandiose and 'above his station' for a monarch in exile who was 'wanted' by the Allies. Eventually they agreed on the former summer palace of the Bishops of Utrecht at Doorn, which came fortuitously on to the market, and this the Kaiser bought. It was, however, a tight squeeze, especially, as we were to find, when one of the best bedrooms in the Schloss itself was devoted to a rather macabre purpose. An orangerie was turned into quarters for the *Umgebung* and guests were housed in the newly built gate-house.

Our rooms in this annexe were very comfortable. We each had a good-sized bedroom, and we shared a sitting-room and a bathroom. The furniture had a distinct flavour of the Tottenham Court Road, and the décor was more interesting than aesthetic. There were a great many photographs of central European royalties all signed familiarly 'Go-go' or 'Bu-bu' or 'Matushka' or 'Nicky'. There were some rather mediocre water-colours of the Achilleon at Corfu and of some men-of-war and of course, the imperial yacht. Bruce, to my envy (though he called it a 'monstrosity'!), had a huge gold-framed montage containing mounted photographs of *all* the Coburgs includ-ing Queen Victoria, but I more than equalled with him in finding on my bedroom bookshelves the official biography of the Prince Consort, which Sir Theodore Martin had written with Queen Victoria practically breathing down his neck, in all the glory of its five volumes, each inscribed: 'To darling Willy with love from Grandmama' – and all of them uncut! We each had a framed text over our bed. Bruce's was 'Watch ye, stand fast in faith,' and mine 'In God we trust.' We had the feeling that we were well protected.

I have said that expatriation and increasing age had mellowed Wilhelm II, and this was true, but even his physiognomy had changed. The beard of exile softened the sharp belligerency of the famous up-pointed moustaches. I found it curious, however, that he should have had himself painted in the full service uniform which he had worn in wartime yet with the beard which he had only grown after abdication. His English was of a definite Edwardian flavour, guttural but fluent, being garnished with such adjectives as 'ripping' and 'topping', and I recall that on one occasion it rather ran away with him to describe someone as 'a damned topping good fellow'. His wardrobe too was of the vintage of 1910, and in his tie he wore an immense tie-pin consisting of a miniature of Queen Victoria set in diamonds.

To a great extent he had put aside the role of play-actor and had become a much more genuine personality. He still cut down trees, but he did it for exercise and not for exhibition. He still delivered sermons on Sunday to his household, but he no longer whitened his face as when, in former days, he had preached to the ship's company of the *Hohenzollern*. He had formed a literary society among the intelligentsia of Doorn and Utrecht to whom he read erudite little papers on such subjects as the origin and development of the palanquin and of the swastika. He gave me a copy of this learned work along with his memoirs, all pleasingly inscribed and bearing the sweeping 'Wilhelm, I et R'.

Our days at Doorn were well filled and well planned. We break-fasted in our rooms and about eleven o'clock a member of the household would summon us to the Schloss, in approaching which we crossed the two moats of the traditional Dutch countryhouse. We were with the Emperor from then until lunch, which was a formal meal at which everyone attended and he 'made the circle', and all bowed or curtsied. After lunch we were free until tea-time and I took advantage of this to write up notes of our morning talks. We drank tea with the Empress Hermine, and then came another session with the Kaiser until dinner, at seven thirty. He and the Empress dined alone, and we with the *Umgebung*. There were six of these gentlemen, chosen from a panel and in waiting for a month at a time. With two exceptions they were exceedingly unpleasant men, combining all the distasteful aspects of the Prussian character with few of its virtues. Though the bluest of East Elbian blood flowed in their veins, they had the manners of wart-hogs and the political intelligence of low-class morons. Moreover it was clear from the first that they were entirely inimical to us (perhaps their introduction to Jeeves still rankled) and made no secret of it. Bruce and I had agreed beforehand that, as they knew that our conversations with the Kaiser were conducted in English, we would give the impression that we spoke very little German and understood less, with the result that they spoke very freely among themselves and made no secret of their admiration for the Führer and for his coming conquest of the Poles. That the Kaiser was aware of the political affinities of his entourage was clear from one of his remarks to us. 'I am a prisoner in my own house,' he said.

We did not look forward to our evening meal, which lasted until eight-forty-five when we had our third session with the Kaiser, but we very soon found that among this odd assortment of humanity were two men of probity and decent conduct. The first of these was Herr von Ilsemann who had married the daughter of Count Bentinck of Amerongen. He was devoted to his master and to his master alone. He loathed the Nazis and said so. His wife had become a close friend of the Empress Augusta Victoria, the Kaiser's first wife. (When she died the Empress bequeathed her favourite hunter to Frau von Ilsemann.) He remained at Doorn throughout the war and died in the sixties, leaving some rather dull posthumous memoirs.

The other exception was the Kaiser's private secretary, Freiherr von Sell, a gentle, friendly creature of transparent loyalty and 'right thinking'. We liked him at once, and the three of us used to walk and talk together in the afternoons. I was later told that, after the Kaiser's death, von Sell returned to Germany and became actively involved in the conspiracy against Hitler, being executed after the abortive coup of 20 July 1944.

The Empress Hermine was what is known as a 'tough cookie', Born a Princess of Reuss (a tiny German principality of which all the heads of all the branches are called Henry and it is not unusual to encounter a 'Henry XXXII') she had first married a Prince of Schönaich-Carolath, who had been president of the *Reichsrat* before the war. On the death of the Empress Augusta Victoria, one of whose bridesmaids she had been, Princess Hermine visited Doorn and made a conquest of the Kaiser. They were married in 1922, and there is no reason to suppose that she did not make him happy and comfortable.

But she was a woman with a grievance, in fact two grievances. The first was that the monarchist movement in Germany would not recognise her as the Kaiser's consort, partly because the Reusses were only regarded as demi-semi-royal and partly because she had married in exile and not gone through the due processes of acceptance of the crown. This rankled very bitterly. Our tea-parties were a series of jeremiads against the cruelty and effrontery of the Prussian nobility. 'They are sadists', she frequently repeated.

The second grievance, with which I rather sympathised, was disclosed to us in a dramatic manner. When we had finished our tea she rose suddenly, and moving rather rapidly, like the Red Queen in *Through the Looking-Glass*, she led us down a long passage, saying in a voice full of emotion: 'Now I will show you the *Todkammer* (Death Chamber)', with which words she unlocked and threw open the door of a bedroom, in shadowy twilight from heavily curtained windows of which the blinds were drawn. We realised after a moment's bewilderment, for she offered no further explanation and stood there like a figure of Greek tragedy, that this was the bedroom of the late Empress, and that it had been left exactly as it had been when she had died there. Toilet articles thronged the dressing-table, family photographs filled every occasional table and covered the walls. A nightdress and a peignoir were laid out on an arm-chair in front of which was a pair of slippers. The bed was turned down, and the only additions appeared to have been a sheaf of immortelles on the bed itself and a wreath of bronze laurel leaves on the pillow. In the shrouded light it all looked very unreal.

After being allowed to gaze our fill, we were led back to the sunlit morning-room in which we had had tea, and rather glad we were. Though the whole affair was conducted in complete silence, it was a silence eloquent of resentment. I confess that the thought did occur to me that to have the best bedroom in one's house occupied by the memory (perhaps even the ghost) of one's immediate predecessor must have been very trying.

III

In our talks with the Kaiser, Bruce, with his usual kindness and generosity, allowed me to make the running. Having performed the office of *entrepreneur* he was content to listen, which he did with great interest, and occasionally to intervene, which he always did to good effect. Our sessions with the Emperor were held in his study which, situated in a tower, had a large series of bow-windows with comfortably upholstered embrasures. The Kaiser himself sat at a large desk with the light coming over his left shoulder and having accessible a cupboard set under the window. He sat on a backless saddle, which swung around like a piano stool, and at eighty years old he could hold this position for over two hours. Happily Bruce and I were placed in more comfortable armchairs.

The Emperor began by asking me why I thought he had agreed to see me, and I said 'I do not know', which was obviously the answer he wanted. 'It was partly,' he said, 'because my old friend Bruce Lockhart here had asked me to, and partly because I had read your life of Hindenburg. You have given the only true and accurate account of what happened at Spa in November 1918.' I was naturally pleased, and I didn't tell him that I knew it must have been pretty accurate because I had got it all from Gröner who had played the key part. But it got us off to a good start.

It was almost immediately apparent that he was consumed with a desire for personal justification, to which end his own literary efforts had been directed. He was supremely conscious of the enigma and the problem which he presented to the historian of the age and displayed an almost childlike willingness to co-operate in the search for a solution. Once launched upon a subject – and he placed no prohibition on any subject for our discussion – he talked fluently, with animation, wit and, on occasion, biting criticism. He had an amazing grasp of dates, but not always such an outstanding respect for facts and their interpretation. Rancour dominated many of his memories of the past, and there were few who escaped the caustic backlash of his reminiscent tongue; on more than one occasion he referred to persons of all varieties, dead and alive, as 'the greatest villain unhung'. We heard this applied to Stalin, Mola the Spanish General (His Majesty was a keen supporter of his rival, Franco) and Sir Sidney Lee, the biographer of King Edward VII, upon whom he vented some of the spleen which he had always entertained towards his uncle.

His most marked hatreds, however, were centred on Hindenburg, who had sent him out of Germany in November 1918 against his better judgement, and Prince von Bülow, the Imperial Chancellor, who had sent him to Tangier against his will – and who incidentally, had summed up his character in the words that 'in peace the Kaiser was a war-lord, in war he evaded taking decisions, and in defeat he fled'.

With very little prodding he gave us a vivid account of the summer of 1914, though what he said added little to what he had already written in his memoirs. He spoke with deluded petulance about the English who had cruelly misunderstood him and had misled him in 1914. He would never have gone to war if he had known England was coming in; he had only wanted to beat the Russians, 'who had started it all', but he brushed aside a question from me concerning the 'blank cheque' he had given to Austria-Hungary in July.

It was, of course, an extraordinary experience to hear all this from the point of view of one of the leading actors, however prejudiced this view may have been or warped by the rationalisation of age and exile. What, however, particularly caught my attention was the fact that in order to refresh his memory on a certain point he would swing round to the cupboard on his left and unlock it. There, ranged in row after row of beautifully bound red morocco volumes, each with its clasp and lock, were his diaries from I don't know how long back. He selected the volume for 1914, unlocked it with a key on his watch-chain, found the particular entry he wanted and thrust it under my nose. To my intense surprise it was written in English, though other pages were in German. I took particular notice of this little cache of history.

Emboldened by the Emperor's frankness and willingness to talk, I decided to take a chance which, whatever answer it elicited, would be of historical importance. No one, I said to him, sitting in my place could resist the temptation of asking him one special question, though I realised that he might not wish to answer it. Had he ever, I asked, regretted dismissing Bismarck? It was the only time during our conversations when he appeared hesitant and discomposed, and my heart sank a little as I thought perhaps I really had gone too far. Then he smiled in a rather foxy way and said, 'I won't give you a direct answer to that, but I will say this: I might not have done it today.'

Because of the delicate state of the international situation neither Bruce nor I felt justified in broaching subjects of a current nature, though we had noted with interest that, whereas on our arrival, there was in the hall an easel which had held a large-size map of the Sino-Japanese war, this had been replaced during our visit by a map of the German-Polish frontiers. But we had no need for such niceness of restraint; the Emperor himself launched forth on the subject of *Lebensraum*. Peoples and nations, he said, were given their allotted living space by Providence. (Incidentally, I noticed that he never spoke of God, only of Providence. The 'Myself and God' period had evidently passed, and it is my private belief that he believed that God, with whom he had claimed so close a partnership, had let him down in November 1918 and had subsequently been demoted to Providence.) It was the duty of these peoples and nations, he continued, to develop this *Lebensraum* and to defend it, if need be, but they must not take more than their fair share. All great empires had failed because their rulers had not been content with their allotted spaces. Others would fail for the same reason. Bruce asked him whether among these future failures he included the British Empire and the Third Reich. He refused to be drawn, however. 'You may take it whichever way you choose,' he replied, and passed on to a denunciation of the Treaty of Versailles, which must be revised – 'either by you, the British, or by Providence'.

IV

Hanging round my neck like a very heavy albatross, I felt the message with which I had been entrusted by the Duke of Connaught. This was mid-August 1939 and I felt quite certain that, in view of the steadily worsening situation between Germany and Poland, and in that atmosphere of hostility and pro-Nazi sentiment on the part of the Household, it would be hideously wrong to give the message in its original form. Relayed to Berlin by willing tongues it would be twisted into something of totally disproportionate importance. The fact that the great-uncle of King George VI of England had sent a personal message by word of mouth to the effect that he was still proud of being a Prussian Field-Marshal would be grist indeed to the Nazi propaganda mill, who would certainly suppress the fact that the Duke was ninety years old and had in all probability long ago forgotten that he had ever seen me.

So at the luncheon table where I sat on his left, I gave him a bowdlerised version. I had, I said, seen the Duke of Connaught shortly before I left England and he had sent his warmest greetings to His Majesty. This worked famously. The Kaiser was in a gay mood and received my news with vivacious pleasure. 'Ach, ja,' he said, 'Thank you very much. Uncle Arthur, *dear* Uncle Arthur! Always my *favourite* uncle. *Very* unlike Uncle Bertie.'

The general cuisine of luncheon was good, though not excellent. There was an admirable Moselle and – of all things – a sparkling Burgundy, which to my surprise the Kaiser drank. I preferred the Moselle. Turning to me, he said: 'I see you drink the better wine. I know this is not first class, but I drink it because I was never allowed to as a little boy.' I thought that for a monarch, even an exiled monarch, to be still compensating at eighty for what he was forbidden to do at the age of, say, twelve was very odd indeed.

It served its turn, however, because at our next meeting that evening the Emperor's mind was running on his early life. The two people whom he had clearly loved most were 'Grandmama' (Queen

Victoria) and 'Grandpapa' (the Emperor Wilhelm I) and he spoke with great reverence and affection of both of them. It was equally clear that he had little of either for his parents, and that in his mind, either consciously or subconsciously, they were associated with his early sufferings in connection with his deformed left arm. He talked freely of this and of the stern régime of exercises and treatments which were inflicted on him and of the inhumanity of his tutor, Professor Hinzpeter, who would make him ride bare-back. His faulty balance often made him fall off and, despite his tears and pleas, he was made to remount and carry on. The result was that he became a perfectly competent horseman, with his reins in his right hand, but he always had to mount his horse from the wrong side. He had also become a pretty good shot, though there was a story (which I did not hear from him) that, as a result of resting his gun on the shoulder of a beater to fire at the game, there were around the imperial hunting grounds a number of retired *Jägers* who were locally known as 'the Kaiser's deafies'.

As a matter of fact, however, it was surprising how little one was aware of the imperial infirmity. Even at table there was no sense of embarrassment as he made use of some specially designed dual-purpose implement which served as both knife and spoon combined. His wearing of norfolk-jackets enabled him to rest his left thumb in the loop of the belt, just as in the old days, when he wore uniform, it rested on the hilt of his sword.

Of all the many stories of his youth which he told us my favourite was one he reserved for our final session *à trois*. His greatest treat, he said, was when his parents were away and he would take his Sunday luncheon with 'Grandpapa'. It would be served on a trolley and the old gentleman would help the boy and then himself. There was also always a bottle of champagne, and the Emperor would pour a glass for himself and one for the boy and then in due course another for himself. Then he would carefully re-cork the bottle and mark the height of the contents on the label with a pencil. The idea of native Prussian thriftiness moving the German Emperor to re-cork a bottle of champagne and also check up on his butler, somehow pleased me not a little.

There was another side to these little Sunday luncheon-parties. The changing of the guard took place in the early afternoon and a crowd would gather each week to watch the ceremony, which on Sundays was a full-dress affair, and also in the hope of seeing the old Emperor and the young Prince as they stood in an embrasure of a corner window of the imperial *Schloss* to view the parade. The onlookers cheered the aged grey-haired monarch and the slim, blond boy enthusiastically, and the young Wilhelm expressed his delight at the loyalty and affection of his grandfather's subjects. 'I can never forget,' replied the old man, somewhat bitterly, 'that twenty-five years ago these same loyal Berliners chased me out of the city and into exile.' The grandson, now himself an exile, commented to us: 'This was my first lesson in the mutability of human fealties.'

I had thought that this could mark the conclusion of these delightful and thrilling talks in which I had felt that not only was I in the presence of history but had touched hands with it. As we said good night to the Emperor, we also made our farewells and he gave each of us some inscribed photographs of himself. Early next morning, however, when the car was at the door to take us to Utrecht, fat old von Dommes came panting down to the gate-house with word that the Emperor wanted to see me again and alone. I went up to the Schloss and found him sitting up in bed, looking very pink and clean, with his hair brushed up into a plume, which gave him the appearance of an elderly cockatoo. He wore a silk nightshirt, smocked across the chest and with the imperial Prussian eagle embroidered in black silk on the pocket.

His greeting was cordial. He took me by the hand and said that he wanted to say once again how much he had enjoyed our talks. 'Come back again and see me next summer,' he said gaily, 'and we'll talk some more.' Then he paused and a look of great sadness came into his face. He said: 'No, you won't be able to, because the machine is running away with *him* as it ran away with *me*.'

V

There were several sequels to this story.

During the Second World War and until his death the Kaiser behaved with supreme rectitude and even nobility – except on one occasion. When the Germans swept into the Low Countries in May 1940, he was almost overwhelmed by invitations for an alternative residence. Queen Wilhelmina offered him continued asylum in one of the Dutch colonial possessions; King George VI and his government made it known that he would be welcome in England; and Hitler proposed that he should return to Germany as the honoured guest of the Third Reich. To all of these offers the Emperor returned a courteous refusal. The Dutch people, he said, had been exceedingly kind to him in his exile and he would not now desert them in their hour of adversity. Besides, he added, he had been accused once before of running away; now he would stay put.

And so he did. When the tide of war had swept past Doorn and the line had been established, a guard of honour of the Wehrmacht was quartered in the gate-house, where Bruce and I had been so happily installed. Almost at once senior officers from all parts of the front found pressing business to be attended to in Holland, which always included a visit to Doorn for a glimpse of their former sovereign. So widespread did this pilgrimage become that the Führer's jealous hostility was aroused. He withdrew the Wehrmacht guard and substituted one composed of crack S.S. men, commanded by a colonel reputed to be two hundred per cent *Führertreu*. This warrior was, however, not proof against the charm of the old Hohenzollern fox. Within a surprisingly short space of time the conquest of the S.S. colonel was complete, and he was standing stiffly to attention, bowing with a '*Ja, Majestät*', '*Nein, Majestät*'.

The untoward incident, the flaw in the Kaiser's correct behaviour, was when Hitler entered Paris on 14 June and received a telegram of congratulation signed by the Kaiser. Whether this was on Wilhelm II's own initiative, or whether it was the brainchild of those East Prussian characters with whom we had dined less than a year before, I do not know, but it created a very bad impression not only abroad but also in the ranks of the monarchist movement in Germany.

The death of the Kaiser on 5 June 1941, passed almost unnoticed. At that moment the attention of the world was centred on the Battle of Crete.

In her widowhood the Empress Hermine returned to Germany and settled down with her sister, the Countess Stolberg, in Upper Silesia, where, in the latter stages of the war, they were duly picked up by the advancing Russian armies. It may be understood that a pair of elderly ladies of obviously aristocratic bearing and background would be of little appeal to the Soviet Occupation Authorities. The two found themselves relegated to a very low category of food rationing and for a while they were in extremely poor circumstances. Eventually some bright young officer on the Soviet General Staff discovered who they were – or at least who one of them was – with the result that the change in their state of affairs was like the transformation scene in a Christmas pantomime. A comfortable villa in Frankfurt-am-Oder was requisitioned for the Empress's use, and such comforts as were obtainable were placed at her disposal. Later, when the hostilities were over, she was allowed to visit the Russian sector of Berlin, escorted by a Soviet and a German adjutant. It is not without irony that the royal honours, which she had so coveted and which the German monarchists had denied her, were bestowed plentifully by the Soviet authorities. She did not live long, however, to enjoy her triumph – if triumph it was – for she died in August 1947.

There remains the sad story of the Kaiser's diaries. I confess that throughout the war I had made it my personal war aim to 'liberate' those beautiful little red volumes in which so many historic secrets must be locked away. I even dreamed of it occasionally. As soon as it was practicable I returned to Doorn to find it wonderfully unchanged though a little run down, but with the loyal Ilsemann and his charming wife still in charge. The property had been placed under seal by the Netherlands Government and its future was uncertain. The Ilsemanns took me all over the *Schloss*, reviving old memories. At last we came to the Tower Room, where Bruce and I had spent so many sunlit hours with the Emperor, it seemed a century ago. I sat in the saddle at the writing-desk and reconnoitred the cupboard below the window. 'That's where the Emperor used to keep his diaries,' I said. 'Have you the key?' Ilsemann silently unlocked the cupboard. It was as bare as old Mother Hubbard's. I realised that my heart had been hammering against my ribs as he had fumbled with the key; it now stopped with a sickening thud and I could have wept with disappointment. 'Where are they?' I asked. 'Did the Empress Hermine take them?' Ilsemann's sad face broke into a brief and chilly smile. 'That she did not,' he said, 'for I searched her luggage myself.' 'Then where are they?' I repeated. 'The Crown Prince took them to Berlin after the Emperor's death. They should be in Charlottenburg.'

This was a ray of hope, and I saw to it that my duties took me to Berlin as soon as possible. It was very soon after the German surrender, and there was much chaos. The Charlottenburg *Schloss* had been occupied and obviously looted by the Russians. There was no sign of the diaries. I utilised every kind of source and facility to trace them but without avail. Nor did I ever find them. This gold-mine escaped me and, what is worse, is lost to history.

I returned several times to Doorn after the war. It is a museum now, and the Orangerie, which in our time had housed that unlovable *Umgebung*, is now a restaurant where one can lunch very well. On one occasion my wife Ruth went with me and we found Ilsemann had died since my last visit. His wife, however, received us most kindly and asked us to tea at her family home at Amerongen. It was a delightful afternoon, but she afterwards told us that her brothers, the Counts Bentinck, were so anti-British that she had had (to use her own phrase) 'to lock them in the cellar'. We could not actually hear them pounding on the door, but there was a strong smell of sulphur!

VI

Within a week of our return from Doorn in August 1939, Bruce and I said an indefinite goodbye, not knowing when we should meet again nor that, as fate would have it, we should spend much of the war together. He departed for a holiday in Scotland and I sailed in S.S. *Normandie* (the last transatlantic crossing she ever made) for my first war station in Washington. But that, as Mr Kipling says, is 'another story', and I hope to tell it in a future volume.

Index

INDEX

INDEX